BROTHERS IN WAR

BROTHERS IN WAR

MICHAEL WALSH

ISIS
LARGE PRINT
Oxford

First published in Great Britain 2006
by
Ebury Press, an imprint of
Ebury Publishing

Published in Large Print 2007 by ISIS Publishing Ltd.,
7 Centremead, Osney Mead, Oxford OX2 0ES
by arrangement with
Ebury Publishing

British Library Cataloguing in Publication Data
Walsh, Michael, 1953–
   Brothers in war. – Large print ed.
   1. Beechey (Family) – History
   2. World War, 1914–1918
   3. Brothers – Great Britain
   4. Soldiers – Great Britain
   5. Brothers – Australia
   6. Soldiers – Australia
   7. Large type books
   I. Title
   940.4'4941

ISBN 978–0–7531–9422–5 (hb)
ISBN 978–0–7531–9423–2 (pb)

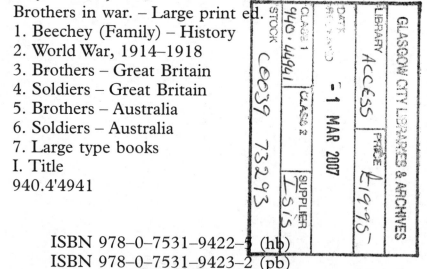

Printed and bound in Great Britain by
T. J. International Ltd., Padstow, Cornwall

To the memory of my mum and dad,
Noreen and Bill Walsh

Contents

Prologue

They shall grow not old as we that are left grow old . . .

Anzac Day, West Leederville, Perth, Western Australia, 1968

In far-off days Christopher Beechey had the looks of a matinee idol. Of the eight Beechey brothers, he was the most handsome, the only blemishes two scars on his forehead. They once made him appear heroic, but most of the heroes he knew died long ago on the shrapnel-scarred beaches and in the bullet-swept gullies of Gallipoli in 1915. He came away wounded, his tall, athletic body broken. As he was convalescing back in England, he found love with the hospital volunteer who helped, encouraged and occasionally bullied him as he learned to walk again. Chris feared he would lose her when doctors advised he return to the warmth of Western Australia for the sake of his health, but Bertha Halsey Nye agreed to become his bride. They were married in a rush on Easter Monday 1916. A breathless letter saying the wedding was fixed for nine the next morning was the first Chris's mother heard of it.

More than fifty years later, on 25 April 1968, Chris sits on the verandah of their bungalow as the early autumn sun climbs over the rooftops. His dark wavy hair has long been replaced by wisps of grey, but the scars on his forehead are still visible amid the lines of age. Anzac Day is dawning and Australia is pouring out its heart and waving the flag to remember the Gallipoli boys. It will be Chris Beechey's last Anzac Day on this earth. He suspects as much himself because he has written to his youngest sister in England, "I'm getting near the last round-up, as Bing Crosby sang many years ago."

Bertha had stopped him going to the official Anzac commemorations long before. It wasn't the pain of having to stand there propped up on his sticks all that time. It was the pain in his heart that was too much. His heart was one part of his body that had not been smashed in May 1915 when the sniper's bullet slammed into him and sent him plunging down a ravine, but it was broken every Anzac Day as "The Last Post" rang out.

So he watches the sun rise from the comfort of his rocking chair while Bertha is still sleeping inside. The faint wail of a distant bugle carries on the early morning breeze. Tears fill his eyes, and dabbing them away he brushes over the small scars on his forehead. Long ago Bertha had asked whether enemy bayonet, bullet or shrapnel was responsible for them. "It was an ambush," was all he said, adding mischievously, "I really don't know how I survived."

Christopher William Reeve Beechey, veteran of Gallipoli, died on 26 September 1968 at Hollywood Repatriation Hospital, aged 85. His last wish was to be commemorated like those of his warrior brothers who never came back and whose final resting places, where known, were marked with name, rank, number and unit. An Anzac to the end, his headstone in Karrakatta cemetery, Perth, Western Australia, carries the rising sun badge of the Australian Imperial Force above the inscription:

1368 Private
CWR Beechey
4 Field Ambulance
Beloved husband of Bertha, father of
Kathleen and Daphne — Requiescat in Pace

Friesthorpe, Lincolnshire, England, 1896

The ambush was set. The two bushwhackers crouched behind the coach house next to the rambling Victorian rectory. Fanny and Frank Beechey had had enough teasing from their older brother Chris, a big, boisterous teenager who delighted in tormenting them when he was home from boarding school. They had made a pact to get their own back. Their young hearts beat faster as they heard footsteps scraping on the gravel. Only one of the Beechey clan could make that much noise merely walking up the long, winding driveway to the large house with its pale yellow brickwork cloaked in golden Virginia creeper. Chris had clumping great feet and wore boots the size of boats.

Fanny and her short but stocky accomplice skulked in the evening shadows intent on teaching their brother a lesson. Fanny was architect of the plan and chief conspirator. Being the only girl among seven brothers for much of her young life had bred a ruthless streak in her. She was small, almost waif-like, but as tough as Chris's old boots. Frank would pounce and hold their victim while she carried out the main assault.

The attack was carried out to perfection. By the time the assailants had been swatted off, the damage was done. Fanny hoisted up her petticoats and she and Frank fled in triumph to the sanctuary of the rectory with its maze of rooms and cubbyholes. Chris was late down for supper that evening. When he eventually appeared, two deep gashes were visible on his forehead where his sister had clawed him with her fingernails. "I fell into a bramble bush," he told his horrified mother. Even as a teenager, Christopher William Reeve Beechey was a gentleman of honour.

There had been seven children in tow in 1890 when the Rev. Prince William Thomas Beechey became the new rector of Friesthorpe with Snarford, a remote and sodden corner of Lincolnshire. It would have been eight but Maud, the first-born girl and her father's favourite, had died aged five. The reverend's own sister, also called Maud, had also died young, and he took his daughter's death particularly badly. The family never sang the hymn "There's a Friend for Little Children" for fear of upsetting him. Another six youngsters came along when they were installed in Friesthorpe rectory, at which point Amy finally banished her husband to a spare bed in the adjoining coach house. On the rare occasions they were all home together, the Rev. P.W.T. struggled to find the right name and ended up reciting each of them in descending order of age, so that the youngest grew up thinking *"BarCharLenChrisFannyFrankEricHaroldKatieDaisyWinnieEdieSam"* was another nursery rhyme.

Barnard b. 26 April 1877
Charles b. 27 April 1878
Maud b. 13 December 1879 (d. 7 December 1885)
Leonard b. 31 August 1881
Christopher b. 1 June 1883
Frances b. 7 February 1885
Frank b. 12 October 1886
Eric b. 28 April 1889
Harold b. 22 March 1891
Katherine b. 2 February 1893
Margaret b. 5 March 1894
Winifrede b. 12 October 1895
Edith b. 7 November 1897
Samuel b. 13 August 1899

Amy, the daughter of an affluent brewer from Linslade in Buckinghamshire, had hectored the church authorities into giving her growing family a more suitable home after years of living in cramped curate's accommodation. It paid off when Friesthorpe came up as a vacancy. The big 1860s house with its eight bedrooms was a boon, but Friesthorpe was a poor living, even with the addition of neighbouring Snarford to the parish. Other than the rectory, Friesthorpe consisted of half a dozen farms and eight or nine cottages, while Snarford, two miles away, was just a few scattered farms. The combined population was less than 160. Church income, topped up by a handout from Queen Anne's Bounty for needy clerics, amounted to under £300 a year, of which a sizeable lump had to go as an annuity to the retiring minister, who remained a burden on the Beecheys for another twenty years. Beechey was so hard up that he immediately informed the managers of the local primary school at neighbouring Faldingworth he would not be able to continue with the one-pound subscription traditionally paid by the church.

Although more pauper than Prince, Amy's husband was a generous soul; too generous at times for her liking. On the days when he had to go to Lincoln, eleven miles away, he came back with boxes of biscuits and cakes for his children. Whenever he sent one of them to the shop in Faldingworth for his pipe tobacco, he would reward them with money for sweets. The rector was almost twenty years older than his wife, and the brilliant mind that achieved an MA at Trinity College, Dublin, was apt to go absent when it came to menial household duties. He would pour buckets of water on the fire instead of into the boiler, and dump the contents of the coal scuttle in the boiler instead of on to the fire. Preaching the same sermon twice in a fortnight might pass by unnoticed, but not so the cheap scarlet handkerchief he flourished from the pulpit after

6

forgetting the clean white one his wife had laid out for him.

As well as coping with her own family, Amy accommodated the children of poor parishioners and gave them rudimentary schooling. Doing this while meeting the already considerable demands of a large family took its toll. When she was struck down by a mysterious illness she was diagnosed as having a weak heart, but it was probably nothing more than exhaustion. One unfeeling relative advised her to buck up her ideas, saying her husband would not want a sickly woman on his hands. Amy escaped to the pretty vicarage of another parish to recover and enjoyed a brief, blissful respite from all the cooking, washing and cleaning. She, above all, epitomised the family motto: *persta atque obdura* — persist and endure.

For over twenty years, there might have been no happier home in England. A photo from 1902 shows a bewhiskered Rev. P. W. T. Beechey perched proudly on a ladder while battalions of his children — only Charles is missing — peer out from the branches of their magnificent tree house, built in the ash that towered over the rectory grounds. There were dozens more trees to climb and ample hedgerows for hollowing out into secret hideaways. There were ditches and dykes for damming and for sailing paper and wooden boats on. The iron railing between the rectory's front field and lawn was the supreme test of balance, with the children queuing to see who could inch the furthest along it. Home-made stilts were another favourite, particularly with the sisters, who would totter along, fleetingly as tall as their big brothers, before spilling into their waiting arms.

The rector fretted over two large ponds in the fields around the house. Whenever Sam or Edith, the two babies of the family, went missing he would peer anxiously into those dark depths, fearing the worst. In fact, Harold, always the most adventurous of the boys, was the only one ever to fall in. The pretend galleon he made from logs lashed together with creeper disintegrated on its maiden voyage and left him clinging to a piece of wood until his brothers fished him out.

All the boys were taught chess by their father but tactfully refrained from beating him. The old gentleman had their unfailing love, devotion and respect. They would sit in awe of him as he expounded on philosophy, astronomy and theoretical mechanics. As they became men, he would accompany them to the Brownlow Arms in Faldingworth, less than a mile away across the fields. But it took only a single pint to loosen the reverend gentleman's tongue and make him a little indiscreet about matters far removed from theoretical mechanics. The family was not known for its capacity to hold its drink.

The idyll ended when the Rev. Beechey was diagnosed with cancer. When he was too weak to preach, the family were shown the door of the huge rectory they had made their home and moved to a two-up two-down in Avondale Street, Lincoln.

The terraced house would not have had room for all the memories of Friesthorpe, let alone the children and their belongings, but only the girls and Harold were still living at home by then. Chris had left for a new life on the other side of the world in 1910. Frank, Charles and Barnard were all schoolmasters. Eric was learning dentistry, Leonard was working as a clerk in London, and Samuel, the youngest of the Beechey boys, was away at boarding school.

Their father died on 5 May 1912. He was 76. "He seems to have been much loved," said the Bishop of Lincoln after the cortege had made the slow journey to Friesthorpe for the funeral service. And he was spared what his wife was not: seeing so many of his sons lay down their lives in the First World War.

CHAPTER
ONE

The Beechey boys

In the charming tree house photo of the Beechey clan, Barnard Reeve Beechey, known simply as Bar, is leaning moodily over a branch brandishing a paper, eight brothers and sisters away from the prim-looking governess who would break his heart. Unlucky in love and life, the most brilliant of the Beechey boys was a middle-aged failure by the time war came along in 1914 to offer some kind of redemption.

Born in 1877 at Pinchbeck, near Spalding, in Lincolnshire, Barnard was the first child of the Rev. P. W. T. and Amy Beechey. At the age of nine, he won a scholarship to St John's Foundation School for the Sons of Poor Clergy at Leatherhead in Surrey, which provided free education along public school lines for those of good church stock who could not normally afford such an extravagance. Epsom racecourse was near by and bunking off each Derby Day became such a tradition that even the disciplinarian headmaster, the Rev. A. F. Rutty, turned a blind eye. Such leniency rarely applied to other misdemeanours. On Mondays there would be a queue of miscreants waiting outside the head's room to be beaten. One unfortunate youth was hauled in and thrashed before he could whimper that he was merely a candidate for confirmation.

Bar, like most of the impressionable St John's youths, had a crush on Nurse Wylie, who looked after the pupils' welfare and had the face of an angel and a figure that became more matronly by the term. But the boys preferred to worship her from afar, for Nurse Wylie's antidote to all ills was an enormous glass of the most foul concoction conceived by human ingenuity — "No ordinary skrim-shanker looking for a few days' rest could face it. You had to be near death, or wishing for it," wrote a school historian. More palatable were the tankards of beer — bought by the barrel load — with which pupils washed down their evening meal.

Bar stood out not merely for being a mathematics prodigy but also for the striking tuft of white in his dark mop of hair. It made him resemble the arch-villain from a Victorian melodrama. But he survived the ribbings, matron's concoctions and the headmaster's summonses. Bar won an open exhibition to study at St John's College, Cambridge, graduating in 1899, before setting out on a modestly paid and ultimately unfulfilling career as a master at a succession of minor public schools in provincial towns. He returned to Friesthorpe often enough to fall in love with the governess, Miss Rawding, who helped look after the youngest Beechey brothers and sisters. But Miss Rawding was being encouraged by her father to wait for someone with better prospects. She spurned Bar.

Six stagnant years at Katharine Lady Berkeley's School in Wotton-under-Edge, Gloucestershire, brought hints of a darker character and signs of trouble to come when the head was summoned by the governors to answer complaints from parents that masters had called pupils names and taunted them in an undignified manner. Two years later, the contracts of all the staff were terminated and offered back to them at reduced salaries. A Miss Webb, the school's first female teacher, who had formed an attachment to Bar, left at once. She would make one more poignant appearance on the scene when a generation of starched and scrubbed Edwardian schoolboys and their duty-bound masters had gone to war. The head also resigned, while Bar quit the following term. He had no difficulty finding a new job in Dorset, which began promisingly enough.

Dorchester Grammar had only a small group of boarders. Most pupils came from the town itself or arrived by steam train from Weymouth or pedalled their cycles from the collection of Piddle and Puddle villages nestling among the hills and folds of Dorset's Thomas Hardy country. Hardy himself sat on the board of school governors. Bar was appointed first assistant master — in effect, deputy head. Living in at the school, he often supervised evening prep sessions. However, his temperament does not suggest cosy evenings in his study where teas were laid on and the smoke from his pipe blended with the delicious smell of crumpets toasting over an open hearth. Bar had apparently become rather too fond of a drink.

The headmaster was Hugh Albert Francis, known to the boys as "Frankie". He had arrived just a few months before Bar and was already showing a sadistic streak. Producing a small bunch of keys from his pocket, he would carefully select the sharpest one and, holding it vertically, dance it on the head of any boy who had provoked his ire. The other masters lived outside the school. Two came in from Weymouth and would put on a thrilling show every morning for boys travelling by rail to Dorchester. One master rode a motorbike, to which the other master, on a pushbike, was attached by a rope. Together they raced to beat the train, cheered on by the cap-waving pupils crammed in the carriages.

The gruff and possibly hung-over first assistant master took roll call, and there would be trouble for any latecomer caught trying to sneak in. At break time, masters joined the scrum when Bugler's bakery sent a boy round with a tray of doughnuts and Chelsea buns at a penny each. Writing of those days, one youngster recalled, "In the higher forms there was a mathematics master by the name of Beechey. He was very knowledgeable but lost control not only of the boys, but also of himself from time to time. He would fly into violent tempers and go almost berserk sometimes, which only made matters worse."

While Frankie taught the junior school the rudiments of cricket and was a great exponent of the forward stroke and the straight bat, Bar guided the fortunes of the first XI at football. He also helped to set up the Officer Training Corps, which schooled the boys in military discipline and drill and marched them out to historic Maiden Castle on manoeuvres. There, on the grassy, terraced slopes of the Iron Age hill fort, they fought mock battles, which would ill prepare them for the carnage to come.

After four years in the school, Bar suddenly and mysteriously left in June 1912. No reason is given in the staff register, but his father had died only the previous month and Bar had been at his bedside for the final, harrowing days to spare Amy the ordeal of watching her husband's suffering. An inappropriate relationship with a colleague's wife was hinted at by some of the family, but Chris, in later life, blamed his eldest brother's fall from grace on the bottle. Under "post taken up after leaving school", Bar's entry in the Dorchester staff register simply states "Unknown", followed in brackets by "Enlisted in 1914" with a question mark. For all his brains, he was unable to obtain another teaching position. The army was also pursuing him for the cost of his officer's uniform from the cadets. His career in ruins, he returned to Lincoln and lived with his mother for a while, eventually finding undistinguished employment with the local education authority.

When the world went to war in August 1914, Bar enlisted as a humble private in the 9th (Service) Battalion of the Lincolnshire Regiment. He was classic officer material — public school background, Cambridge graduate and a leader of young men in the classroom, on the sports field and in the cadet force — but he was also thirty-seven years old. The upper age limit was thirty in the earliest days when recruiting sergeants were almost trampled in the stampede to join up. It soon went up to thirty-five, or forty-five for ex-soldiers and anyone who had led their school OTC. Perhaps because of his experience of assaulting Iron Age hill forts, he would get a crack at the enemy sooner than most.

Charles Reeve Beechey, or Char

A midsummer evening in the 21st century and the boys from two English public schools are playing out an age-old rivalry on the cricket field. Stamford versus Uppingham is the most eagerly awaited fixture of the season. A spiralling shot to mid-wicket looks a certain six for Uppingham until a Stamford youth scampers round and makes a flying catch an inch inside the boundary. It is a moment Char would have warmly applauded, and today it might be rewarded with the C. R. Beechey Cup, which is still presented to the best fielder from the cricket team at Stamford Grammar School. The ever-thoughtful Char bequeathed a sum in his will to pay for it.

To his mother, her second son was her "rock", the one upon whom she could most rely in a crisis. He never married and there is little suggestion of a love in his life beyond the boundaries of Stamford, where he had been pupil and master. He was the archetypal Mr Chips character. "Of a modest, retiring disposition, he was content to live for the school and in the school," his headmaster said of him. One former pupil of long ago remembered the time a maths class was interrupted by the arrival of a telegram for Mr Beechey. He glanced at it, tucked it into his pocket and continued teaching without pause. Only at the end of the lesson did he inform the boys that one of his brothers had been killed in action.

Char was also born in Pinchbeck, and named after his mother's flamboyant brother, Charles Reeve, an intrepid Victorian gentleman who had been a missionary in India, where he had built a hospital and pioneered solar power. Edith, or Edie as she was usually known, the youngest of the Beechey girls, recalled how he visited the family in Lincoln in belted khaki suit and puttees, "making us all proud and Mother nervous. He'd take short cuts through people's gardens, down drives, through back gates, in an outback spirit that made us feel he was altogether too large for our country."

Char inherited a love of the natural world that would have made his eccentric uncle Charlie proud. The unconventional army unit he ended up with would also have appealed to his uncle. The 25th Battalion, Royal Fusiliers, known as the Legion of Frontiersmen, was the most bizarrely romantic regiment to leave Britain's shores to fight a war, and included within its ranks elephant poachers, cowboys, explorers, circus strongmen and lion tamers, a lighthouse keeper from Scotland, an opera singer and an Irishman who had been sentenced to death by the president of Costa Rica. It would eventually welcome gentleman soldier Private C. R. Beechey, armed with the personal compass and miniature chess set that were as vital to him as his Short Magazine Lee Enfield rifle and iron rations.

16

Born a year and a day after Bar, he would forever be bracketed together with his brother as "Bar and Char", more like a music-hall turn than the earnest, scholarly sons of a man of the cloth. At the age of eight, Char was packed off to his first boarding school, in Warwick. He went on to spend seven years as a pupil at Stamford where Latin and Greek had to be studied six mornings a week, with mathematics on four afternoons. Chemistry, French and geography were hardly taught and barely tolerated by a headmaster who insisted that the concentration on classics and mathematics should not be condemned "simply because they are of no actual use in counting house or office".

Char had his own room with a window and the freedom to sit round the fire in the school hall and to enjoy a daily cold bath. New boys at Stamford had to face one of those familiar, character-building initiation rituals beloved of the public school system. "Kissing the Old Man" required the victim to be hoisted up by two prefects to kiss a stone head over a doorway while being barracked, pinched and buffeted by the rest of the assembled school. Char came through the ordeal and went on to excel at mathematics as well as playing football and cricket. He followed Bar to St John's College, Cambridge, but he was not brilliant enough to gain an open exhibition and went instead as a sizar, a hard-up student who received free food and tuition and subsidised lodging. In return, sizarship scholars like Char might have to carry out menial college tasks, such as waiting on dinner tables. It led to the same uninspiring career route as his brother around the backwaters of England, drumming Euclid, algebra, trigonometry and arithmetic into the heads of young gentlemen. Returning happily to Friesthorpe for the holidays, Char would indulge in his two great passions of playing tennis and studying natural history. He instructed the younger children in bird-watching and butterfly-hunting, taking off on solo jaunts to inaccessible bird haunts and climbing perilous cliff faces to steal not only a closer look, but also an egg or two.

Edie describes him as shortish, thickset and formidable. His love of tennis made him a stickler for level lawns — "He was always at it, taking out sods and putting them in." Char was the practical one: the keenest gardener and an expert carpenter. He constructed a hexagonal summerhouse on the front lawn with bench seats all round and shutters that could be fixed open, but it was no substitute for the tree houses and hedgerow hideouts that bordered the rectory grounds. It struck Edie as unbearably pathetic that whenever Char was invited to a tennis party he would be down on his knees by the front door, rubbing the ageing tennis balls on the mat to try to restore some of their original, long-tarnished whiteness.

In May 1913, unmarried and thirty-five years old, Char returned to Stamford as mathematics master. An energetic young head, Canon J. D. Day, had arrived the previous January and set about building a new, dedicated staff. The school magazine reports the setting up of a Natural History and Photographic Society, with Mr Beechey as president. Thanks are expressed to Mr T. Sandell for "a gift of Australian insects and reptiles (dead)". Char was also playing cricket for the Masters XI and, like Bar before him at Dorchester, running the First XI at football. Summing up a lacklustre 1913–14 football season, he finished with a call to arms for the faint hearts in the team:

> Most of the bigger boys had left in July and had to be replenished with some very small and light forwards. In the first few matches these recruits hardly made their presence on the field felt at all, serenely waiting for the ball to come to them, and then giving it a gentle kick in the direction of the opponents' goal line . . . One more piece of advice — there is no disgrace in being knocked down, and very often a forward must either shoot and be charged over, or lose his opportunity of shooting at all.

At a school concert on Thursday 26 March 1914, a tone-deaf Char gave an unaccompanied recitation entitled "Perils of Invisibility". Within a few months, brothers and colleagues were accepting that their duty lay elsewhere. In the summer of 1914, three of Canon Day's four teaching staff at Stamford immediately abandoned their careers to enlist. However, Char was in no great hurry to swap black cap and gown for khaki. It would be a difficult time.

Leonard and Christopher William Reeve Beechey

The Rev. P. W. T. Beechey meticulously recorded the arrival of each new child, with date of birth, baptism and godparents, in a huge family bible. So many came along that the births would eventually spill on to the page headed "Deaths", bordered by images of angels and the resurrection. Leonard arrived in 1881 and Christopher in 1883.

As with Bar and Char, there was a neat symmetry about their lives from childhood through to making a living in the Victorian world. Both attended Christ's Hospital, the famous "Bluecoat School" founded in the City of London by Edward VI in 1552 for the education of poor children. When their parents unexpectedly visited them there one day, they found Chris sporting two magnificent black eyes. The perpetrator was recovering in the infirmary.

Len was the opposite of his ebullient brother, quiet and studious and seldom getting into scrapes. He was eight years old when he was admitted to Christ's in June 1890. For the next six years he wore the distinctive uniform, largely unchanged since Tudor times, of long blue coat fastened from neck to navel with shiny buttons and red leather belt that looked as if a sword or a dagger should be dangling from it. Underneath, they sported breeches, tucked into knee-length stockings. The puritan-style bands around their necks gave them the appearance of trainee monks.

Before either of his sons could be accepted into such an exclusive establishment, the Rev. Beechey had to lay his finances bare and prove to the Christ's Hospital governors that he was a man of sorely limited means. The records show his annual income at Friesthorpe dwindling from £294 and 12 shillings to a mere £136, 11 shillings and sixpence after deductions, including the burden of providing £70 per annum pension for the previous rector. It was noted that proceeds from tithe rents had slumped on average by £10 a year for the previous ten years and were expected to go on shrinking. Leonard and later Christopher passed the means test and met the school's paramount condition that a child's parents or guardians must be in need of assistance towards his or her education or maintenance.

Next came the medical hurdle. On his school presentation forms, Len was reported as being clear of child-killers such as diphtheria and scarlet fever. He had been vaccinated and had never had fits, been ruptured, suffered discharge from the ear or been prone to wetting himself. The only blot on this otherwise clean bill of health was a case of measles, which he had contracted in November 1885 at the age of four. He recovered fully, but Maud had caught it from him and died the following month.

The rector filled in presentation papers for Chris on 17 August 1895, but ten months would pass before another of his sons was allowed to wear that quaintly unique uniform. Chris had caught ringworm, an infectious fungal condition that attacks the scalp and makes the hair drop out. The school was not prepared to risk its bluecoat boys walking around with unsightly bald patches. Not until 29 June 1896 was a Dr Aldersmith of Upper Wimpole Street, Cavendish Square, able to confirm, "C. W. Beechey is now free from ringworm and can pass into the London school."

On leaving the school, Len had a year at Stamford, while Chris, just one month after his sixteenth birthday, entered the offices of Messrs D. J. Dunlop, Burmese Merchants of Bishopsgate in London. Their career tracks crossed when both began working for the Railway Clearing House, whose role in the great age of steam was to sort out the mess resulting from so many different rail organisations. With the rapidly expanding track, two or more competing companies would often overlap, creating the problem of who gets paid for what. The clearing house cut through the tangle. It was the final arbiter of fees, producing incredibly detailed diagrams of the network that showed company territories and track and plotted every milepost, point, junction, station and installation.

In the great halls at its offices in Euston, Len and Chris sat among more than 2,000 clerks, silently shuffling a daily mountain of ticket stubs and receipts, poring over ledgers and scratching columns of figures on to sheaves of light blue paper. The more senior staff were paid £140 a year and received a fortnight's annual holiday, plus Good Friday and Christmas Day. By working extra, unpaid hours beforehand, Chris and Len could also add Boxing Day and the Saturday after Good Friday to their leave, which made the 300-mile round trip back to Friesthorpe just about worthwhile.

Long hours and the fact that the clearing house was an all-male preserve until 1912 were not conducive to meeting the opposite sex, but it had its own sporting club and literary society, and a subsidised restaurant was opened to discourage clerks from going to the pub for their half-hour lunch break. Alcohol was only one antidote to the tedium. Another was pestering colleagues as they worked in monastic silence. A Mr Tyson had his fortnight's holiday revoked for lobbing an apple at another clerk, while a Mr Russell was found guilty of making peculiar noises, but the Beechey brothers were too conscientious for such behaviour. Chris let off steam instead by enlisting in a Territorial Army unit in West London. Two colleagues, Messrs Metcalf and Glover, were also part-time soldiers with the Third City of London Rifle Corps and liked to practise platoon drill in the office before work, until the morning one of their guns went off and winged the great clock that hung over the hushed hall of clerks. They got away with a 50-shilling fine and were ordered to pay compensation for the damage.

After the intricacies of the RCH, Len would laze in bed all day when he returned to Friesthorpe. Edie recalled his lovely smile and kind face and told of him dancing for her and the other little sisters on the stone floor in the vast rectory kitchen, ". . . all thin long arms and legs that seemed to go all ways at once."

Chris, however, grew tired of working as a railway clerk, and when he saw the colonies were offering assisted passages for people wanting to emigrate, he decided he would prefer a life on the land in Western

Australia. He left London and the Railway Clearing House behind and headed back to Lincolnshire to learn something about farming from the Olivants, family friends who lived at Snarford. He had long since earned the love and respect of his one-time attackers, Frank and Fanny. The younger girls all looked up to him as their tall, dark hero. When Winnie got stuck in a tree after trying to reach a magpie's nest, Chris, who was strolling out with a baker's daughter, heard her screams. He took off his coat and handed it to the young lady, whom he had brought from London to meet his mother, before clambering high into the branches and carrying his stricken sister to safety on his broad shoulders. Edie marvelled at his strength and chuckled at the absent-mindedness he inherited from his father. Carrying a great millstone out to the coach house, it was still on his back when he staggered back to the rectory for the hammer he had left behind.

In early February of 1910, Chris said his farewells and journeyed to Antwerp in Belgium to board the steamship *Gneisenau*, which docked at the port of Fremantle in Western Australia on 29 March. Chris was a world away from Friesthorpe and did not know when he would see his family or his home again.

Frank Collett Reeve Beechey

Another daughter came before Frank. Frances Mary Deverell Beechey — Fanny to everyone — had been born in February 1885, ten months before Maud died.

For a long time she was the only girl, until in 1893 the first of four sisters arrived, one after the other, over the course of five particularly fertile years at Friesthorpe. Back in 1886, however, the modest accommodation that went with the curate's position at Pinchbeck was sorely stretched with the arrival on 12 October of Frank, son number five. Some breathing space was achieved when Bar and Char were packed off for their first terms at boarding school.

Amy Beechey began to despair of her husband's prospects in a parish where the sitting vicar was part of a dynasty. The Rev. Canon West Wayet's father and grandfather had been incumbents at St Mary's Church, and a clergyman son was waiting in the wings to continue the family line that stretched back to 1792 (and ended only in 1923). Canon Wayet came from a well-to-do family and generously funded a new church with its own school and vicarage to the west of Pinchbeck, but Amy's husband remained a humble curate.

All of the Beechey boys were given their mother's maiden name as a Christian name. As well as Reeve, Frank also inherited Collett from his great-grandmother. Like Bar before him, Frank went to St John's, Leatherhead. During his seven years there the school gained a reputation for fever epidemics and noxious smells. Fee-paying numbers plummeted as doctors advised parents to avoid St John's and the better-off clientele sent their boys elsewhere. One parent hurriedly withdrew his son and asked for a refund because of the risks of catching something fatal.

Neighbouring residents of Leatherhead complained and the county surveyor was moved to write to the headmaster about the "bad smells around the school". Sons of the impoverished, such as Frank, simply had to hold their noses and remain grateful for a free education.

From St John's, he went on to De Aston School at Market Rasen, the nearest town to Friesthorpe. The Beechey boys regularly walked there and back to play hockey or take part in tennis tournaments. Frank was an all-round sportsman, excelling at football, cricket and tennis. He did not quite have the brains for Cambridge but matriculated in English, Latin, French, mathematics and higher mathematics at the University of London examinations of January 1907. Following his two oldest brothers into the teaching profession, Frank set out to improve the minds of what Char called the "little beasts" at various prep schools, beginning at Horsham, then Hornsea, back to De Aston and, finally, from 1912, at the Lincoln Cathedral Choir School.

Although only 5 feet 7 inches tall, he was a giant on the sports scene, captaining the famous old Lindum Cricket Club, keeping wicket for the county and at one time being rated best tennis player in Lincolnshire. His smiling generosity despite a permanent lack of personal funds endeared him to his young sisters, particularly Edie. When he had the money and the time to spare, he used to visit her while she was at Bank House School in Bakewell, Derbyshire. One of the greatest thrills of her young life was when Frank took her out to a posh hotel where they dined on baked trout. Afterwards, he hired a pony and trap and drove her through the grounds of Chatsworth.

Girls and motorcycles were Frank's undoing. He could never afford the first, and had trouble staying on the second. His passion for two wheels was in no way diminished when he fell off a hired motorbike on the way back from another trip to Bakewell. His problem was finding the funds on a schoolmaster's modest salary to indulge his love of the fast life. The only way Frank could pay for such extravagance was through visits to the pawnshop. His suitcase, his pocket watch and his gold-tipped stick all went.

When the girl he worshipped announced she was getting married to his best friend, Frank scraped together enough cash to attend the wedding by pawning another of his possessions. Within a week, he was writing to Edie to give her the news that he was engaged to someone else and had chucked in his job at the choir school. One month and one day later, Britain declared war on Germany. Overnight, prospects improved for an unemployed and betrothed Frank Collett Reeve Beechey.

Eric Reeve Beechey

Eric was son number six, and the last to be born before the move to Friesthorpe. He was educated at De Aston and at Katharine Lady Berkeley's School, where Barnard taught. Like his brothers, he would return to the rectory for the holidays and sit in the kitchen or housekeeper's room making ammunition for his air rifle over a roaring fire while his sisters stewed gooseberries. With so little money around, parish events were always being held to help supplement church funds. For one parish dance, Fanny persuaded Eric to dress up as a girl. He went along in frock and wig, padded out in all the right places, and was the belle of the ball, receiving iced buns and offers to dance in the muscular arms of unsuspecting farm boys all evening.

After schooling, Eric began a dental apprenticeship in Lincoln. Edie remembered how he would return home at weekends, shout "Hello, mater!" and throw sweets to the little ones before chasing them around the rectory. He was the first of the boys to marry and the first to have children. Around the same time as his father died, Eric married Mary Elvidge, the pretty daughter of a farmer from a neighbouring village and the only girl in a family also with eight sons. It was said that Mary could have had her pick of the Beechey brothers, who fell over themselves to please her. She and Eric were wed in 1912 and within a year they had their first child. They named her Amy after Eric's mother, but she did not survive into infancy. She was followed by a son, christened Thomas in honour of the Rev. P.W.T.

Harold Reeve Beechey

Harold was the first Beechey to be born at Friesthorpe. The rambling rectory with its surrounding wide-open acres was perfect for a youngster straight from the pages of *Boy's Own Paper* or a Mark Twain tale. He got into more scrapes than the rest of the boys put together. On his first day at De Aston boarding school, Harold fell in the baths and nearly drowned. He was ever after known as the Rat — as in drowned rat — to school chums. But for all his buccaneering spirit, Harold was a sensitive soul. He once shot a robin with Eric's airgun and then sobbed with remorse. His younger sisters learned that a hefty kick on the shins could usually reduce him to tears.

He hated it when the older ones left him behind to go off on bike rides, to chase after the hunt or to embark on pole-jumping expeditions over the dykes and channels that drained the low, wet Lincolnshire farmlands. Brothers and big sister Fanny would disappear for a week in summer on a cycling tour. The first time Harold was allowed to join them his little legs gave up a mile or two out of Friesthorpe on an unseasonably cold spring day and he was left shivering by the roadside while a message was relayed back to the rectory. A pony and trap had to be sent to fetch him and his mother coddled him back to life and scolded the others.

Born in 1891, it was two years before Harold spoke, but he always preferred action to words. With the eldest brothers away at school and the Rev. P.W.T. not the most useful person to have around in a domestic crisis, the cry would go up . . . "Harold! The water's coming in," or "Harold, the horses are in the garden again." Amy Beechey could depend on him to grab the tin baths and buckets when rain began pouring through the leaky roof or to round up their neighbour's great lumbering carthorses if they got into the kitchen garden and threatened the rector's precious vegetable patch or Char's immaculately rolled tennis lawn.

While everyone else took the staircase to bed, Harold shinned up a rope ladder to his room. He once chopped off the top of his thumb with an axe and walked in white-faced clutching the severed piece, which was bandaged to the stump and later stitched back together by a doctor. It was just as well that he wasn't listed among the winners at De Aston school sports during his days there in the early 1900s when triumphant pupils were handed fruit knives as prizes. There is a Christmas 1902 picture of the whole school in which the rather serious young face of Harold Beechey can be picked out among the ninety boys and a solitary little girl, sitting in white dress on the end of one of the rows. She was the daughter of the headmaster, a Mr Elliott, who might have been more circumspect regarding official photographs, considering he had sneaked her into the all-male school and was having her taught there without the blessing of the governors.

Harold passed the preliminary Cambridge local examination in 1905 and achieved some sporting recognition by turning out for the school cricket team and scoring 0, 0 and 1 in three innings. He went into apprenticeship with an engineering firm in Lincoln after leaving De Aston, but the taste for adventure made him decide to give it up and join his brother

Chris in Australia in 1913. The Olivants again obliged with some basic lessons in farming, but the dull, damp landscape of Lincolnshire — "the most brute, beastly and sodden shire in all my realm," according to King Henry VIII — would soon be remembered as a paradise compared to the cruel, parched environment of the Western Australian wheat belt. Harold would face one ordeal after another — all with the courage and dash of a true *Boy's Own* hero.

Samuel St Vincent Reeve Beechey

Called "Tom" by the father who fussed over him and was in his mid-sixties when he was born in 1899, sometimes known as "Vincent", other times as "Sam" or, rather obscurely, "Peter", the last born of the Beechey children had a name for every occasion. Four more daughters were sandwiched between Harold and the youngest Beechey child — Katherine, Margaret, Winifrede and Edie. But Sam/Tom/Vincent/Peter was his father's pet. It made him a confident, arrogant child, and when the venerable rector was looking the other way, his sisters took particular delight in knocking some of the "intolerable bounce" out of their spoilt little brother.

Fanny, in particular, stood no nonsense. She was detailed to keep the little ones in order, having first taken charge of domestic duties at the age of twelve when her mother was away convalescing. She organised everything from bedtime stories to picnics, where she would pack large currant buns for the youngest and make sure they were eaten to the last crumb before passing round the more mouth-watering treats in the basket. Fanny would bath the youngest children in a tub in the warm kitchen and then tell them fairytales in front of the fire as they ate baked potatoes covered in dripping. Then she would shoo them up the stairs to bed. Sam resented her authority, but he reserved the greatest enmity for brother Eric, the generous one who always came home laden with chocolate and sweets. Sam hatched a plan to put poisonous juice from the fruit of the snowberry bush in Eric's tea, but never carried it out.

The highlights of his Friesthorpe days were the holidays in Bridlington on the Yorkshire coast, when there was just him and Edie and their parents. Their mother was nearly fifty and their father almost seventy by then but between donkey rides and ice creams the years fell away and, for Sam at least, the bonds grew stronger. He appreciated his mother as a "great person", although she was never the most affectionate of parents. He recognised that his father, despite his age and occasional forgetfulness, possessed a remarkable brain — the older boys inherited their mathematical brilliance from him. The old man was also fair game for childish pranks. Sam and Edie would hide his glasses, baccy or stick so he thought he'd mislaid them, and only give them back when he offered tuppence to anyone finding them. When their father died, Sam was only twelve and Edie barely a teenager, but she later recalled: "I never had any real contact with him. I remember driving seven long, cold, bitter miles with him in a cab to a church where he had to preach. We never spoke a word. I can see him now — an old gentleman wrapped in so many cloaks that he had great difficulty in getting into the cab, and looked four times his normal size."

When the war came, Sam was still nine days short of his fifteenth birthday. He was a pupil at De Aston for most of those turbulent years but was impatient to swap his school uniform for an army one. He left for cadet training in February 1918 and had earned a temporary commission as an artillery officer by the middle of August. He sailed for France from Folkestone on 17 October. The war would be over in twenty-five days. He would have just over three weeks to survive before the killing finally stopped.

CHAPTER
TWO

A place of much water

By 1913, Chris Beechey had been in Australia for three years. He was used to the heat, the hard graft and such perils of the bush as redback spiders and poisonous snakes, which made even a trip to the dunny fraught. The wheat belt of the west was brutal and unforgiving pioneer country. Living rough, eating whatever you could shoot and slaving outdoors until the sun went down was a huge culture shock for a product of the English public school system who had spent his working life in collar and tie behind a desk.

Bagging kangaroo, emu and rabbits for the pot was not the only sport to be had. Baiting the Poms, who were often clueless in the harsh environment, was another local pastime. Hapless Englishmen became the stuff of legend. Take the newcomer who ran screaming from the dunny convinced he was dying after being bitten on his bare backside. Doctors were thin on the ground — so scarce that one medic had to remove his own grumbling appendix — and when one eventually arrived he scratched his head at what looked like beak marks rather than the punctures of a snake or spider bite. An inspection of the outhouse revealed the culprit to be a broody hen. Another tale concerned a Pom who had been warned to make sure he gave the waggon wheels a spin or two to check they were properly back on the cart after removing them for greasing. A neighbour found him five miles down the road with the heavily laden cart precariously jacked up. Asked if he was having trouble, he replied, "I just remembered I hadn't given the wheels a turn."

Harold, who packed in his engineering apprenticeship to join Chris in this wildest of wests, was grateful to have an older brother to put him right in the ways of "cockeying", as their kind of bush farming was known. Snakes of the human kind preyed on many unsuspecting amateurs who had severed family ties for ever and crossed the world with the promise of £4 10 shillings a week wages, only to find they were not paid even half that.

Chris was thirty in 1913 and more like a father figure to Harold, almost eight years his junior. In a state that was eighteen times the size of England and Wales, there was only a tiny fraction of the population. Gold-diggers, driven from even more hostile mining territories like Kalgoorlie and Yilgarn when the precious metal ran out, joined the trickle of British immigrants who settled in an expanding wheat belt stretching out for hundreds of miles with the city of Perth as its buckle.

The Beechey boys were living near the small town of Dowerin, named by Aborigines as "a place of much water", 102 miles north-east of Perth. The only thing it could claim to have in common with their Lincolnshire home was its isolation. But Chris could still find a game of tennis, a sport most of the Beechey brothers loved and played with varying degrees of skill. A makeshift court fashioned from flattened and rolled anthills was a magnet for the Englishmen on their Sundays off. The wife from one homestead where Chris had been clearing land and burning off stumps was so used to seeing him blackened and filthy that she didn't recognise him when he turned up washed and scrubbed wearing the immaculate tennis creams he carried around in his battered backpack.

The brothers could earn decent money labouring for the local farmers. They got plenty of work with Gus Hagboom, the son of a Finnish sailor who had jumped ship in Victoria and married a local girl. Augustus Hagboom senior had turned his back on seafaring and taken up farming. Gus junior was the eldest of his four children when, one wild night, gales brought a tree crashing down on their flimsy home. Augustus and his wife were killed. In 1904, the orphaned Gus headed west where land was cheap as long as a man wasn't scared to work himself into the ground trying to make it pay.

Chris, discontented with pen-pushing in the railway office at home, had been attracted to this life. He had visited the Western Australian state immigration office in London, which altogether gave assisted passages to more than 50,000 "mainly well chosen" individuals ready to face the challenges of the bush. He wasn't to know that with his health wrecked by the war, he would end up spending the rest of his working years cooped up in another railway office. But in 1913 there was much work for him and for Harold, with the prospect on the horizon of being able to afford their own farm and become their own masters. By the light of a candle in a bunkhouse for hired hands, he lay on his bed of straw and sent news from the other side of the world to his mother.

5 October 1913
Ucarty, Dowerin, Western Australia

I'm afraid this seasonable letter will be a week late for the Christmas mail but very many wishes for a merry Christmas and a happy and prosperous New Year to you all, including Mrs Eric Beechey. I'm here at Hagboom's again for the harvest and will be until next February, I suppose. Harold and I finished the axe work on a clearing contract of 61 acres here for Watson about a month ago and Harold is working at Watson's now for the harvest. He and I are buying out a farm with 160 acres cleared on it and a dam full of water and will be going on to it after we burn off Watson's job in March. I'll get about 60 or 65 acres in next year and fallow the rest and clear some more ready for fallow. I suppose Harold is writing you so you will get news from him. Give my best seasonable wishes to all friends at home.

Ever your loving, Kris

Huge expanses of the west were still mostly gum trees and thick scrub, but areas were gradually being cultivated and the exhausting axe work went on from dawn to dusk. Wildflowers flourished on the sand plain, native birds such as mopoke, bookok and mating wagtail flitted from tree to tree and the vast skies provided wonderful sunsets. Char would have marvelled at the natural wonders, but all that untamed beauty went unobserved amid the daily grind under a baking sun. Such glories hardly merited a line in letters home.

Watson was James Cecil Watson, a farmer who had arrived from Ballarat, Victoria, in 1905 and built himself a small shack on a plot off the old lake road at Nambling before moving to Ucarty to be closer to the railway, which reached Dowerin in 1906. The line would have arrived sooner but for the stubbornness of a local blacksmith whose forge blocked the way. When he refused all offers to relocate, the rail company was forced to make a detour round him. By the time the looping track was completed, the smithy had realised business would be better in town after all and decamped to Dowerin.

With the railway came expansion. Mrs Ayling opened the first bakehouse and Mrs Allen provided an almost genteel dining room, offering a pleasant alternative to bush staples like boiled mutton and kangaroo-tail soup. The Grace brothers founded the Dowerin Trading Company and George Allanson opened his Emporium, so that by the time Chris arrived the long trek to Perth to stock up on essentials for the farm and for mere survival was a thing of the past. Everything, from a case of "dog" — the name given to tins of corned beef by the gold-miners of old — to tools and rifles, could now be purchased locally. The railway also allowed greater contact with the outside world. Newspapers were a day old instead of a week old. The mail came up by train from Perth to be sorted in Mrs Stacey's post office and popped into individual pigeonholes for collection the next time a settler was in town.

An influx of families as well as solo farmers meant a schoolhouse was needed. Lessons were held in the Agricultural Hall until it was flattened by a cyclone one day while the pupils were at lunch. Children who came in by horse and cart from miles around were then accommodated in the premises of Mr Angel, the reassuringly named undertaker. But the teacher, Miss Avery, one of the few eligible women around in Chris's time, was forced to write to the Board of Education complaining of a corpse being left so long in the adjoining room that it was "quite enough to give fever to all in school. All the children complain of feeling sick."

Despite the gradual arrival of civilising influences, it was still another planet compared to Lincoln or London. Chris told the folks at home how he and Harold had to work like "threshing machines". It was no exaggeration — but labourers like them could earn more over a year than the farmer who employed them. The one thing young Sam Beechey later recalled about his older brother who went off to Australia was his superhuman strength. Chris needed every ounce of it. Clearing the land took toll on every muscle and sinew.

Today, you can stand on a red dirt road in the wheat belt with the hot, dry wind blasting you like a blowtorch and see hardly a tree for miles around. There are corners where the bush is still wild and tangled and there is the occasional clump or copse to break the monotony, but when Chris and Harold were paid £1 or 25 shillings per acre for clearance work much of the country was still untamed. It was money hard earned — it might take all day to clear an area they could barely spit over.

Home for anyone buying virgin land was usually a tent, or else they slept under their waggon. As they began to get a foothold in the country they built a "humpy", a more permanent residence made from the trees felled when clearance work got under way. Tough gimlet posts at each corner and walls made of saplings and manure bags with sheets of corrugated iron perched on top kept out the elements and the flies. A stone fireplace provided warmth on chill winter evenings.

As the hired hands, Chris and Harold were provided with some kind of roof over their heads. For bedclothes, they had a wogga, a kind of quilt made out of four corn sacks. They lived and learned the hard ways of the bush — ring barking to kill off the salmon gum and gimlet trees that defied the sharpest axe, putting the "burn" through areas of felled timber and mallee, digging dams and wells for precious water supplies, fencing off the cleared areas and handling majestic teams of heavyweight Clydesdale horses for ploughing, seeding and harvesting.

So, in 1913, the Australian Beechey brothers were making a fist of it. They had a clear if daunting future mapped out ahead of them, even if the inhospitable spot where they had chosen to settle would be hard to find on any map. Ucarty was honoured with a name but the few dirt tracks and scattered shacks did not amount to anything that was recognisable as a place. The 160 acres Chris wrote home about was a homestead block, half a mile square, the traditional size of an initial plot taken up by farmers. They would need 400 to 600 acres just to become self-sufficient, before they could even think of making a living.

The gruelling existence bred a comradeship among the scattered settlers — a "mateship" the Australians called it — which helped overcome every privation. It would also see them through the desperate times to come at Gallipoli, when the terrors of a redback in the toilet would be remembered as a minor inconvenience compared to a Turk armed with a powerful German Mauser rifle.

The Commercial Hotel had opened in Dowerin in 1909 and its public bar was *the* place to meet on the one day of the week when the settlers put down their axes. The rest of the time, socialising depended on whether they still had the strength left after work to walk miles to their nearest neighbour's for a yarn or a sing-song. But the boys were usually too wasted even to eat supper.

The one big event that brought everybody together was the "burn", the clearing fire put through a patch of ground before it was ready to be ploughed. It was carried out in late autumn when the air was cooler and the grasses still dry before winter rains arrived. Chris spoke of it in letters home, but in the damp, flat Lincolnshire farmlands it must have seemed a strange concept. Settlers came from all around to lend a hand. Branches of wattle and "strawberry-jam" tree were set alight and the sweet smell of strawberries wafted across the burning landscape as the felled salmon gum and gimlet trees were gradually engulfed. If the wind was strong enough the stumps burned right down to the ground, saving much hard labour later.

As for world events, they mostly passed Dowerin by, so the occasional newspaper from home was particularly welcomed. Chris, with memories of fist-fights from his school days, saw that a charismatic French teenager called Georges Carpentier had knocked out British challenger Bombardier Billy Wells to win the heavyweight boxing championship of Europe. In the same month of June 1913, suffragette Emily Davison threw herself in front of the King's horse Anmer at the Derby and died in hospital four days later. The failed and ultimately fatal heroics of Scott of the Antarctic made Chris proud to be British, the same pride that would burn fiercely until his dying day. In a few months, when the call came from across the ocean, the Beechey boys would be ready to abandon everything they had slaved for. But for the time being, in the scorching midsummer heat of Christmas 1913 in Western Australia, they were engaged in an altogether different fight for survival.

CHAPTER
THREE

Oh, by the way, did I ever tell you that I was married?

Christopher to his mother:

> 1 April 1914
> Ucarty via Dowerin, W.A.

I'm afraid you've been thinking us both very thoughtless in not having written to you in answer to your many letters, the last one wishing Harold a happy birthday. We both of us wish you the same for yours. We are camped together on our own land next to Watson's where Harold was working during the harvest. We paid the owner £25 for it and there was another £26 due for back rent and interest to the Agricultural Bank. We have been burning up about 60 acres of Watson's that we felled and scrubbed last August and September (winter months). We've just about finished — only the holes to fill in and anthills to knock down, two or three days' work and then I'm going back to

Hagboom's to work off 60 acres of crop that he is going to put in for us. Harold is going to stop on our own place until harvest when he is under contract to go bag sewing — a penny a bag and his tucker, if we can manage to find tucker for him till then. We've also taken up 1,800 acres about four or five miles east of here just inside the rabbit-proof fence, pretty well all good land but a rather bad track, two or three miles of sandy road, but that's only until the roads board gets a bit stronger.

We've also bought a spring cart capable of carrying a ton, cheap for £8, and Harold has to have a new suit and is going down to stay a week in Perth with some friends and we also have to buy a good few things like roofing iron and Harold will have to build a bit of a home and bush stable with scrub roof. We had 60 acres of scrub and mallee (small gums) rolled just before Christmas and we put the fire through one hot Sunday afternoon (about 105 in the shade) and had a clean burn of about 40 acres — only want the anthills knocking down to make it fit for putting in the crop.

So you see if we get anything like a decent season we ought to be stronger this time next year and be able to stay on our own place and not have to go out to work. We shall apply for a loan to clear 100 acres on the other place about midwinter when there's plenty of water about and after Christmas apply for a loan to get a team of five or six horses. The Agr. Bank allow £150 stock loan when a man has 300 acres of land cleared and I think I could pick five good light to medium draught horses round here for that. Horses that I know have been driven (I've driven a few since I've been out here, from a one- to an eight-horse team).

To my brothers and sisters, love and greetings. Duly received last three weeks a London Sunday paper for which thank Len and say I'm cogitating a letter to him and one on Nat. History to Char. Love from us both, Chris (for Harold)

Even now, ninety years on, the land that Chris and Harold bought is still known locally as the Beechey Block. It is skirted by one of the few bitumen roads in the area and there is a line of gum trees offering a welcome hint of shade. The parched, wide-open expanses look like desert, with the smaller trees just husks and clumps of dead wood littering the roadside ditches. A horseshoe-shaped mound 100 yards into the fields is a dam. They are dotted everywhere. Now, as in Chris and Harold's time, they are built on the gentle slopes to catch and conserve enough of the winter rains to keep a farmer going through the dry months from late spring until early autumn. Unless they had a well or a spring, the brothers would have had to cart their drinking water from miles away in a 250-gallon drum and then heave the precious commodity off the waggon without spilling any.

Bag-sewing, the job Harold was signed up for when he had built them somewhere to live on their own plot, was grim work that numbed hands and mind. The 180-pound bags were made of jute and when full to bursting had to be tied to keep grain in and mice out. Threading stitches through the rough, heavy jute left the bag-sewer's hands raw and painful. By the end of the day, Harold could hardly pick up the piece of rough home-made bread or "damper" that accompanied just about every meal in the bush. Once all the bags were sewn up they were loaded on to carts for the journey to town where they were heaved aboard freight waggons by "lumpers", who had to be as strong as oxen with the balance of a ballerina to negotiate the narrow gangplank to the rail truck.

The summer of 1913–14 brought a decent enough harvest for established settlers like Watson and Hagboom. There was plenty of sewing needed and no shortage of other work for Chris and Harold between clearing their own land and putting a rough roof over their heads. Harold had even found a girl in Perth, no mean feat when the ratio of men to women was around eleven to one. However, his opportunities for courting were restricted by distance and the workload at Ucarty. And by the time they had their own crop planted, the wheat belt would be in the grip of drought, and yields would shrink from a healthy eleven bushels an acre to less than three.

The winter rains on which everything depended never came in 1914. The dams remained empty. When the sun went down, the brothers sat in the glow of a campfire and recalled with a smile how lack of rain was never much of a problem back home in Lincolnshire where cowslips, cuckoo pint, orchids and rushes thrived in the saturated earth. They remembered sailing boats in the puddles left behind by overflowing drainage channels and feverishly damming up the ditch that ran down one side of the front field at Friesthorpe. How they must have longed for rain as they looked at the canopy of stars in a clear Australian sky.

In England, while war clouds were massing over Europe, Frank Beechey wrote of the pressing reasons why he would not be able to make it to Bank House School in Bakewell to see sister Edie, whom he fondly called "Slave". None of the reasons concerned the imminent threat from Germany. His last jaunt to Bakewell had been by motorcycle. Frank parted company with the machine on the way back to Lincoln, where he was a master at the Cathedral Choir School, otherwise known by its ancient name of Burghersh Chantry. The accident might have contributed to his unspectacular sporting achievements so far that summer. But the main problem was he was broke and had run out of things to take to the pawnshop. Edie, looking forward to another visit from her dearest brother, would have to be disappointed, but Frank let her down gently in teasing, tongue-in-cheek manner.

End of June 1914
Burghersh Chantry, Lincoln

Slave

You are indeed an artful little hussy. Your Latin is shaky so you deliberately wait till the 14th of the month to write to me, as the Ides are the only Latin date you know. As for your request [for

Frank to visit her], I fear me 'tis imposs. For many reasons, which I will enumerate in order, beginning with the least important. (1) Tuesday is a full working day and exams being only four weeks hence it is rather difficult to get off. (2) A motor-bike is one of the few things that men habitually refuse to lend (you can't even hire one under about £2 a day). (3) I am broke to the wide wide world — my watch is being repaired (!!) till the end of the term, my bag is in the same state and I have nothing else of any value so that I have no choice.

I should love to come for several reasons. Firstly because the direct route from here to Bakewell takes one through the finest scenery in England almost, and at the prettiest time of the year. Secondly, because I want to have another go on a motorbike to prove to the world that I can stick on, and thirdly because I should like to see Bank House and its weird inmates.

But life is full of disappointments as I say to myself when old potatoes come in day after day here instead of the new ones for which my soul is languishing. As for young Thomas [baby son of brother Eric and his wife, Mary], he grows and that is all — he smiles and says "goo" if one tickles his cheek after a successful meal. After that he sleeps and after that cries out for more food, gets it and smiles again and so on in a circle. He does not yet know his commandments in Hebrew perfectly, but we mustn't expect too much yet. As for cricket, I am dead off at batting this year — a 29, 27 and about 10 scores of under 12 — but my wicket keeping has been much better than last year. My tennis shows lack of practice, though the googliness of my "google" serve is increasing. My candidates for the Locals [school examinations], Clarke and Haslam, are very backward but should just scrape through.

PS Madge is going to be married on July 25th to R. G. Ash and I am probably going to the wedding at Horsham — if I can borrow a top hat and the needful bullion. Wedding at 1. Reception 2. Cricket afterwards at the school — dine with kings and sleep at school — return Sunday night. I am playing for "old boys" at De Aston on July 1st so must raise 2/6 somehow — even if I have to rob a bank or slay a little baby for the coral on its neck, or forge a little cheque.

Madge was the girl who had once melted Frank Beechey's heart. Now she was marrying his close friend Dickie Ash. Frank was twenty-seven years old and his personal life was as parlous as his personal finances. On 28 June, Archduke Franz Ferdinand of Austria had been assassinated in Sarajevo, lighting a fuse that burned for another five tense weeks before exploding into all-out war. But Frank was only fussed about finding a penny for a stamp to go on his next letter to Edie, which carried unexpected and sensational news about himself and intriguing gossip about brother Len.

I write now, not because it is my custom to write to you once a week, but because I have some more or less interesting news to tell you. First then I must give you formal notice that your duties as slave will no longer be required after about 3rd or 4th of September. So I advise you to send in your application for another post immediately. Of course, I will give you a good testimonial and answer any questions on your behalf. You will naturally ask what you have done to merit this sudden dismissal, but it is the way I have said for some time that I should either get a motor-bike or get married this year — and as I can't afford to get a motor I must get married. So I have engaged myself to a girl in Lincoln — one Doris Robson, whom I think you will like — and have chucked my present job and am looking out for a non-resident post at a minimum salary of £100 p.a. If I get this I am going to take the bull by the horns and time by the forelock and have a small wedding at the beginning of September, take a cottage some 3¾ miles from the school to which I may be appointed, furnish on the hire-system and live there a staid and serious married man.

I shall keep a hen (not two, because the girl doesn't like eggs), a bee, a rabbit, a cat, a dog and a pig, also an elephant or two perhaps. We shall plan to live on 30/- a week, so as to give us a chance really to exist on £2 a week. Bread and butter on weekdays and jam on Sundays — and meat on pay-day. It will be a charming little cottage with roses all over the front (all the year of course) with insects falling off down your neck, a nice little bit of garden — not too big because I shall have to dig it. At present we will only furnish three rooms — kitchen room! and 1 bedroom — so that you can't come and stay as yet awhile, unless you bring a folding bed and washstand in your pocket. I reckon that we can furnish three rooms on about £20. Of course I haven't got it (in fact I shall have to borrow a penny from Mrs Coombes to post this letter) but I can get father Robson (I think) to pay the first instalment and be my guarantor for the monthly payments. They are, so they say, very badly off for ready money, but he is a partner in a fairly good printing firm in Lincoln, and she is the only child — so there may be something to come to her when her parents peg out. I can't say that I know much about house-keeping on 30/- a week, but I daresay I shall learn. She is a goodish cook (for which many thanks), a very fine needle-woman and I think a good manager — slightly extravagant in dress, but she will have to make most of her clothes in future — I shan't be able to buy her many. I am afraid I shall have to give up my bachelor habits — dances, tennis (tournaments anyway), cricket, footie etc., smoking cigarettes, beer, motor-bike rides — and take up instead the married man's virtues — getting up early to light the fire, shopping for bread etc. Well, I won't write any more till things are more settled. Write to me and say what you think of the prospect, and when you get home try to like my Doris and make her feel to some extent one of the family. It is rather an ordeal for a girl to become one of the huge Beechey tribe.

Apart from this have you heard that you have a new sister? Len, apparently, has been married some time. If Mother doesn't tell you — don't let on that you know. He said in a postscript to his last letter — "Oh, by the way, did I ever tell you that I was married?" They have no children but have been spliced some time — perhaps three years. Does all this news startle you a bit, old sport? You see that our already fairly large family is rapidly growing — when all 13 are in double harness with large families what a tribe we shall be! Write as soon as you can.

Ever thine, F.R.B. — PS I can't quite imagine myself married.

Frank's sister-in-law Mary, Eric's wife, remembered in later years how his prospects always seemed so promising but never materialised, and how his career was being upset by "that awful girl called Doris, who managed to get herself engaged to him". When the relationship finished, as suddenly as it started, Edie admitted, "We were all so glad."

And Len, despite the bombshell he dropped in his letter to Frank, was not married. However, "Len's Annie" was duly introduced to the rest of the family as the new Mrs Leonard Reeve Beechey, complete with wedding ring. If Frank's information had been reliable, his secretive older brother would have been wed long before the war, and there was no reason for anyone to suspect otherwise when Len finally brought Annie home to meet his mother. Edie remembered her as kind and delightful, and Amy was just pleased to see her quietest son rescued from loneliness. Mary once stayed with Len and Annie for a week at their London flat and was struck by how close and how happy they were. One evening, she was with Annie at the window as Len strolled up the street on his way home from the office. Spying the two women, he stopped, raised his bowler hat with a flourish and out dropped a red rose he had bought to give to Annie, the love of his life. She laughed with joy until the tears ran down her face.

Five years older than Len, "Annie" was in fact a widow, Mrs Frances Smith. In each other they found love and companionship, and were content to live together while putting on a show for Len's family, who would never discover the harmless deception. Amy welcomed Annie into her home like a new daughter, and was happy to accept that her son had simply been anxious to pay off his debts and set himself straight before revealing his "bride" to the family. The coming war would eventually force Len and Annie to marry, but that wouldn't be for another year or more.

The third of August 1914, the day before war was declared, was a Bank Holiday Monday in Britain. In Lincoln, trains chugged off to the coast from early morning packed with day-trippers. Many locals preferred to stroll the walks and parks of the city between the scattered showers, which soon scurried away, leaving a perfect afternoon for the annual cricket match between the Lindum club and the Rest of Lincoln. F. C. R. Beechey batted low down the order and was bowled Buttery for five as Lindum fell more than 33 runs short of the Rest's modest total of 112 before a huge crowd. Kirke White's restaurant did a roaring trade in afternoon teas and sticky buns. The Pearls of Music packed them in at the Palace Theatre that evening. A world war was twenty-four hours away, but nothing was allowed to disturb the holiday mood.

On Wednesday 5 August, the *Lincolnshire Echo* reported, "His Majesty's government declared to the German government that a state of war exists between Great Britain and Germany from 11p.m. on August 4." More shocking to many was a report that a schoolboy named George McNeill had been killed in an accident with a cow while riding his cycle. But the war would soon capture the imagination, with men rushing to join up and an outbreak of panic buying that emptied the shops of meat, sugar and other essentials. Amy Beechey, with her limited means, would no doubt have agreed with the expert authority who declared: "It is the very people who can best afford to keep calm who are spreading the panic. They have lost their heads and are giving the poor people no chance." The Mayor of Lincoln appealed for calm, for the public to refrain from hoarding food and for shopkeepers to avoid profiteering.

First news of casualties came with the sinking of HMS *Amphion*, a British cruiser, which struck a mine in the North Sea and went down with the loss of 131 lives. Plans were announced to turn Lincoln Grammar School into a military hospital and Harrison Photographer advertised free sittings for anyone wearing the King's uniform. Reports that a prominent member of Lincoln Constitutional Club had been expelled for drinking a toast to the Kaiser were dismissed as "an abominable falsehood". The suitably sentimental play *The Old Folk at Home* began a run at the Theatre Royal, while the Palace determinedly went for escapism with *Abomah*, the African ragtime giantess, standing 8 feet tall and weighing 24 stone, with Francis Alfred "and his assistant in science and drollery" as supporting act.

Within days, euphoric young men crammed recruiting offices the length and breadth of the land fearing the war might all be over by Christmas. Frank's engagement undoubtedly was over. Free of Doris Robson and out of work, he immediately announced his intention to join up. On 11 August Kitchener made his famous "Your King and Country Need You" appeal. On 12 August, Frank was at the recruiting office. Two days later he was in the town of Beverley applying for a temporary commission with the East Yorkshire Regiment. Having already had soldiering experience with the Territorial Army, which he had left just the previous March, he was confident he would be accepted as an officer. A colonel in the East Yorks endorsed his application and a doctor passed him fit for service.

Eight days later a corporal in the Royal Irish Dragoon Guards fired Britain's first shot of the war in Europe near the Belgian town of Mons. The following day the highly trained but numerically challenged British Expeditionary Force took part in its first battle and was soon in headlong retreat from Mons. As it fought for its existence, Frank despaired of ever getting a commission. Days and then weeks dragged by without word from Beverley depot, so he lowered his sights and, on 14 September 1914, enlisted as a private in the Lincolnshire Regiment. The attestation papers he had filled in more than a month earlier at Beverley were messily amended until they resembled the corrected essay of one of his errant Choir School pupils.

On the other side of the world the pioneer life was turning sour as the drought continued. Work had dried up like the dusty, cracked landscape, where crops were shrivelling and dying. Things were so desperate in the wheat belt that Harold had to rely on the charity of his girlfriend's mother. Stores were refusing credit and in the remotest areas people were reduced to a diet of boiled wheat stalks. Lives as well as the livelihoods of 75,000 settlers were in the balance. For Harold, at least, the war offered an escape from this ruinous state of affairs.

On the first day of recruiting Down Under, more than 4,000 West Australians signed up for what they called the Great Adventure. The new Australian Imperial Force (AIF) could afford to be selective and a fifth of the hopefuls were marched straight back out for having rotten teeth, crooked toes or some other physical deficiency. Bad teeth were a particular problem. The finest figures of Australian manhood hardly dare open their mouths for fear of rejection and an ignominious return to the communities that had waved them off as heroes when they left to enlist. Special dental centres, dubbed Chambers of Horrors, were later set up so that rather than being turned away, strapping lads could have their offending teeth fixed.

Chris Beechey, aged thirty-one years and two months, 5 feet 11 inches tall, weighing 160 pounds with a 38-inch chest and two small scars on his forehead, was passed A1 and accepted into the 11th Battalion. "These first recruits of 1914 would be remembered as great big fellows who came down from the bush at first bugle call — men said to be capable of killing a running kangaroo at 300 metres and who could ride anything on hooves," was how one historian described them. Meanwhile, Harold was kicking his heels in Perth and desperately hoping the war would last when he sent word to his mother.

14 August 1914
220 Lake Street, Perth, Western Australia
I am very sorry I have not written before. I have no excuse to offer. Things are in a terrible state here — no hope of any harvest at all anywhere in the state. No work at all. Kris is in camp ready to leave any time and I am now in Perth waiting till they leave when I shall go into camp with the second lot. I have passed the medical exam last Wednesday.

I am staying with my friends — it is awfully good of them to put me up as I am absolutely broke. Mrs Bailey has lent me clean underlinen, handkerchiefs etc. as I had only one shirt to my back.

I only hope the war will last long enough for me to get away so I can get a few quid. They pay 35/- a week while we are in camp here and 42/- directly they embark. If we come to England I shall be able to come and see you.

Will write again soon, Harold

Mrs Bailey — she was Mrs Boyce before her first husband died and she remarried — delighted in mothering the polite young Englishman who was far from home and verging on the destitute with the backside almost out of his trousers. The Bailey household in Lake Street was where Chris and Harold lodged whenever they were in Perth. The family had arrived from England in 1908 with two sons and two daughters, the eldest of whom was three years younger than Harold and took an instant shine to him. Diana Boyce or Bailey — Chris was never quite sure what to call her in his letters home — was pretty with straight black hair. This being Australia, everyone called her Curly. Harold was chuffed to call her his girl.

Disasters, both natural and of man's own making, had combined to wipe out any progress the brothers were starting to make, building their own homestead, sowing their first crop, planting roots that might have survived for generations had the war not called them. In the Dowerin district alone, 176 men left the land to take up arms. Almost a third of them never came back. They swapped one desperate struggle for another that, for once, could not be blamed on any spiteful twist of nature. Gus Hagboom stuck it out on the land, found himself a nineteen-year-old bride and, when conditions improved, employed other labourers to replace the ones who had felt honour-bound to join a fight thousands of miles away. His grandsons still farm in the district today. Dowerin felt the loss of so many good men, but remained mostly untouched by war, although the arrival by rail of a government shipment of wire stamped "Made in Germany" later provoked understandable outrage in the town.

Chris's attestation papers give 10 September as the day he joined up. In fact, he was in uniform and, with his experience as a territorial back in England, had been made acting sergeant before August was out. The 11th Battalion set up camp on the slopes of a rounded hump in the foothills of the Darling Range, sixteen miles from Perth. Recruitment for the AIF had commenced on 10 August and the government promised it would be armed, kitted out and ready to sail by 21 September, six short weeks away. Chris wrote to his mother, certain that he would be seeing her again in the not too distant future.

29 August 1914
No. 1 Section, G Coy, 11th Battalion
Australian Imperial Expeditionary Force
Military Camp, Bellevue, Western Australia
No doubt the news I could write to you would be

59

stale regarding the war. I for my part think it may be the war of the world so often prophesied. I never dreamt of it on or about July 27th or 28th when the old pensioner cooking at Hagboom's said that Austria had declared war against Serbia and that Germany was preparing to assist Austria, and France, Russia and England preparing to oppose them. I sent my name in to the military commandant for W.A. volunteering in any capacity for the first contingent. I walked out to Harold at our camp to tell him and of a reported British victory in the North Sea. He was away up at South Ucarty and so as I was busy I left it until Sunday. He heard it the first Friday in August and on the first Sunday in August came over to Hagboom's in the afternoon saying he was going. We talked it over and he said he would wait for a bit to hear from me as I had training and he had not.

For once in my life I saw duty clearly in front of me and could not do otherwise. I waited for five days and then saw in the paper that they were enrolling in five or six centres personally so followed my letter to Perth. They had my name down from my letter all right but had spelt it wrong. I had to wait for two days for the doctor's inspection. I was as sound as a bell and two or three inches every way over the required measurements. There were 4,444 volunteers for 1,370 men in the contingent so they made the doctor's certificate pretty severe, turning men down for flat feet, bad teeth, varicose veins etc. We have been training here in camp since Monday week (today is Saturday August 29th) and will be here for a fortnight yet I expect, but whether we shall sail with the South Australian, Victorian, New South Welsh or Queensland contingent yet or on our own is not known. Today's paper says that all colonial troops are to make one army corps of 100,000 men but that may be a rumour. I don't think Kitchener would let them take part until they've had proper training. Even our destination firstly is unknown but my opinion is one of the training grounds in England and then through France to the front. So I may have a chance to see you all before my baptism of fire. It's no use answering this letter, but write to Harold. I want him there until harvest anyway. Then if the war is thick and results dubious he will probably follow. I have obtained a postponement of rents, interests and conditions from the minister of lands until I return or get killed but could not get it for the Grazing Lease Harold and I took up as he will be there. All loan money from the Agricultural Bank is suspended but then we may have a moratorium so that creditors cannot close on us in time of war.

They made me section commander and acting sergeant straight away and I've been drilling my section of 30 men ever since, working like a threshing machine. They asked me to join the Field Hospital but I thought that if any squarehead German pots at me I'll pot back at him and I'm a fair shot with a service rifle. I don't think there is any chance of my not being made sergeant anyway. We sail round the Cape of Good Hope, I believe, so will be in Europe probably the end of October. Love to yourself, all my brothers and sisters and tell the boys to meet me on the firing line and as Paul of Tarsus said, "Quit you like men; be strong".

Ever your loving son, Chris W. R. Beechey

Chris's five years with the West London Rifles and his time in the bush, where a dingo scalp was worth a 20-shilling government bounty, had made him a crack shot. 21 September came and went and the 11th Battalion sat stewing in their camp near Perth while a cat and mouse game was being played in the Pacific. Two daring German sea raiders, the *Scharnhorst* and the *Gneisenau*, were picking off ships with alarming ease and could have played havoc with any troop convoy. In the meantime, eager recruits from all over Australia and New Zealand were kept bottled up in their home states until the coast was clear.

Harold was keen to be with his brother in arms, if only to earn some money and not have to worry where his next pair of pants was coming from. The farm was a hopeless cause in the continuing drought and so, with Chris's blessing, he enlisted on 9 September. The vital statistics on his attestation papers are given as height 5 feet 8¾ inches, weight 148 pounds, green eyes, dark hair and a scar on his left front thigh. He was twenty-three years old. Harold was thoughtful enough to go into a photographer's studio and have his picture taken in his smart new uniform. He posed informally, perched on the edge of a table looking self-consciously proud and not a little dashing. The distinct Australian slouched hat is at a slight angle, pinned up on one side by the AIF badge of the rising sun and with the strap clinging on just below his bottom lip. Polished brown boots, immaculately wound puttees and stylish Norfolk jacket with four big pockets made up an ensemble that would before long be caked in Melbourne mud and, in time, reduced to feeble rags at Gallipoli. One photo would be for Curly to keep while he was away. The other was for his mother.

Harold had enlisted in the 16th Battalion of the AIF and he and his brother were together in camp at Blackboy Hill, which Chris refers to as Bellevue. It was between the local landmarks of Bellevue and the old Swan View Tunnel and comprised a couple of lots of the Blackboy Hill Estate, owned by a Mr Woods but commandeered by the Commonwealth government as a training camp. They named it after the Blackboy trees that grew there. The men lived in bell tents and slept on bags of straw. A rainless August and September meant great clouds of dust were whipped up by the wind. It got into everything: in the tents, in the men's eyes and nostrils and in their food, turning the daily dinner of mutton into a mud stew. Bread and jam were the other staples but a few little extras could be bought at the tuck shops that sprang up around the camp as private enterprise swooped on a captive market.

Life was tough and monotonous — a long, fast march or physical jerks before breakfast followed by squad drill, rifle exercises, signalling, gun drill and trench digging, all to be repeated in the afternoon. Occasionally, they took to the hills for mock fights or headed for the Helena Vale sports ground to practise embarkation and disembarkation, using the grandstand as a pretend troopship. Shirkers and weaklings were quickly found out by the gruelling routine and unceremoniously sent packing. On one particular day, the 16th Battalion was lined up to witness a dozen or so shamed comrades stripped of their uniforms and summarily dismissed for going AWOL with the first month's pay. For recreation, there were occasional concerts and field sports for the troops and the camp was thrown open to visitors on Sundays. Friends, relatives and sweethearts arrived with their picnic baskets and hampers by rail from Perth and the wheat belt settlements to spend a few hours with menfolk who might be packed off to a war on the other side of the world at any moment. Finding a quiet, secluded spot under the shade of an old gum tree was a challenge for Harold and Curly, but, just like Friesthorpe, Blackboy Hill had its secret hideaways.

Chris to his mother:

24 September 1914
No. 1 Section, G Coy, 11th Battalion
Australian Imperial Expeditionary Force
Military Camp, Bellevue, W.A.

We have been in camp here nearly six weeks and rumours are still about as to when we sail. The latest rumour is October 2nd and I think there is some foundation for it as we are only waiting to complete our transport. I threw up my stripes [went back to being a private]. The captain is too rough-tongued and too hard a curser and he blames and curses every NCO when things go wrong, whether we're wrong or no, and as I'm too well disciplined to answer back and too thin skinned to take it lying down, I let them go. Crops are practically a failure — all through the wheat belt only four inches of rain since Christmas round where we were. So I got an exemption from rents, residence and conditions on the 500 acres we bought and made it over to Harold. I sent for Harold three weeks ago and he is now in camp in the 16th Battalion of the 2nd WA Expeditionary Force. I have claimed him as a younger brother according to the King's Army regulations during active service to my own company and regiment so we shall be together. We've been out on a bivouac yesterday and today. I unfortunately cannot give you a permanent address but we will wire it to you as soon as we can. I hope sincerely all things are well with you and my younger brothers and sisters and that you have not any hardships to bear.

Ever your loving son, Chris

PS We get the daily paper here 15 miles from Perth and have just heard of the loss of three English cruisers. Some of the yarns and reports of the doings of the English Tommies are stirring enough and equal to the best traditions of the

English army and, please God, we bushmen from WA will do our best and hold our own with all of them — C.W.R.B.

After the sinking of the *Scharnhorst* and the *Gneisenau* by the Royal Navy off South America, troop carriers from all around Australia and New Zealand steamed for the little port of Albany, Western Australia, where the force was massing in one of the world's great natural harbours. The 11th Battalion was given a last spell of leave and then a heroes' farewell as they embarked from Fremantle to join the convoy. But Chris was not with them. He had injured his back in camp, and by the time he recovered another fit man had filled his fighting boots. Instead, he joined the Australian Army Medical Corps (AAMC), becoming a stretcher-bearer with the 4th Field Ambulance.

Over the period of the war around 32,000 men trained at Blackboy Hill. Ten of them were awarded the Victoria Cross. The most famous member of the AIF to pass through there was another stretcher-bearer, John Simpson Kirkpatrick, who won immortality rather than any medal, though the lack of official recognition for his bravery remains a contentious issue to this day. A teenager from South Shields on Tyneside, he arrived in Australia as a stoker aboard a merchant ship — at about the same time as Chris was taking his first steps ashore — before bedding down in the Immigrants Home at Fremantle. Today, outside Canberra's Australian War Memorial, a sombre, magnificent

Antipodean Taj Mahal, stands a sculpture of the character most identified with the Anzac legend — Simpson, the Man with the Donkey.

After the landing at Gallipoli, he was one sight guaranteed to gladden and stir a soldier's heart, plucking wounded from the firing line day and night and hoisting them on to the back of a donkey he'd commandeered from an Indian artillery unit. He would lead Murphy and its pitiful cargo down through snipers and shrapnel to a clearing hospital on the beach. The young man who had joined up only in the hope of achieving a free passage back to England lived a charmed life for a little over three weeks before being killed by a Turkish machine-gun bullet that hit him in the back and exited through his stomach. "If ever there was a man deserve the Victoria Cross it was Simpson," proclaimed Australia's official war historian, C. E. W. Bean. Simpson's name was put forward for the highest gallantry medal and turned down.

Like so many of the veterans who came through Gallipoli, Chris saw sights he never spoke of in later life, even to those dearest to him. To this day, close family, unaware of the letters to his mother, would be astonished to have heard him say, "If any squarehead German pots at me I'll pot back at him." They were convinced he had become a medic on high moral principles, that he felt it was his duty to go but not to fight and kill. Bertha perpetuated the myth after his death, but it is clear that Chris would gladly have exchanged his field dressings and water bottle — the stretcher-bearer's only weapons — for an army service rifle.

In the end, delays surrounding the departure of the 11th Battalion and Chris's subsequent injury and transfer to the field ambulance almost certainly saved his life. After living and training with them over those grimy, uncomfortable months at Blackboy Hill, he watched his mates heading off to war with a sense of disappointment and frustration. Six months on they would suffer appallingly as one of the first battalions to land on a hostile shore. For now, Chris and Harold had little news for their mother as they sat in camp together awaiting their fate.

11 November 1914
4th Field Ambulance
AAMC
Military Camp Bellevue, W.A.

I've transferred as you see by the heading. I was in the first contingent 49 days and strained myself heavy lifting and was attending Perth General Hospital for five days and when I came back my place was filled and so I joined the AMC attached to the 2nd contingent of which A Coy, 16th Battalion, the one Harold is in, is part. I joined the AAMC so as to continue my nursing drill and am attending nursing daily at Fremantle Public Hospital. Rumours flying around as to our date of sailing but they'll tell us nothing. I'll try to get into Harold's regiment very likely before marching to the front but am not particular. Harold is sitting opposite so I'll hand the letter over to him.

Dear love to you and all at home, Chris

[Harold writes:] Having a pretty good time and getting into good trim; the weather is a bit too warm for comfort. There is going to be a patriotic concert next Wednesday, which we are going to, I think. I have really very little to say except that I expect we shall get home some day, but no idea when — hope everybody in the pink.

Love to all, Harold

By November 1914, the war raging far across the seas had degenerated into a stalemate that would last for most of the next four years with opposing trench lines snaking from the Swiss border to the English Channel. The Australians were expecting soon to be part of it. But another twenty months would pass before they experienced the miseries of the Western Front. Two unrelated factors found the first contingent of the AIF pitched up in a city of tents in the shadow of the pyramids instead of in Europe. First, Britain had declared war on Turkey in November, and then an Australian medical officer had successfully argued that it would be criminal folly to pluck thousands of men from the heat of a southern hemisphere summer and, after a long and stifling voyage through the tropics, dump them under canvas on bleak Salisbury Plain at the start of an English winter.

On 21 November the men of the 16th Battalion crowded aboard a troop train bound for Fremantle docks, 12 miles south-west of Perth. A few days earlier they had been given final leave to dispose of any personal effects and settle their private affairs — a chilling reminder that they might never return. It was Harold's last chance to see Curly. She promised to wait for him. As anxious weeks turned to months and then years, she would remain true to her word.

Harold's outfit steamed out of Fremantle on the SS *Indarra* and docked at Melbourne a week later after a rough crossing. The 16th joined up with the rest of the 4th Brigade at Broadmeadows camp, where the swirling dust was every bit as bad as Blackboy Hill, until torrential rain turned the ground into a bog. At first there was nowhere to wash but eleven showers were eventually provided for a brigade of 4,000 men. Even then it was a mile's slog to the nearest shower and a man would return dirtier than when he had set off.

Training was cranked up to include day and night battle manoeuvres, digging trench systems, communications in the field and more intense musketry coaching, with regular lectures by officers and NCOs about what was expected of the men. But they were still mostly clueless about where they were going and whom they would be fighting. Brigade sports were held on one of the few fine days and the 16th finished runners-up. They came first and second in the "VC race" where a competitor had to run 50 yards to a wounded comrade and carry him back to the starting point. It was a game that would be played out for real and without victory ribbons in the months to come at places of infamy such as Bloody Angle, Quinn's Post and The Nek.

70

On 17 December the whole brigade turned out in full fighting order to march through the streets of Melbourne where the Governor General, Sir Ronald Munro Ferguson, took the salute from the steps of the Federal Parliament. Afterwards he applauded the fine physique and soldier-like bearing of the troops. Five days later they were on the march again, sloshing through pouring rain to Port Melbourne for the next stage of their journey into battle. The 16th Battalion war diary records, "Weather for two days preceding embarkation very bad, continuous rain fell. Camp at Broadmeadows was in a very bad state, mud several inches deep. All ranks embarked thoroughly wet and with symptoms of a great prevalence of influenza . . . the health of the battalion suffered severely during the time at Broadmeadows."

Caked in mud and weighed down with full kit, Harold slithered along with the rest of his pals in A Company until the bedraggled troops lined up at Port Melbourne's Railway Pier to board the magnificent 18,500-ton White Star liner *Ceramic*, which would be their home for the next six weeks as they sailed for Egypt. Each man was given a special sea kitbag — big enough to hold a pound of sugar — in which to keep all essentials for the voyage after packs and rifles were stowed. They were also issued with blankets, hammocks and eating utensils. Sleeping quarters were improvised below deck and until the patriotic concerts got into full swing the chief source of entertainment was sabotaging a neighbour's hammock so he was sent crashing to the ground when he tried to clamber into it.

Chris was still in a bell tent at Blackboy Hill when he wrote home in early December — huts were not provided until the following winter after a recruit froze to death while he slept and all but one of the tents were flattened by a gale.

> C Section, 4th Field Ambulance
> AAMC, Military Camp, Bellevue, W.A.

My dear mother

You must think that I have been an unkind and undutiful son in not having written for so long. But you know quite well it has not been thro' any want of affection on my part. I have been meaning to write many a time but things seem so unsettled. We worked pretty hard; all sorts of rumours about our embarkation; but now I don't think it will be until the last week in December or first in January.

Harold went over to Broadmeadows camp near Melbourne about a month ago and I have not heard from him since. All the 2nd contingent are training there now, including the A and B Sections of our Field Ambulance. So are the transports and battleships I believe and they are supposed to pick us up. Harold is a fine, healthy, upstanding lad and keen on his work and I'm hard as nails and nearly impervious to all diseases so we both have a high resisting power against germs and should not fear any illness during the campaign. Even if disease does catch us we ought to recover and become fit for service again quickly. You have probably seen long before this reaches you that the first

Australian contingent landed and are training in Egypt and the second contingent will probably join them and all form part of Kitchener's army in the spring.

I see that those German barbarians lost to all sense of Christianity, Humanity or Civilisation are breaking the Geneva Convention wholesale and that the list of wounded among doctors and RAMC men is very heavy considering what a small unit they are, so rumour says that all hospitals will probably go straight to France.

Words can't express the hatred I feel for such a nation as the Germans have proved themselves to be, and, pray God, though the war be long or short they will be so severely crippled as to make such treachery, brutality and arrogance impossible for hundreds of years and that England will be the nation to do it. But the hardships of those left will be appalling.

Love to all at home. Ever your loving son, Kris

On the Western Front, enemies who had spent the summer and autumn months killing and maiming each other famously marked a frosty Christmas Day 1914 by playing football matches and swapping cigarettes and souvenirs in No Man's Land. Harold, one of 3,000 troops aboard the *Ceramic*, was feeling like a pincushion after lining up for inoculation but he suffered no ill effects and was able to enjoy Christmas dinner of pork followed by plum pudding.

As the rest of the 4th Brigade sailed across the Great Australian Bight and eventually weighed anchor off Albany, C Section of the 4th Field Ambulance finally left Blackboy Hill behind for the last time and steamed out of Fremantle on the troop transport *Ajana* to join the fleet. There were 343 men on board and 268 animals belonging to a contingent of the Light Horse, distinguished by the emu feathers they wore in their slouched hats.

The convoy of eighteen ships crept from the shelter of Albany on 30 December with the Australian Navy submarine *AE2* as a lone escort. From the *Ceramic* to the *Ajana*, men lingered long on deck quietly thinking of home and loved ones as they watched Australia slowly vanish off the horizon. Many would never see their chosen country or land of their birth again.

CHAPTER
FOUR

Trust we may all come safely out of this

A momentous new year began with a burial at sea. "Unto Almighty God we commend the soul of our brother departed, and we commit his body to the deep," intoned an Australian padre. Troops crowded the deck rails to honour the first of their comrades to die, struck down by pneumonia. Less than two days out of Albany the whole fleet halted for the 15-minute service. There would be few such opportunities to give a mate a decent send-off. As the wrapped corpse was swallowed by the darkness of the Indian Ocean, a bugler sounded "The Last Post", his sombre notes echoing off the lines of silent ships before turbines resumed their steady rumble and screws turned once more.

The war was five months old. Mons, Le Cateau, the Marne, the Aisne and first Ypres had already ripped the guts out of the British Expeditionary Force. In terms of arrows on maps, this small, highly skilled army had played a vital role in delaying and holding the enemy juggernaut. But a third of the BEF's seasoned soldiers and reservists — men called back to the colours from civilian life — had been killed by the beginning of 1915 and many more would never be fit to fight again. The elite 7th Division, so quick and deadly with a rifle that the Germans thought they were facing machine guns as wave after wave of enemy attackers were mown down near Ypres, was reduced from more than 12,000 officers and men to 2,500 in one month. Eager, patriotic recruits from Lincoln to Dowerin need not have worried about the war being over by Christmas.

Amy Beechey now had five sons in uniform, but the Beechey boys had yet to fire a shot in anger. It was Eric's good fortune that the Royal Army Medical Corps was desperately short of dentists. Not one had gone to France with the BEF in August 1914 but 800 were serving with the British forces by the end of the war. Eric had been trained as a technician rather than a dentist but he was needed in the front line of the battle to fix teeth shattered by army biscuits. (It was rumoured that warehouses full of biscuits as hard as shrapnel had been left over from the Boer War.)

In 1915 Eric was posted to the Mediterranean island of Malta with the dental section of the RAMC, and while he was there Mary gave birth to their daughter Joan. Eric's mother, concerned how Mary would cope, despatched daughter Katie to live with her sister-in-law.

After giving up on a commission and enlisting as a private, Frank was posted to the 7th Battalion of the Lincolnshire Regiment. They were part of Lord Kitchener's new volunteer army, which usually had to make do with broom handles for guns and, if they were lucky, postmen's cast-offs for uniforms until proper equipment could be provided. The day before Frank joined up, the authorities raised the height limit from 5 feet 3 inches to 5 feet 6 inches to try to thin out the numbers besieging recruiting offices the length and breadth of the land. The required height soon reverted to 5 feet 3 inches and shrank to 5 feet 1 inch when the pressing need for more troops led to the formation of so-called bantam battalions, made up of men big in heart but small in stature. Frank was elevated to corporal on 11 November 1914, but it would be another eighteen months before he got the front-line posting he so desired.

Bar, at 37, somehow got round the age restrictions and just met the height requirement — with less than an inch to spare — in the early days before the staggering numbers of dead demanded that restrictions be eased. Photos of the football First XI at Dorchester School for the 1911–12 season show several boys towering over their unsmiling master with the bristling moustache and greying, centrally parted hair. But his chances of making officer had been blighted when war was still just a distant rumour. An announcement in the *London Gazette* of 30 June 1914 — two days after Franz Ferdinand's assassination in the Balkans — had stripped him of his moribund commission with the Officers Training Corps at Dorchester Grammar. Just a month before hostilities broke out, the military were still pursuing him for the debt he owed for his OTC uniform. Only later did they decide, "It is no use prosecuting this claim now unless we get in the police, which is inadvisable . . . the £13, 6 shillings and 8 pence must be written off as a claim abandoned." But it remained a stain on his record. Like Frank, Bar enlisted as a private and was posted to the 9th (Service) Battalion of the Lincolns, another New Army unit, who were being turned into soldiers at Whittington Heath camp near Lichfield in Staffordshire.

Of all the Beechey brothers, only Chris and Harold were fated to serve side by side in the front line. In the Indian Ocean, the fleet carrying Australians and New Zealanders steamed on towards Egypt, although those on board remained frustratingly ignorant of where they were going. At the end of the second week in January they were anchored off the island of Sri Lanka, then known as Ceylon, just inside the breakwater at the port of Colombo. After being cooped up for a fortnight, there was widespread irritation at not being allowed off the ships. Many sat and wrote letters to catch the mail boats heading back to Australia, but a few dozen daredevils slid down ropes over the side of the steamers and bribed local people to row them ashore. Despite reports of men rushing around the streets drunk, hatless and coatless and singing songs at the tops of their voices, all those who went AWOL had returned to face the music by the time the fleet sailed on two days later. None the less, no leave was granted at Aden, the next port of call, though Harold went ashore with a firing party for the funeral of the 16th Battalion's first fatality, a Private Robinson who was another pneumonia case. Dealing over the side of the ships with local people selling fresh fruit and cotton vests at a shilling each provided a welcome diversion for those left on board.

When the fleet steamed onward, Egypt loomed as the likeliest destination and there were now daily distractions to relieve the monotony. The *Ceramic* almost collided with a New Zealand troopship, the first mail arrived from home to lift morale and there were new wonders to behold — the thrill of entering the Suez Canal and of seeing an aeroplane for the first time. Gurkhas who were dug in along the canal to defend it from Turks gave the newcomers a rousing cheer. Harold, wary of censors, gave little away in a letter written before they docked in Alexandria.

> 200 HR Beechey
> A Coy, 16th Battalion
> 2nd Australian Imperial Expeditionary Force
>
> I have been very remiss in writing. I got your last letter in Melbourne. We went there to join the rest of the brigade at a big camp some 10 miles from the town, stopping there three weeks and then coming on here. I have had very good luck in the health line and seen a little bit more of the world. I am only drawing 1/- a day, letting the rest accumulate in my name at the bank, payable in London if I ever have the luck to reach England. I can't let you know what we are doing or going to do — I don't know myself except we are told we are going to finish our training here and then go on to the front, but where the front is I couldn't

say and the censor forbids us to say anything of our proceedings and military life.

[On the same letter, he included a brief note to Char]
Very sorry I have not written before — hope to see you before we go on to the front and have an idea we shall get home for a spell. Just finishing a long sea voyage. Hope you have not forgotten the semaphore as I have become fairly proficient in it and am put down as a reserve signaller.
　　Good luck, Harold

Frances, Katie, Daisy, Winnie, Edie, Sam — good luck from loving bro Harold

Alexandria was the first time most of the men had touched dry land in six weeks. One soldier, who could not wait for his ship to dock, shinned down a rope and, to the hoots of watching mates, sprinted for town pursued by military police. Others had to wait for days while the great transports were emptied of human and animal cargo. After disembarking, men were put on to rail waggons for a 100-mile journey to Cairo that took seven hours. They marched the final few miles to a base that had been prepared for them on the fringe of the desert at Heliopolis. By 6 February, the 16th Battalion and the 4th Field Ambulance were settling in with the rest of the 4th Brigade and Harold and Chris found themselves camped within a couple of hundred yards of each other. A homely touch was added to the scorching sands when the troops fashioned a large map of Australia from stones and shells. Above it fluttered a Red Cross flag and the Union Jack.

The soldier's life in Egypt was a punishing round of route marches across strength-sapping desert sands and rampant, sometimes riotous, recreational pursuits. There were an estimated 35,000 prostitutes working in Cairo and, as one historian points out, "It certainly was asking a great deal to expect angelic behaviour from thousands of adventurous young men, half a world away from their families, with little opportunity for polite female company, and spending what was for many the last months of their lives on exhausting military training." There are no black marks on Chris's or Harold's army records to suggest they sought out the pleasures that landed many a young comrade in hospital with a sexually transmitted disease and his pay stopped. After a hard day's graft, Chris and Harold preferred to practise their signalling, or "flag-wagging" as it was referred to by some less conscientious members of the AIF. They also set off in search of wondrous sights, such as the Grand Palace Hotel at Heliopolis and the pyramids. Built at a then staggering cost of £3 million, the palace with its 1,300 rooms and magnificent ballroom was meant to be a casino but became the sultan's residence after it was refused a gaming licence. It was now the swishest of military hospitals.

There were other civilised corners that appealed to the more refined tastes of the Beechey brothers. At the American Mission they could sip coffee, write letters and postcards home and read out-of-date English newspapers, with just occasional interruptions from missionaries warning against the temptations to be found elsewhere. No such hazards awaited them at Café Saulte, where they could nibble pastries and sip tea from elegant gold and china cups while a small orchestra played softly in the background.

Harold and Chris took a taxi to Mena, the huge Australian encampment sprawling across the desert at the foot of the pyramids. There, they marvelled at the sights of antiquity, including the Sphinx, which would later lend its name to one of Gallipoli's rocky landmarks. They also caught up with Chris's old pals from the 11th Battalion. There were plenty of hard-luck stories of comrades facing repatriation and disgrace after catching a sexually transmitted disease.

Leave days and free evenings were spent exploring other famous sights — donkey rides to Memphis, Nile river trips, excursions to the Apis Mausoleum. Even hours of marching across the desert sands could offer enlightenment. Chris and the stretcher-bearers of the 4th Field Ambulance trudged four miles to the native village of Matarich and drank from the Virgin's Well, where Joseph, Mary and the baby Jesus supposedly stopped for water on the flight from Jerusalem. Alongside was the petrified tree where the holy family had sheltered almost 2,000 years ago. It was long dead and had been wedged upright between rocks.

Special passes were required to visit Cairo, just a few minutes' tram ride from the sophistication of Heliopolis. Harold ventured there to look for a gift to

82

send back to Curly. Unused to the sights and smells, he was shocked and repelled. Urchins selling the local paper loudly proclaimed its superiority over all others with cries of "*Egyptian Mail*! English paper no fucking good!" or "*Daily Telegraph*! The colonel is a German!" Silk and vases were the most popular gifts for sending home, with vendors starting off by demanding fabulous amounts before settling for a few piastres. Every shop and street-corner stall sold liquor that could leave a man blind as well as drunk. Just a day or two before Chris and Harold's arrival in Egypt, authorities had sent 130 of the worst disciplinary cases and diseased men home. The history of the 16th claims, "nothing happened in Cairo that would give the battalion a bad name, something for which all ranks were to be congratulated for there was no control of drink traffic." This proud boast must have been sorely tested by the infamous "Battle of the Wazza" that was soon to come, in which, the battalion historian concedes, "men from every Australian and NZ regiment were probably involved". Harold gave his mother a glimpse of what Cairo was like when he wrote home in February 1915.

A Coy, 16th Battalion, Australian Imperial Force
Heliopolis Camp, Cairo, Egypt
I am camped — Chris as well — in Heliopolis, a suburb of Cairo and superior in every way to Cairo itself, being quite modern. Most of it consists of some very fine buildings which have been erected during the last five to six years, built on the edge of the desert. A huge hotel, put up as

a rival affair to Monte Carlo, second largest in the world I believe, and beautifully designed, failed to get the government sanction for the scheme and is now being used by our troops for a hospital. There can't be another like it.

Our camp is just on the desert and all our work is done over the sand. I shall not be sorry when we leave as the dust and heat combined are somewhat trying on the long marches. I think we shall not be long before we see some fighting now as we are in as good nick as we shall ever be.

I have seen the pyramids and climbed to the top of the big one, done my devoir to the Sphinx and its temple, squinted into excavations, been told sumptuous lies by guides and turned deaf ears to cries of "baksheesh", eaten countless oranges, and encountered diverse stinks in my wanderings through Cairo. It's a city of filth in every way and I hope the British government will take a few drastic measures and introduce a few common laws of hygiene into the town. In fact I am dead sick of the place and hope to soon get out. We are only now waiting till the time is right to hop into the firing line as our training is complete. We shall see no fighting in Egypt. I can see when we came through the Canal that the Turks have no chance as the defences were elaborate and very strong.

Harold was correct in his prediction that they would not be staying to fight in Egypt. Britain had been at war with Turkey since November 1914. The Royal Navy was attempting to force a passage through the Dardanelles, whose craggy shores bristled with gun emplacements while shoals of mines lurked in the depths. The aim was to drive a stiletto into Turkey's heart at Constantinople, compelling the country to capitulate and opening up a supply lifeline for Russia from the Black Sea to the Mediterranean. But after the navy began losing ships and scurried for safety, it was decided to make an amphibious landing on the Gallipoli peninsula. The British would storm ashore at the southern extremity of Cape Helles, with the Australians and New Zealanders landing on the western shore in the region of a promontory called Gaba Tepe. Conquest of Gallipoli would allow the navy a clear run through to Constantinople. Secrecy was paramount, so it was an ominous sign when news of the Allies' Constantinople Expeditionary Force hit the newspapers.

The AIF, still training hard and playing hard, remained oblivious to the grand scheme of things. More practical concerns were troubling the boys from the colonies. They were desperately short of kit and Harold was again forced to rely on handouts for his undergarments. This time it was brother Chris coming to the rescue, rather than Curly's mum. Egypt had also given the colonials their first taste of British army food — mostly unappetising bully beef and biscuits. What was good enough for the British Tommy was not enough to satisfy big Aussie and Kiwi appetites. The ravenous legions kicked up a stink and were granted sixpence-a-day allowance to supplement the meagre fare, but they had to spend it in the Lipton's canteens that served the military. As one of Chris's 4th Field Ambulance colleagues admitted, "He pleased himself what he gave us — the general opinion was that someone was making a fat thing out of this war." But at least the Australians were earning six times more than Britain paid its would-be heroes — six shillings a day compared to the solitary shilling a Tommy received.

Chris found himself drafted in to help out in the cookhouse between training exercises and nursing instruction. As the day of action neared, preparations intensified. Training went on through sandstorms and locust plagues of biblical proportions. Divisional manoeuvres brought 12,000 men together in early March to practise defending Cairo against a pretend force of 30,000 Turks. In toughening-up exercises a day or two later, the 16th Battalion filed out of camp at 9.30a.m., returning at 4p.m. They sat down for supper before being ordered back on to their feet for an all-night march with periodic halts to entrench in the bitter cold under a clear Egyptian sky. The following day was spent in mock fighting, and the most wearying 48 hours of their young lives ended with another 10-mile, sweat-drenched slog back to camp.

General Sir Ian Hamilton, head of the by now more subtly named Mediterranean Expeditionary Force and a veteran of the 1881 battle of Majuba Hill and other minor Victorian conflicts as well as the Boer War, paid the men a visit and pronounced himself pleased with what he saw. He had been put in charge of the Gallipoli invasion just two weeks earlier and would have less than four more weeks to plan the operation. Chris still had no inkling of what was to come when he wrote to his mother.

12 March 1915
No. 1368, C Section, 4th Field Ambulance
4th Australian Infantry Brigade
On active service

We're here camped on the sand near Heliopolis. The Pyramids are about 11 miles the other side of Cairo and there are over 20,000 Australian troops there. I went over to see them last Sunday week. We're practically working like threshing machines in the cookhouse — two of us, the Corporal Cook and myself, cooking for about 100. We only have about 3lbs of wood per man per day and it's wet, green acacia and won't burn.

Harold is about 200 yards away, just the other side of a hard made road through the sand. I see him frequently. We can both signal now and practise in the afternoon if all's going well. We have a much better chance in our Field Ambulance of getting kit, especially flannel underclothing, and I've just refitted him with underclothing before we move off again which I believe won't be long now.

We may not get or be able to send mail for about three months after we leave here so accept my assurance of my dear love and respects and hopes for the well being of all at home with you.

Trust we may all come safely out of this after
Victory is with us.

The air crackled with excitement and expectancy in the
camps of Egypt. On the morning of 2 April, Good
Friday, Chris and Harold found themselves on
opposing sides when the 4th Field Ambulance played a
rousing game of football against the 16th Battalion at
Heliopolis Sporting Club, the medics winning 3–2.
That evening the tension that had been building up in
the powder keg that was Cairo finally exploded in the
Battle of the Wazza, named after the city's most
notorious red-light district. Drinking dens and brothels
were ransacked and set ablaze by drunken troops taking
revenge on behalf of mates locked up in isolation
compounds after catching STDs. Egyptian fire waggons
came clanging through the narrow, crowded lanes only
to have their hoses chopped into pieces by the rioters.
Beds, exotic garments and a grand piano were hurled
from windows of eight-storey blocks into the streets
below where the soldiers fought running battles with
military police.

All leave to Cairo was immediately stopped. But the
time for revelry was over anyway. Men were ordered to
have their hair cut short for action. At the 4th Field
Ambulance camp, anyone resisting the chop was
frog-marched into the tent of the transport sergeant
who ran a clipper across the centre of their head leaving
a kind of reverse Mohican, which then had to be shaved
off completely. Emergency rations were issued,
comprising tinned beef, biscuits, tea and sugar, which

would sustain a man for 48 hours on the battlefield. Preparations halted for an afternoon when a man from Chris's unit, yet another to be struck down by pneumonia, was laid to rest with comrades and a firing party from the 16th in attendance. Afterwards, the victim's belongings were auctioned off to raise money to send home to his family.

The order went out that men would only be allowed 20 pounds of personal effects, so bulging kitbags, weighing twice that, had to be emptied of all souvenirs and extra little luxuries, although some contraband could be salted away in rolled-up blankets and greatcoats. The camp cobbler was in demand to repair boots worn thin by the constant marching. A few lucky ones were issued with a new pair.

Finally, on 11 April, they struck camp and were herded on to troop trains for Alexandria, where a convoy of more than 120 transport ships was waiting to ferry an army to war. The 4th Field Ambulance boarded the *Californian*, the cargo steamer that had failed to respond to the distress flares of the sinking *Titanic* exactly three years earlier. Chris, who was among 500 troops and a similar number of horses packed on to a vessel with accommodation for seventy men, had to bed down on the floor in the horse stalls.

Harold's battalion were to sail on the *Haida Pascha*, a captured German ship so lacking in basic amenities that the men had to camp out on the quay until the following day while toilets and cookhouses were installed. Christened the "iron ship" because of its iron decks, iron rule and iron rations, the old tub crawled with cockroaches and rats. A day out to sea the men lined up to be paid. There was nothing to spend it on.

In twos and threes, the sluggish, overcrowded, uncomfortable transports edged through the Aegean until they reached Mudros harbour off the island of Lemnos, main staging post for the coming assault on Gallipoli. Men gawped in awe at the fine fighting ships gathered there — the *Queen Elizabeth* with her great guns, HMS *Agamemnon* with her battered funnel hanging over the side and her bridge badly damaged from trying to force the Dardanelles on 18 March. The *Agamemnon*'s crew gave the Australians a cheer as the *Haida Pascha* steamed past.

While men practised sliding down ropes over the sides of the ships into smaller craft, the fleet continued to grow. Over the next few days the number of vessels anchored off Lemnos swelled to more than 200. Those longed-for letters from home arrived almost on a daily basis and there was a sense of impending drama and tragedy in messages sent by return. Harold dashed off a postcard to his sister Margaret, which is undated but the Gallipoli landing would have been only a matter of days away.

On Active Service

This is the citadel at Cairo, a very fine building of alabaster. I cannot tell you where I am writing this from but it may be some time before I am able to write again. Tell mother to write to me and put On Active Service besides my Coy, Etc.

Harold

A censor's thick black crayon obliterated some of the few lines Harold then scribbled to his mother, but allowed him to explain that he had fixed his account in her favour.

Harold, Amy's most adventurous of sons, her hero from stormy nights battling floods at leaky Friesthorpe Rectory, was about to face the greatest test of all. All she could do was pray for her sons in Australian uniform and trust that Chris continued to watch out for his younger brother.

CHAPTER
FIVE

Tell all the women and girls to send their men

As the sun rose over Gallipoli on Sunday morning, 25 April 1915, havoc and horror were painted a glorious shade of gold. The first whitewashed communiqué was issued by the War Office and Admiralty two days later, stating, "The disembarkation of the army, covered by the fleet, began before sunrise at various points on the Gallipoli Peninsula and in spite of serious opposition from the enemy in strong entrenchments, protected by barbed wire, was completely successful."

Turkish sources contradicted bombastic British accounts and spoke of hurling the invaders back into the sea and capturing many of them. By 1 May, newspapers from Lincoln to Perth were reporting how Australian and New Zealand troops on the lower slopes of Sari Bair to the north of Gaba Tepe had "pushed on with the ultimate boldness" and "been engaged almost constantly with the enemy who made strong and repeated counter-attacks, which were invariably repulsed . . . casualties have necessarily been heavy". Then Amy received dramatic word from Chris.

92

7 May 1915
Gallipoli

I am down here in a gully near the sea resting after having had about three days and two nights continuous work under shrapnel fire and fire from snipers along the track from our first dressing station to where we bring the wounded — a distance of about two miles, a very rough stone track. We had to carry the stretchers during the night over the last 48 hours on account of snipers during the day inside our own lines.

I suppose you will know more about our fortnight's fight than we do. We know very little. The Australian troops behaved with great gallantry, charging hills of rough sandy country covered with scrub and no roads. Looking at it after the first landing it seems incredible. I've hardly seen a flinch among any of our men and some of 'em just lads and I've been right up to most of the Australian trenches. Harold was safe and sound up to last night. Most of the men in our field ambulance know him by sight now and bring me word. His company were given possession of a hill very dangerous to hold and with snipers to their left rear, losing 23 out of 50 in his platoon before they were relieved on the fifth day, but no one shifted unless killed or carried down wounded. I found their position on the third day and made it my field of work until they were relieved. I then specialised another hill where the casualties were heaviest.

It seems to me nothing but divine providence that neither of us are hit, men being hit all around us and we stretcher-bearers not being able to take cover like the infantry.

One doctor and two of us were sewing up an officer's bowels when they hit the man holding the needles. Things are quieter now. Our section is out for 24 hours. I'm off duty resting for the 24 hours on account of falling on some rocks on my knee with a heavy patient but will be able to go next time all right.

About the wounds, some of them are terrible. One soon gets callous — lots of men with part of their brain knocked out we leave to go quietly though they may breathe for several hours. I think their snipers are using explosive bullets or turning the broad end of the bullet to the front, making it turn broadside on when travelling through the body, otherwise I can't account for the huge gaping wounds. I'm pretty good at dressing and stopping heavy bleeding.

Let me have news of you all and any friends who are fighting — after we'd been here a week and seen what it means it seems inconceivable to me that men can stay out of it.

PS Harold is a clever and gallant soldier and a credit to our name.

The brothers had been spared the dawn chaos of 25 April when the first British, French, Australian and New Zealanders stormed ashore. The 16th Battalion remained aboard the *Haida Pascha*, anchored out of range of guns blazing away at the invasion force from the Turkish forts. Sunday church parade went on as normal accompanied by the distant rumble of battle. If Harold and his company were hoping for inspiration from their chaplain, it was patently lacking in a sermon beginning, "Well, boys, I know you are going into action today and some of you will never see another sunrise." But they could take heart from the stirring words of General Hamilton, whose special order declared, "The whole world will be watching our progress; let us prove ourselves worthy of the great feat of arms entrusted to us."

Harold's A Company would lead the 16th Battalion attack. Weeks of clambering down the Helena Vale grandstand and the sides of the transports in Mudros harbour were finally put into practice as the destroyer *Ribble* inched alongside the *Haida Pascha* to take the men in closer. From the *Ribble*, they transferred to lifeboats for the latest leg of a journey that had begun at Blackboy Hill almost eight months earlier — fifty raw, untried troops in each open craft edging towards a hostile shore amid a devil's symphony of bursting shrapnel and flying bullets. A Lance Corporal Mackenzie was running around one of the boats with his bayonet making out he was bayoneting Turks.

A few yards from the beach they splashed overboard to find the chill Mediterranean up to their waists and the seabed carpeted with the bodies of Western Australians of the 11th Battalion, cut down in the first wave before dawn. Weighed down with backpacks and with rifles hoisted above their heads, they reached the beach with just half a dozen casualties. One of Harold's comrades recalled only a single shot troubling his party, while those leaping from another bobbing lifeboat were astonished to hear an immaculately turned-out English artillery officer telling the last soldier off to hand him his hatbox.

Ellis Silas, a 16th Battalion signaller, later recounted his experiences from the last moments aboard the *Haida Pascha* to the first steps into the unknown . . . "The Assembly is sounded — there is a large cheer as we gather together in the hold [of the ship]. Here for the last time in this world many of us stand shoulder to shoulder. We are descending on to the destroyer *Ribble*, which is alongside us. Noise of the guns is frightful. Colour of the sea beautiful. We are packed very tightly on the destroyer. Getting nearer to the shore, Turks pelting us like anything. We are transferring into the boats — it is raining lead. Every burst of flame, every spurt of water means death and worse. It was a relief to get ashore. In jumping ashore I fell over, my kit was so heavy. I couldn't get up without help; fortunately the water was shallow at this point. These chaps don't seem to know what fear means — in Cairo I was ashamed of them, now I am proud to be one of them. The beach is littered with wounded. It is commencing to get dark — we are now climbing the heights."

Unpredictable currents and questionable navigation had swept the Australians and New Zealanders more than a mile off course and dumped them on a sliver of sand a few hundred yards in length, backed by towering cliffs. Harold stumbled over the dead, dying and wounded begging for water on the beach and reached the shelter of the steep walls of sandstone. He ditched his kit and was ready to start climbing, though this was not going to be like scaling the great ash tree at Friesthorpe. Shots and lumps of shrapnel whistled past as men scrambled through gullies and across razor-backed spurs. Amid the firing and confusion it was every man for himself and units became hopelessly lost and entangled. The only cover was provided by clumps of scrub a foot or two high with the consistency of barbed wire, which tore puttees and trousers to shreds. With night falling, ships' searchlights bounced off the shadowy heights trying to pick out an unseen enemy. Shells from the 15-inch guns of the flagship *Queen Elizabeth* roared overhead like a hurricane, thundering into imagined targets and knocking the wind out of men as they clung on to the cliffs by their fingernails.

Harold's A Company was directed to fill a gap in the line between units that had landed earlier and been butchered as they stubbornly hung on at the top of a steep valley. In failing light, the men of the 16th filed up a gash in the cliffs made slippery by a sudden heavy shower. It was Broadmeadows all over again, with the additional hazard of being sniped at. Between two forks at the head of the valley rose their objective, the dark mass that would later be named Pope's Hill after the 16th Battalion's commander.

At this precise time, senior officers were expressing grave misgivings about the prospects for holding on.

Requesting an immediate evacuation, they were ordered by General Sir Ian Hamilton to "Dig! Dig! Dig!" The boys of A Company creeping up on to the jagged spur of Pope's Hill through a rattle of Turkish rifle fire did not need telling. They dug.

Throughout the night the Turks poured a hailstorm of lead on to this ragged new section of line. Enemy marksmen on an adjacent hill were able to pick off the attackers from behind. A boy bugler acting as a runner for the 16th had a close shave when a single shot knocked out the two men sitting beside him — the same bullet went straight through the stomach of one and hit the other in the testicles.

The horrific sight of huge, gaping wounds sparked rumours that the enemy were using exploding dum-dums. In fact, it was nothing more sinister than a combination of the powerful German Mauser rifles and the closeness of the combatants that inflicted such damage on flesh and bone. Some snipers infiltrated gaps in the line dressed in uniforms stripped from dead Australians — they were bayoneted without mercy if caught. One who had been holed up on the rocky outcrop christened the Sphinx was pinpointed and brought down by a lethal rifle burst. His hideaway contained water and provisions for several days plus a basket of carrier pigeons for sending messages about troop movements back to his own lines.

By dawn of the second day the men from A Company and other embattled units on Pope's Hill had dug down to a depth of three or four feet in the loose, damp, sandy soil. Some would recall the sound of birdsong as the sun came up on a scene of carnage. Still, there was no chance of rest and no respite from the fire raining down on them. Shelling from warships broke up some of the organised Turkish resistance but the enemy could not be dislodged and, with the opposing lines so close, shells fired by the Royal Navy miles out at sea were just as likely to explode on their own troops. The Turks threw in reinforcements and maintained their strategic advantage, looking down at the exposed Australians and New Zealanders on the slopes below and picking them off almost at will.

In the heat of the day, lips cracked and tongues swelled for lack of water. Many men had ditched full packs on the beach, water bottles included, rather than be encumbered with them as they stared up at 300-foot-high sandstone cliffs. Those deprived of their dubious emergency rations were fortunate — nothing was guaranteed to provoke a rabid thirst more than salty bully beef and dry biscuits. Bringing up water, ammunition and stretchers was a near suicidal mission. Everything had to be hauled up the steep rear slope of Pope's Hill, a difficult climb even for a soldier unburdened by supplies. A sturdy rope borrowed from the navy was secured to a bush on top of the hill so that a man could pull himself up. Machine guns to replace the two of the 16th Battalion knocked out by the enemy also had to be dragged up and one of those was quickly hit and put out of action again.

From the decks of the *Californian*, Chris Beechey had watched antlike figures fighting and falling through the smoky haze of battle for two long days before duty called. Men of the 4th Field Ambulance were awoken on the morning of 25 April by the sound of gunfire and saw the British mounting their ill-fated attack on Cape Helles, at the toe of Gallipoli. As the *Californian* steamed past, they were far enough away to declare it a wondrous sight.

At around midday they anchored off Anzac Cove* and heard the crackle of rifles and the booming of the ships' guns all day and into the night. At 1a.m. on the 26th a party of bearers was ferried towards the shore but had to return because no picquet boat was available to guide them in. All the next day they remained passive spectators, watching troops and stores being landed under fire and a growing number of casualties crowding on to the beachhead. Even the novelty of seeing a seaplane and observation balloon above the scene wore thin as another exasperating day of inaction dawned. The only excitement was when a burst of shrapnel sent red-hot shards of metal fizzing into the depths 100 yards from their ship. It was close enough for the captain to retreat a further mile out to sea.

Then the waiting was over. The medics boarded a tug at 7.30p.m. on 27 April and chugged to within 400 yards of the shore, where they were kept waiting another two hours for the small craft towing a line of boats that would finally land them on the beach —

---

* *This name, coined by Anzac Corps commander Lieutenant General Sir William Birdwood, passed into legend and was officially recognised by Turkey seventy years later in 1985.*

raked by shrapnel and rifle fire the whole time. Chris's C Section stayed on the beach until daylight but another section was immediately despatched to the front line via places where only goats had trodden until a couple of days before and which were soon honoured with names that would never be forgotten — MacGlagan's Ridge, Shrapnel Gully, Monash Valley.

There had already been much work for the stretcher-bearers, whose Red Cross bands on their sleeves gave no protection against bullets and made them easy targets — "From the time the first boat grounded on the beach it was recognised that the toughest men on the peninsula were those carrying the wounded down the gullies in the blistering heat of the day and the dark stumbling abyss of night," wrote one historian. The 4th Field Ambulance worked a deadly manor. Their pick-up point was the dressing station just below Quinn's Post, almost a mile up into the serrated hills. The drop-off spot was the beach dressing station built of timber, tarpaulin and sandbags at the foot of the cliffs. The bearers earned the admiration of all. As well as the unceasing fire, there was the obstacle course of a journey through the gullies — piles of kit dumped from the initial landing, holes desperately dug for water, mud and slush to wade through, communication wires to ensnare or almost garrotte them. There was also little protection against snipers in the first fortnight before the track was widened and sandbags piled up in the more exposed areas.

Cornelius Joseph Lawless kept a diary that mentions several of his C Section comrades, including Chris. He

101

tells of their first trip up into the firing line to begin the task of bringing down the wounded — "[It] took us over an hour to get back owing to the shells bursting to the tune of a ragtime all around. We are forming a first aid post. We worked like hell all day and it is a nasty trip. The snipers are popping at us all day but none of our crowd has been hurt yet except Jack Rayside got a smack on the foot from a splinter of shell and Abe Shaw got his hand hurt while ducking out the way of a grenade while he was rescuing a wounded man from just outside the trenches.

"Camped that night on the beach and it rained like blazes. Next morning took up position again in the firing line. Shells still rained and bullets whistled around us but nothing of event happened. I boiled a billy on the beach and had a cup of strong tea which set me up . . . the first I had drunk for 48 hours or more. When I got back we had orders to cut off our brassards as they were too much of a mark for snipers. One of the 2nd AMC got killed, shot through the head while carrying a patient down the track. We had tea and turned in. There was only one alarm for wounded and it was not our turn. Beechey, Jones and a few more went and searched the hill but couldn't find anything."

Chris kept a lookout for Harold and relied on colleagues to send word of his brother whenever they were taking wounded from the forward positions. The Beecheys had so far been lucky but they were not the only Gallipoli brothers fretting over each other's safety. Three Foss boys were from the wheat belt as well. They

102

had flipped a coin to see which one would stay and take care of the land while the others went off to war. Ernest lost but, like Harold, he didn't want to miss the Great Adventure and joined up with Henry and Cecil, who won the MC at Gallipoli. None of them came back. Carl and Ernek Janssen had sploshed through Broadmeadows like Harold and were hardened up in the heat of Egypt. A piece of shrapnel ripped Carl's throat open as he waded ashore on the first day of the landing. Ernek took it badly but there was hardly time to mourn let alone bury a brother. He fought on until reported missing a few weeks later, never to be seen again. Others died side by side, like the young man killed by a sniper as he placed a wooden cross over his brother's grave at Shrapnel Gully.

Chris was relieved to find Harold still in one piece at the head of that valley of death where the bearers carried out their strenuous and dangerous work almost on a knife-edge. One wrong step could send a man down a deep ravine. All around lay the dead and the wounded. From their dominant vantage points the enemy blasted away at anything that moved. Chris wondered how he ever survived and how Harold came through those hellish first days, going without sleep, with so little food and water, and fighting around the clock to retain a toehold in trenches hacked out of formidable heights.

For five days without a break, Harold had remained one of a dwindling force that fought thirst, hunger and Turks, surviving enemy sniping and shrapnel as well as misdirected high explosive from their own side. The general who described it as a "dog's life" was hardly doing it justice and he would have been nowhere near close enough to experience the worst of it. Even General Hamilton conceded, "There is no square inch of ground the Australians hold which is really safe from shell and rifle fire."

On the afternoon of 27 April, the Turks had launched an attack in six waves but were driven back with fearful casualties. Then a line of about 300 of the enemy emerged from a gully and charged forward. At their head was an officer brandishing a flashing sword in one hand and revolver in the other. The line of shattered men of the 16th at last had something more than shadows to aim at. The Turks were annihilated.

Further misery and discomfort for those dug in on Pope's Hill came on 29 April. They had left their waterproof sheets and warm blankets behind on the ship so they had no protection from a cold wind and driving rain, which left them soaked. Not until the evening of 30 April were they finally relieved. Under cover of darkness, the remnants gladly gave up their trenches to another battalion, slipped over the precipitous sides of Pope's Hill and trekked down to a place in the gully officially designated as rest camp. There the killing would go on but at least a man did not have to die hungry or thirsty.

Relieved from the front line, Harold dug himself a shallow "possy" hole for protection against snipers hiding in the scrubby hillsides and snatched whatever sleep he could. During two days out of the line in rest camp the 16th Battalion lost a further fifty men. The nearby watering hole was a particular death trap where anyone stooping to drink risked a Mauser bullet in the head or chest. Bodies piled up there and lay unburied for days. Harold managed his first wash for a week and made running repairs to the disintegrating uniform in which he had once posed so proudly. Dysentery was also starting to take effect, but sick and haggard sufferers were reluctant to go to the medical officer and abandon their mates. Many would shortly be put out of their misery.

They had landed on an impeccable Sunday evening. Exactly one week later, another sunny Sunday evening would take many more from the battered 16th. Ordered to drive the Turks from one of the ridges at a point known as the Bloody Angle, they set out with the latest stirring message from Lord Kitchener ringing in their ears. "Good luck, Australia," declared the great man. "You are the pride of the world." In the gathering gloom they climbed the sheer face of the valley head — "like going up the side of a house" — and poured on to an exposed ridge where the enemy were waiting to machine-gun them into oblivion. Falling back into the gully below the Bloody Angle, they rallied beneath the ridge and clambered back up the slopes, taking turns at fighting and digging while almost completely surrounded. "God it was frightful," Harold's comrade Ellis Silas recorded in his diary, ". . . screams of the wounded, bursting of the shells, ear-splitting crackling of the rifles. In a very few minutes the gully at the foot of the hill was filled with dead and wounded. It rained men in this gully. All round could be seen the sparks where the bullets were striking. Our artillery was firing into us as well." And ammunition was running low. Soldiers fell across the heavy boxes, cut down by machine guns as they tried to drag up fresh supplies.

Survivors holding the ridge at bayonet point were in danger of being cut off completely. Turks fired into them from front, left and rear. Then just before daybreak the enemy came yelling over the top in a suicidal full-frontal assault to be scythed down with staggering losses. The thin ranks of the 16th were ordered to subdue an enemy position 80 yards away across the ridge and were further decimated by fire from a hill to their left. Another perfect Mediterranean dawn lit up a sandy hilltop carpeted with the dead and dying from both sides. The Turks made one more attempt at pushing the Australians off the ridge but were again shot to pieces.

The quiet of the graveyard that descended on the hill was suddenly shattered by a bombardment — the Australians were being blown out of their makeshift trenches by their own artillery. A contingent of Royal Marines sent up as reinforcements were blasted to bits while Harold and the rag-tag remnants of the 16th, huddled on the crest of the ridge, could only watch. The position was hopeless.

Under the covering fire of a solitary surviving machine gun the remaining men gradually began evacuation, darting from their holes in the ground in twos and threes and tumbling down the hillside. Their abandoned trenches were swiftly overrun and a

Sgt-Major Harvey, lying there wounded, was bayoneted by the Turks and tossed over the parapet for dead. He crawled away as night fell and three days later reached the sanctuary of his own lines only to die of his injuries. Of the 645 officers and men who remained of the 16th and took part in the action, 307 were present when they paraded back at rest camp.

Their commanding officer, Colonel Pope, never ceased to be amazed at the courage of his men — "The spirit of those who were left is in no way diminished — all were proud to belong to the 16th and more than proud of its share in the fighting," he wrote. There was no chance of even compiling a proper casualty list. Many of the dead lay rotting on the high ridges, pay books that would identify them still tucked into tattered pockets and impossible to retrieve without risking further losses. The survivors of four companies were reorganised into two threadbare new ones and sent back into the firing line the next night at the point widely accepted as the most wretched and dangerous at Anzac — Quinn's Post.

As Harold fought for his life at the Bloody Angle, Chris was working the gully below with the bearers of the 4th and 3rd Field Ambulances, including the Man with the Donkey. They, too, were under constant fire as they tended the stricken, crouching down to retrieve the iodine ampoule carried by every man, snapping off the end and emptying the contents over cotton wool used to plug the wound before applying a field dressing and perhaps a tourniquet which would have to be released every 20 minutes to prevent gangrene. Then there was the long haul down the valley — two men to a stretcher instead of four — in a game of cat and mouse with Turkish crack-shots.

Stretchers were in short supply, vanishing into the recesses of hospital ships where the sick and wounded were laid out in rows. The bearers had to improvise, more often than not lugging a casualty down the gullies in an oil sheet. With so little grip, aching hands soon seized up with cramps. If they were lucky there might be a welcoming cup of tea waiting for them when they reached the beach dressing station before they had to turn around and scramble back on another mercy mission.

A member of Chris's company had been shot dead during the night of the Bloody Angle assault and two others were wounded by shrapnel as they grabbed some rest in a dugout. As the disastrous action was petering out, further shells exploded over the Field Ambulance leaving another man dead and twelve wounded. Any guilt Chris might have felt about the medic's role being a soft option must have long since vanished.

At Quinn's, the 16th immediately began to haemorrhage more men. The half-strength companies were sent into the line with just half a dozen officers between them. One was shot through the head and killed and another hit in the lungs on the first day and there were several casualties in the ranks. "Nothing could cleanse the smell of death from the nostrils for a fortnight afterwards," said one visitor to Quinn's. In front, the Turkish trenches were a few yards away on rising ground. Peering over the parapet in daylight meant certain death so makeshift periscopes were constructed from mirrors donated by the navy but these were easily smashed by rifle fire. Five yards behind the Australian line was a sheer drop into Monash Valley.

The narrow divide allowed Turks to lob over hand grenades in the shape of cricket balls while the Australians replied with jam tin bombs, invented by a master of improvisation in their depleted ranks. Jam was one of the more acceptable staples of the Gallipoli diet, even though the baking sun often turned it to liquid. Men spread or poured it on everything, from biscuits to lumps of cheese. When the tins were empty they were packed full of nails and explosive with a short fuse attached. At Quinn's the two sides were never more than 10 yards apart, and were about to get even closer.

Another Gallipoli Sabbath brought another trial for the boys of the 16th. The 9 May operation was billed as a reconnaissance mission but the Australians were expected to overrun the enemy line at Quinn's and then hang on at all costs. The 16th went in as support for the attacking battalion who succeeded in seizing the opposing trenches. Parties armed only with picks and shovels were sent out into the maelstrom of No Man's Land to try to link the two lines. The Turks counter-attacked, cutting off the Australians in their trenches, while their machine guns, firing from the flanks, tore into the digging parties.

Harold's company had gone over the top to the sound of their leader singing "Tipperary" through a megaphone. A rifle bullet hit Captain Margolin alongside Harold but it embedded itself in the thick notebook in his chest pocket and he managed to stagger back when the 16th was told to withdraw.

Hand-to-hand fighting continued into the night and two officers from another company were ordered to take forty men and try to relieve their comrades. Both were killed in the charge and only a fraction of the small force reached the enemy parapet. For the rest of the night the survivors helped bring back the dead and wounded. One working party reported burying thirteen and a half enemy dead. When queried by battalion HQ, they assured them they had disposed of thirteen corpses and half of one. The figure was duly recorded and officially forwarded to brigade.

For the 16th there was another pitiful roll call. "How heart-breaking it is," wrote Ellis Silas. "Name after name is called; the reply a deep silence which can be felt despite the noise of the incessant crackling of rifles and screaming of shrapnel. There are few of us left to answer our names — just a thin line of weary, ashen-faced men." The 16th, which had landed with 959 soldiers and had been further reinforced after its earlier losses, was now down to 200 men.

The "reconnaissance" had achieved the seemingly impossible — it had made Quinn's even more deadly. The partly dug trenches between the two lines meant it was easier for the Turks to creep up at night and hurl their bombs. In effect, the two sides now shared the same trench. Another fifty men were killed or wounded in a failed attempt to fill it in a few days later. But by then Harold was on his way to hospital. He had dysentery and pneumonia, either of which might accomplish what Turkish bullets had so far failed to achieve. But Chris was confident he would pull through when he wrote to their mother.

14 May 1915
Gallipoli

I'm still well but have had a rather rough time, a touch of fever or ague following on 96 hours of heavy duty. But then came 48 hours spell [of rest] then 24 hours duty then 48 hours spell — now we go on for 24 hours tonight. I missed one 24 hours through a badly bruised and swollen knee through falling with a stretcher on a heap of stones. The work is still dangerous through shrapnel fire and snipers. One chap has had six or seven shots at me and missed every time, sometimes by inches. Harold's health has broken up and he is going back to the base hospital. He's had a hell of a time, lost everything on landing and fought and slept for days with only what he stood up in. The regimental doctor of the 16th diagnosed pleuro-pneumonia and he's pretty bad. I saw him off to the boat 10 minutes ago this forenoon. I'm rather pleased in a way as I think his constitution will pull him through all right and he may come out fitter than ever and it takes a certain amount of anxiety off my mind. All his mates speak highly of him and his work. Shrapnel and snipers got six of us on our last 24 hours work. One man lost his leg. It's only my habit of never travelling in a bunch that saved me. When I'm not actually carrying a stretcher I go forward or hang back about a chain [22 yards] on the idea that if it gets me it misses the squad and if it gets the squad it misses me.

Let me know when Bar, Frank and Eric are going and try all you can to send every man. Tell all the women and girls you know to send their men. I'm at one with Sir Edward Grey [Britain's Foreign Secretary] and would rather perish or hang than live under German Kultur. What it was in Belgium it would be 10 times worse in England if ever they got a landing.

The situation here is a blank book to us, but still the fighting spirit of the men is fine. They'd take anything on earth I believe if put to it.

Harold was brief and matter-of-fact, considering what he had been through, when he sent a postcard home from his sickbed in Alexandria. The English parson's son was evidently very much an Australian now after his adventures in the bush and with the AIF — Amy and the girls waiting at home for news would have been puzzled to read he'd been a "bit crook". Harold was obviously on the mend and showing no qualms about being sent back to Gallipoli.

28 May 1915
On Active Service
My dear mother, I have been away from the firing

line for a week or two a bit crook, but hope to get back now in a day or so. Things were a bit solid at first on shore but look fairly healthy now. Kris still going good.

Love, Harold

Medical arrangements at Gallipoli were as chaotic as the military situation. Sick and wounded lay in rows on the beach, waiting to be loaded on to barges and ferried out to a hospital ship after dark when the shelling died down. Every verminous old tub, however unsuitable, was pressed into service to cope with the casualties. This grim fleet earned the macabre nickname of the Black Ships. Men, caked in mud and blood, were left unattended with just a bedpan between hundreds in holds still foul from their previous cargo of horses and mules.

Ellis Silas, also evacuated because of illness at the same time as Harold, was one of 600 cases aboard a ship with space for 150. He wrote in his diary, "Patients are lying here just as they were when they left the trenches with all the filthy and blood-soaked clothes still on them. Handsome-looking fellow has lost his left leg up to the thigh; he tries to throw himself overboard — but generally the patients are showing wonderful fortitude." Silas had the good fortune to end up amid the splendour of the Palace Hotel in Heliopolis while Harold was sent to the less salubrious Deaconess Hospital in Alexandria. But anywhere with a comfortable bed, crisp, clean sheets and visions in white to

113

administer to the sick or wounded seemed like heaven after Gallipoli.

Chris had mentioned how easy it was to become callous in the midst of so much horror where there was no escaping the stench of corpses and the sight of maimed young men. Nurses throughout the chain of military hospitals stretching from Lemnos and Imbros islands to Egypt and on to Malta saw the same suffering and could hardly remain insensitive to it. From one Egyptian hospital a nurse tells of being moved to tears by a man badly smashed up at Quinn's — "He was very tall and he had multiple wounds. Compound fractures of the legs as well as other wounds and he wasn't conscious. We didn't have a bed long enough for him so we put him on a mattress on the floor and the poor fellow died just as a gramophone in the ward struck up God Save the King — it seemed a fitting end for this brave man. Another time, a beautiful young fellow came in and they just said to me there is another patient over there, sister, in a pretty bad way and when I went over he was just going. He was such a fine-looking fellow, beautiful physique and everything and he just went before I could do anything for him and I think I broke up then. They had marvellous courage. I don't know how they did it but they never thought of themselves. It was always, 'I can wait, sister, that chap needs you more.'"

Harold was in Curly's thoughts as she read of the Gallipoli heroics. The first scraps of news had been in the papers on 1 May. Under the heading "Australians

114

in Action", it was reported that, "As soon as the House of Representatives met today, the Prime Minister announced that he had received the following message from His Majesty: 'I heartily congratulate you upon the splendid conduct and bravery displayed by the Australian troops in the operation at the Dardanelles. They have indeed proved themselves worthy sons of the Empire.' (Cheers)." A leader column in the *West Australian* on Monday 3 May, headed "The Blood Tax", declared, "These are anxious moments to the relations and friends of the Australasians at the front; and who among us counts not some friend or relative among the gallant fellows who are fighting our fight . . . the casualty lists are incomplete and it would be self-deception to deny that they are likely to be heavier."

Initial reports gave no clue to the losses being suffered. In early May, when Anzac casualties already stood at 8,000, the first list to appear in the newspapers totalled a mere fifty-five names. By 20 May, the publicly acknowledged death toll had reached 291, whereas 500 had been killed on the first day alone.

With the time it took for letters to get back to Australia, Harold might have been dead for weeks or even months by the time Curly received word that he was "in the pink". Despite the ominous bulletins filtering back from Gallipoli, she never gave up on him. On Saturday 8 May, Perth papers carried the first eyewitness account, filed by noted British war correspondent Ellis Ashmead-Bartlett. Though yet to set foot ashore he was able to declare, "I had never seen anything like these wounded Australians before. Although many were shot to bits and were without hope of recovery, their cheers resounded throughout the night . . . they were happy because they knew they had been tried for the first time and found not wanting."

While the fighting continued in a distant land, there were reports of improved prospects for farmers in the wheat belt where rain was forecast at last. Having given up on the drought-stricken land for a life or death struggle, Chris and Harold might have appreciated the irony. 1915 would turn out to be a boom year for those farmers who stayed at home — "It is now fairly certain that the Australian harvest will yield a surplus of 100,000,000 bushels for export, and it will require 1,000 ships to carry away that surplus," reported *The Sunday Times* in Perth.

All those with loved ones at war were moved by the story accompanying a bullet-torn picture of two little boys in toy soldier uniforms. A Western Australian soldier found the crumpled photo on the Gallipoli battlefield. It must have fallen out of a man's pocket as he was being carried away, either to hospital or for burial, and the paper thought it reasonable to conclude that the two bonny boys were his sons. "Articles like these," it went on, "are usually kept by soldiers in the left breast pocket of the shirt or tunic, so the fateful bullet, after piercing the photo, probably passed into the unfortunate man's body, inflicting a severe if not fatal wound. When the man was being searched the picture apparently dropped out and was subsequently picked up — if it were not so fraught with dread possibilities, the story would be a romance; as it is, it is a tragedy, and the bullet-torn picture is but a grim reminder of Gallipoli."

Chris went on rescuing casualties from the battlefield around the clock. But his luck was still holding out. Continuously shot at and showered with shrapnel as they toiled out in the open, the bearers were not even safe when they got back to the sanctuary of their dugouts. One of Chris's section was wounded when a shell cap embedded itself in his thigh while he was shaving. The 4th Field Ambulance had a lucky escape when a huge 35-pound shell, fired from one of the Turkish forts, landed in the middle of their camp but failed to explode. "Had it not been so tragic," one medic wrote in his diary, "an amusing incident occurred. The shell buried itself in the earth unexploded and one of our men ran and picked it up, carrying it to where a crowd was taking cover. They all ran away shouting for him to bury it. He put it down at his feet and looked amazed, evidently wondering where the danger lay. Three more of our corps were wounded this evening."

The Turks remained intent on driving the invaders into the sea. On 19 May they attacked along the entire line with 42,000 men until a wall of bodies lay out in No Man's Land. Keen not to miss out on such easy targets, 12,500 Anzacs jostled with each other for shooting space on the parapets and, for once, suffered few casualties themselves. Five days later an armistice was called from 8a.m. to 4.30p.m. to bury the heaps of dead. Chloride of lime was hauled up to the front to combat the stench and the threat of disease with one officer declaring, "The smell of chloride is of violets compared to the smell of old Turk."

The Australians *were* driven into the sea but only by their fondness for a dip. Swimming was about the only available recreation and it made life faintly tolerable under a baking sun for troops black with grime and crawling with lice. Even after an enemy shell had knocked out eighteen men and turned the water crimson, the bathers — from humblest private to highest-ranking generals, recognisable by their well-fed bellies — remained undeterred. The day after the brief armistice to bury the dead a British intelligence officer visited Anzac and noted, "The first impression from a boat is that of seeing the cave dwellings of a large and prosperous tribe of savages who live on the extremely steep slopes of broken sandy bluffs covered with scrub which go up from a very narrow sandy beach to a height of 300 feet . . . the place is like an ant heap of khaki ants, the whole exposed to shellfire. All here agree that it is the most amazing thing they ever saw."

That same day, men out bathing, on fatigue duties along the shore and huddled in their holes in the ground on the Anzac ant heap witnessed an awesome and awful spectacle — the sinking of the British battleship HMS *Triumph*. Hit by a torpedo from a German U-boat just after midday, she turned turtle in fifteen minutes and lay two miles out to sea with her great propellers in the air. In another thirty minutes the great leviathan disappeared completely beneath the waves, taking seventy-five of the crew with her.

On 30 May, Chris's good fortune finally ran out. At first opportunity he sent his mother a pre-printed, army-issue field service postcard:

NOTHING is to be written on this side except the date and signature of the sender. Sentences not required may be erased. If anything else is added the post card will be destroyed.

I am quite well.

I have been admitted into hospital

{ sick } and am going on well.
{ wounded } and hope to be discharged soon.

I am being sent down to the base.

letter dated
I have received your { telegram ,,
parcel ,,

Letter follows at first opportunity.

I have received no letter from you
{ lately.
{ for a long time.

Signature only. } Yr loving Son Chris

Date 1 · 6 · 15

(Postage must be prepaid on any letter or post card addressed to the sender of this card.)

Field postcard from Chris telling his
mother he has been wounded

119

CHAPTER
SIX

We all wish the thing was over

From the village of Whittington in Staffordshire, the three lofty spires of Lichfield Cathedral, its walls cut from yellow sandstone like the cliffs of Gallipoli but smeared and blackened by the centuries, could be seen spearing the horizon. On dreary Whittington Heath, peppered with wooden army huts, khaki figures drilled and marched day in, day out and through the night. Among them was Lance Sergeant Barnard R. Beechey. Bar had shrugged off past shame, curbed his drinking and fitted smoothly into the humdrum military routine. Most of his fellow volunteers were only a year or two older than the pupils with whom he had occasionally lost his rag at Dorchester. His age and experience of leading schoolboy soldiers on weekend manoeuvres singled him out from other raw recruits in the battalion's motley ranks and earned him his stripes.

Before 1915 was out, some of that great tide of civilian volunteers being turned into fighting men at Whittington Heath and other camps from Salisbury Plain to Scotland would be sorely needed. Winter had hardly turned to spring before lethal stirrings were aroused on the Western Front. The battles of Neuve Chapelle, Aubers Ridge and Festubert — all fought within a damp and featureless few square miles of each other — cost the British Expeditionary Force nearly 40,000 casualties. Flanders mud soaked up more British blood after a poison gas attack by the Germans at Ypres on 22 April. The desperate defence of the Belgian city dragged on until the end of May and claimed a further 60,000 dead and wounded.

Bar read of the Gallipoli landings and waited anxiously for word about his brothers fighting with the Australians. Writing home about his exertions with the 9th Lincolns, he predicted his turn in the front line would come soon enough.

7 June 1915
9th (Service) Battalion, Lincolnshire Regiment
The Camp, Whittington Heath, Lichfield
I am writing this from the Sergeants' Mess. I got promotion to Lance Sergeant yesterday, so can get my meals now in a more or less civilised fashion. We have got the statement of pay from the pay office and I find I am about 25/- in credit, so if we get it next Friday I shall be able to send you a sovereign. I have seen the quartermaster sergeant about allotting pay and the papers will be here in a few days, but they are very slow in this battalion. I see the Australians have been engaged again at Gallipoli, so hope Chris and Harold are all right. I have finished range firing and go to Newcastle

under Lyme either this week or next for field firing. We shall be there a week. They have been working the service company very hard this week. We come in as tired as can be every day with no inclination to go out for the evening. Last Monday we marched out 13 miles in full kit with packs, did two or three hours trenching, had a night attack where we got to bed in the open, did an hour or two's skirmishing the next morning and marched home. It looks as if they are hardening us this time.

Lichfield offered few of the exotic pleasures of Cairo or Colombo. Despite emergency laws brought in to restrict opening hours, public houses like the Malt Shovel and Angel Inn were still the chief attraction. But Bar had sworn off the drink and, anyway, was too worn out from his army exertions to lift a pint. Lord John Sanger's Royal Circus and Menagerie came to town for one day only at Bowling Green fields, and while crowds marvelled at the bareback Cossack riders, Bar could not help wondering whether such magnificent horseman-ship might not be better employed defending Russia from the Hun hordes. The Sisters Della-Casa and their wire-walking elephant were the circus showstoppers, but even this jumbo spectacle paled against a surprise visit to Lichfield by the revered Secretary of War, Lord Kitchener. Thousands flocked to Whittington Heath "for the privilege of a lifetime" to gain a glimpse of the great man, who spent forty minutes inspecting his New Army battalions. After expressing his satisfaction at their progress and steadiness on parade, Kitchener was driven off in a cloud of dust with a cursory wave to the crowds.

While Bar was knocking his section of men into shape in the English countryside — close enough to Lincoln to get there and back to visit his mother in a day whenever time off allowed — his Gallipoli brothers were in Alexandria. Chris wrote to his mother confidently expecting the bullet that had his name on it would turn out to be his passport to a pleasant few months away from the fighting. As he lay in bed helpless, hardly able to move, he was more worried about Harold. He had no idea that his brother was being cared for in another military hospital in the same city.

8 June 1915
Greek Hospital, Alexandria, Egypt
I am being nursed in the above hosp. for paralysis of hips and legs through a fall following being hit by bullet in shoulder. Am lying on my back. Treatment starts tomorrow, maybe for two or three months. Haven't heard of Harold. Please write per return.
Your loving son, Chris

After five weeks of dodging Turkish crack-shots and flying shrapnel, Chris had finally been nailed by a sniper on the crest of one of the ridges. The impact of the Mauser bullet sent him spinning over a precipice into the ravine below. As gently as the rugged conditions and enemy fire allowed, his own C Section comrades carried him down to the beach dressing station. One of them, a Private Boyle, still sported a bloody bandage where the medical officer had extracted a ricochet bullet from his thick skull a day or two earlier. The hole in Chris's shoulder was a nice clean one but the fall had damaged his spine and internal organs. Paralysed, racked by bouts of fever and hollow-cheeked from lack of a decent meal, he was too weak to lift a pen or pencil except to add the briefest of footnotes to a message to Amy written by one of his nurses.

> 17 June 1915
> Greek Hospital, Alexandria, Egypt
>
> Your son Chris is still here. Although he is able to move his foot a little he is afraid it will be some time before regaining the use of his legs. He's now awaiting electric treatment. I am one of the night nurses in charge of him — I hope soon to see him well again.
>
> Yours faithfully, Ethel H. Gibson

> [on the end] Love to all at home — send news of others. Haven't heard about Harold.

In fact, Harold had a new uniform to replace the rags that nurses had cut off him and was waiting to be sent back to Gallipoli. By the time he discovered his brother had also been in Alexandria, Chris was being shipped out to a hospital in England. They missed each other by a matter of hours. Mindful of the censors, the only clue to what Harold had been through came in a short postscript to his mother where he expressed a selfless pride in his battalion.

> 10 July 1915
> Alexandria, Egypt
>
> Just a few lines to say that I am fairly well. I am now in the base camp near Alexandria but I suppose I shall be going back to the Peninsula soon. I was there three weeks from the first day and came away knocked up a good bit in all — dysentery, tonsillitis etc. I am not A1 yet but hope to pick up again my old condition. I am working here at present. Chris has gone away to England, hurt in the back, but progressing favourably I believe. I was very sorry to miss seeing him before he went. We both knew each other was away somewhere but could not find out where. When I did find which hospital he had been sent to, he had gone the night before to England. I suppose you will be able to see him at home in England. I have not had any letters since before we landed. Let me know what Frank, Bar and Eric are up to.
>
> Yours, Harold
>
> PS Our Brigade made a name for themselves, and the 16th especially. We did not take part in the landing of the morning but landed just before dusk.

After a week of convalescence, Harold was put to work at base camp while he awaited a ship that would ferry the next draft of reinforcements to Gallipoli. He was far from fit but a new offensive was planned. Every available man would be needed for a last throw of the dice against a stubborn enemy who had defended a barren splinter of their homeland with such ferocity. In the melting heat of a Mediterranean summer, Harold could expect a warm welcome back.

By the middle of July, Chris was in England and making plans for his mother to visit him at the 2nd Western General Hospital in Manchester. It had been five years since he sailed for Australia, five years since Amy had seen him. She would hardly recognise her son.

14 July 1915

2nd Western Gen Hosp., Manchester

If you have received the postcard saying what hospital I'm in no doubt you were surprised but I wasn't too well looked after during the day time in the Greek hospital so when one day a captain in the RAMC came round he said (I was nearly asleep at the time), "No need to worry about moving him, he's getting slowly better" I woke up and said, "Where were you thinking of me going anyway?" and he said, "Why? Where do you want to go?" And I said England. In a day or two, to my surprise, they said I could go on the next boat and the next day I was on board.

They only gave me a milk diet in the Greek Hosp because I had a bit of a temperature each afternoon and I got as thin as a rail and weak. When I got on board the English doctor made me lie quiet in one position on my back all the voyage because the injury to my spine was not quite healed. He also put me on a full diet and told me to order what I liked. The fever left me in a couple of days and I gained a lot in strength. I can move my legs a bit now but they keep moving themselves a lot through nerves and circulation coming back, I suppose. I'm afraid it will take a good while before I can walk but thank God it will come back in time. I haven't drawn any pay for three months so will write to the authorities for it and send you rail and hotel expenses to come and see me. Have you heard from Harold? I haven't since I saw him on to the hospital boat.

Love to all, Chris

PS Manchester was the nearest I could get to Lincoln.

Bar could have made it to Manchester and back easily enough to see Chris, but events were moving swiftly. He had hoped for one last day trip to Lincoln, taking the train from Lichfield, having a few hours at home and being back in camp before nightfall, but he could not escape camp duty. Then he learned he would be leaving for the front in a rush to join the 2nd Battalion of the Lincolnshire Regiment, a regular army unit that had been in Bermuda when war broke out. It had since suffered badly in the trenches and needed new blood, particularly NCOs. Details of the latest draft for France were pinned up in the orderly room by the orderly sergeant, whose own name was near the top of the list. Bar had only a few hours to pack his kit. He let his mother know he was off to war.

> 27 July 1915
> Whittington Camp, Lichfield
>
> I could not get away last Wednesday as I have been orderly sergeant for the week. Work all day from 4.30 to 10.30. I thought I was going this Wednesday but leave has been stopped as we have two drafts going out. I am in the draft for the 2nd Battalion and we are going out tomorrow. I should have written before but was not quite sure whether I was going or not. I have left arrangements settled to allot to you 6d per day of my pay. They managed to get the papers when they found it had to be done in a hurry. I feel quite confident of coming back all right and will let you know how to address letters etc. when I get out. Very busy packing. With love to all.
>
> Your affectionate son, B. R. Beechey

The next day he was writing from across the Channel after an uncomfortable crossing on a grey-painted steamer with a destroyer escort.

> 28 July 1915
> 3rd Infantry Base, Rouen
>
> Have arrived here, but we should have gone

somewhere else, so we are standing by waiting for orders. Not allowed out of camp so have seen nothing of the city but the streets we marched through. Was seasick twice in the Channel, but had a beautiful boat trip up the river. Will send new address if possible when I get there.

Citizen soldiers were pouring into France to reinforce the worn and torn regular units. They suffered their first painful blisters from clattering over hard, uneven cobbled streets in unforgiving army boots with full kit on their backs, and made their first interminable journeys on troop trains that were no more than cattle waggons, lurching along at walking pace. Bar took half a day to travel from Rouen to Le Havre, less than 50 miles away.

> 30 July 1915
> 3rd Infantry Base Depot, Havre
>
> Here we are at last. This is our proper base, and we shall probably join the Battalion some time next week. We had about 6 hours in a French train today. Please send any letters to same address as I gave before starting. Please send some buttons for clothing as I am always shedding them, Bar

Harold, classed as fit enough to fight, had returned to Gallipoli by the beginning of August, when the flies had reached plague proportions. A man could not lift a crumb to his mouth without it being smothered in the bloated bluebottles that fed off the decay all around.

The big push was imminent and Harold was confident of its success, even though he felt obliged to tell his mother it might be the last she hears from him.

3 August 1915
Gallipoli

I have been back here about a week. I saw a letter from Chris in which he says he's in hospital in Manchester so I suppose some of you will be able to see him. It is very hot and dusty here, practically no rain at all. I am lying in a dugout, the flies keep me from sleeping. I was over to see the 4th Field Ambulance to find out how Chris was hit. He was where he was not supposed to be as is often the case when a chap stops one. He was on the skyline and got it in the shoulders and fell down backwards and hurt his spine somewhere. You will see that this letter put me on my honour not to say anything about our movements. But I will stretch a point — we shall be into the thick of it I think in a day or so and one stands a good chance of going under. This is worth it. We shall finish this affair up finally this time. I believe they are having a good season in Australia this year — it will be the saving of Australia.

Well good luck, your loving son Harold

He hardly recognised the mates he'd left behind a few weeks ago: unshaven, half naked and emaciated from illness and fatigue. It would not take long for Harold and the fresh, clean reinforcements who arrived with him from Egypt to look just as ragged, even though the food had improved since he was evacuated in May. Instead of never-ending bully beef and biscuits, there were sometimes rissoles for breakfast, fresh meat and dried vegetables for dinner, followed by a tea of stewed figs with boiled rice.

Harold's passionate sense of duty was about to be tested once more as his battalion was assigned to help capture a strategic hill in a major new assault on the Turkish defences. Three fresh British divisions were to be landed at nearby Suvla Bay while Australians, New Zealanders and Gurkhas would push north from Anzac Cove to link up with them. On the evening of 6 August, the men of the 16th marched in file along the beach and cut inland through unfamiliar gullies to reach the heights where the Turks lay in wait for them. The order had gone out for everyone to empty rifles of all ammunition. Any man found with a bullet in the magazine faced severe reprimand — the fighting would be done at bayonet point.

In France, Bar was still in a base camp and concerned about the lack of news from home. He wrote to sister-in-law Mary, Eric's wife, in early August, though the letter is undated.

Sgt BR Beechey
2nd Battalion Lincolnshire Regiment
8th Infantry Base Depot
Havre, France
I am still in camp here and we are still doing drills etc. Have not had a letter since I reached France,

but it may have been because I put 3rd instead of 8th in the above address. This is a fine place for scenery etc. but we do not get out of camp much. I have only been down town once as yet. Shall be glad to hear any news that is going about any of the brothers. If Chris is still in hospital I should like his number and address as I have lost them. Also where is Eric now and has Frank gone out yet? I was sorry not to get leave but I never had the chance. I was reckoning on four days but we were taken by surprise and our preparations were hurried, not to say feverish. Every single article of clothing, equipment etc. had to be issued to us afresh. I left a kitbag full of stuff for a pal of mine, Corporal Gilbert by name, to send home for me. Hope it arrived safe.

Am getting a bit lonely here for want of any news so please write a gossipy letter if you have time. Give my love to young Thomas (he ought to be talking now) and say I will write home immediately I get a letter.

Your affectionate brother, Bar

On the day Harold was scaling the Gallipoli heights and steeling himself for a hand-to-hand, eye-to-eye confrontation with the enemy, Chris was making final arrangements for his mother to visit him in hospital.

6 August 1915
C1 Ward Western Gen Hosp, Manchester
I see by today's paper vouchers for half-fare tickets

are issued for distance over 30 miles; will try and get some. Limit is four. Len and a chum came Sunday last. Let me know when you or Char or any of the others are likely to come.

Your loving son, Chris

He sent another short note a few days later.

9 August 1915

I enclose a voucher for two adults (not 4) to exchange at the booking office. Fill in the date. They've started massage on me here so I won't be moving for a bit. Bring one of the girls with you.

Chris

PS I'm improving slowly and surely.

By then, the 16th Battalion's involvement in another Gallipoli shambles was over. The new British divisions had landed largely unopposed at Suvla Bay but failed to press on and take the undefended high ground. Instead, they sat on the shore while their commander, fresh from a spell in charge of guarding the Tower of London, did nothing. When the troops were finally sent into action, the Turks had had plenty of time to strengthen their positions and the British were routed.

The 4th Australian Brigade, which included the 16th Battalion, had been directed to take Hill 971, a commanding peak overlooking the whole of Anzac. But there was a fatal flaw in the plan. Amid the scrubby summits and plunging ravines, the accessibility of the hill, even its exact location, had been badly misjudged — hardly surprising when the whole Gallipoli enterprise was launched without proper maps of a terrain that was a defender's dream. Sir Ian Hamilton was said to have had nothing more than an out-of-date tourist map to plan the entire doomed operation, and it was rumoured that his staff had bought up boxes of Baedeker's from a Cairo merchant, only to find they contained maps of the Rhine Valley instead of Turkey.

Harold and his comrades were sent into action wearing white patches, eight inches square, on their right shoulders and six-inch-wide white bands around each arm. As well as making them identifiable to the troops following on behind, they also provided excellent targets for the enemy on a brilliant moonlit night. Simply marching along the beach that sultry summer evening made a refreshing change for men who had been holed up for so long. By 3a.m., the beach had long been left behind and they were clambering over stony ridges and through dense scrub that provided cover for Turks who had to be winkled out at the point of a bayonet. Dawn revealed Hill 971 to be an impossible, unachievable goal. It lay nearly a mile away still, across fractured country commanded by Turkish snipers and machine gunners at every high point. The commanding officer of the 16th would later have to answer for a lack of offensive spirit but he could see his troops were too ill and too exhausted to go on. He ordered them to dig in. Many did not even have the strength to gouge out a possy hole and were caught in

134

the open by bursting shrapnel. The expected order to withdraw never came. The 16th was instructed to press forward to the next spur from which the final thrust to Hill 971 would be attempted at 4.15 the next morning. As they rose from their shallow scrapes in the ground, Turkish fire stopped them dead in their tracks. A Captain Heming was hit in the leg and the thigh before being killed by a bullet through the brain as a medic dressed his wounds. The dead and dying littered the ravines. Suvla was another disaster.

In Manchester, Chris had taken a worrying turn for the worse. After the emotion of seeing his mother and Char he had been in high spirits. All the Australian adventures came pouring out — life in the bush, heat, hardship, spiders, snakes, how well Harold had knuckled down to it, his delightful young lady, Miss Boyce . . . or was it Miss Bailey? And then the war, how Harold was going to stay behind and take care of the farm, but every man had to stand up to such German barbarity. Char shuffled uncomfortably at his paralysed brother's bedside. Chris insisted he would make a full recovery and was looking forward to going home and visiting old Friesthorpe friends like the Olivants and the Slingers. The fever that laid him low after his mother's visit was something he would get used to. He had little of the bodily strength he used to have, but he had enough moral strength to see him over this crisis and many more to come. For now, a nursing sister had to write home on his behalf.

To Mrs Amy Beechey
16 August 1915
Military Hospital, Whitworth St, Manchester

Dear Madam,

Your son wishes me to write to let you know he is a little better today and hopes in a few more days to be almost well again.

Yours etc. J. Warne (Sister)

Bar's desperate plea for gossip from home and news of his brothers brought a response from youngest sister Edie, but, apart from some mild excitement about aircraft, she had very little to report.

17 August 1915
14 Avondale St, Lincoln

How are you getting on and how do you like Havre? It is a long time since I have seen you. We have had an aeroplane buzzing around this morning for a trial trip and this afternoon it flew away to Farnborough. Several of its predecessors have done the same. Rustons are turning them out pretty fast, and we've got a beautiful, multi-coloured aeroplane shed on the West Common. We haven't had an air raid here yet, though we've had two on the East coast and one on the West quite lately. Chris is progressing and Harold is well according to the latest. Mother and Chas went to stay a few days in Manchester last week. No more news.

Your affectionate sister, Edith

Bar was no nearer the front line after three dull weeks at Le Havre where he received only the sketchiest of information about his brothers. He had obtained one of the army's special green envelopes, which put a soldier on his honour not to give away any military secrets. In return, he could expect it to wing its way past the censors unopened. Such envelopes were distributed so sparingly that there was a thriving black market in them — one man was reputed to have paid two francs for a stolen consignment that lasted him and his pals the rest of the war. But Bar was too much of a man of honour to abuse the privilege. He was able to sign the back, certifying the enclosed letter contained nothing but private and family matters, with a clear conscience. Tunic buttons and the plight of Monks Abbey Tennis Club were topics unlikely to earn the wrath of staff officers at base even if they did decide to open it.

> 21 August 1915
> No. 3 Coy, 11th Entrenching Battalion
> British Expeditionary Force, France

Dear Mother

You see by the above that there is another new address and I have changed my battalion again. We cannot give any details of our movements owing to the censorship though this letter, being in an official green envelope, will not be censored by our own officer and is only liable to censorship at headquarters.

I have been at Havre three weeks now and we

have had it very hot all the time with cold nights. Glad you sent Chris's address; I will write as soon as I have the time. I have been doing Orderly Sergeant again and it means a lot of running about. I am glad Chris and Harold are going on all right and Frank seems to have got a decent berth.

I have been down town once or twice on pass and it is quite a nice town with boulevards and squares planted with trees.

Most of our old 9th Battalion Lincolns have been broken up into drafts for the service battalions now and I believe there are very few of them left at Lichfield. I think the buttons will reach me all right now if sent to the address I have given.

Is Frances at home for the holidays? Expect the Monks Abbey Tennis Club is fairly defunct this year. I am always glad to get any letters here as one gets out of touch and should like to get the Lincolnshire Chronicle every now and then.

Your loving son, Bar

Chris was able to write a line to his mother to tell her he was improving.

26 August 1915
Western Gen Hosp, Manchester

That attack kept me ill for nearly a fortnight, temp. 105 for some time, normal now but no appetite and weak. Will write soon.

★　★　★

A day later, Bar was on the move. He just had time to dash off a postcard, which could not have been much comfort to his mother as he embarked on the last leg of his journey to the front — "Panorama pris du Cimetière du Mont-Gargan" was the legend on the picture of a Rouen graveyard.

> 27 August 1915
>
> En route. Will let you know how to address letters in a day or two, Bar.

Chris was still recovering from his bout of fever, but there always seemed to be an attentive woman around to write home on his behalf.

> Sunday, 29 August 1915
> C1 Ward
>
> I am a bit weak and tired after my illness and very little appetite, but I am slowly improving and no temperature, and soon hope to be as well as when you saw me when I will write again. Love to all at home, Chris. PS I have received several of your letters addressed to Egypt since I saw you. (Written by B. Rae)

There was still no word from Harold. It was almost a month since he wrote saying he would be in the thick of it again soon. Longer casualty lists seemed to be the only result of the Suvla Bay debacle, but H. R. Beechey was not among the names. While the family held its breath over the fate of Harold in Gallipoli, Bar was settling into life in the front line. He was with the 2nd Lincolns in Flanders by the end of August.

Sgt BR Beechey 13773
No. 6 Platoon, X Coy
2nd Battalion Lincolnshire Regiment
British Expeditionary Force, France

Dear Edie

I am writing this on the back of your letter so you will see that I got it. Also because where I am it is all the paper I can get. I am writing this from a dugout in the trenches. I have as you see joined my own battalion now and am where the work is going on.

You may imagine me when we marched here. Half way we had a rest and you might have seen me laying in the middle of the road — and the night — to get the easiest position possible after marching a good distance in the fullest of marching orders. NB It was raining and the road was wet.

My present residence is a charming one, about 9ft x 7ft, and holds three comfortably. It's a lot better than the billets we had before we came in as there the rats used to sit on you while you slept. I have only received one letter from home yet so I suppose there are some wandering about Europe trying to find me. Please keep sending news as some may reach me in time. Love to all at home. I am quite well and comfortable.

Your affectionate bro, Bar

★ ★ ★

For the next few weeks Bar alternated between spells in and out of the line at Bois Grenier, just to the north of that sodden, low-lying corner of France where much of the BEF had been sacrificed for so little gain earlier in 1915. He took the usual mud and miseries of trench life in his stride and was probably unaware that a new, greater attack was being planned in which the 2nd Lincolns were set to play a supporting role.

5 September 1915
Sgt BR Beechey 13773
No. 6 Platoon, X Coy
2nd Battalion Lincolnshire Regiment
British Expeditionary Force, France

Dear Mother

I am now writing from my billet in a village behind the firing line. I have just come out of the trenches; we were in three days and it rained most of the time. The experience is interesting and, in normal times when nothing much is going on, quite harmless. You go in by night and come out at night and it is then you are likely to get hit if any time. You hear firing from artillery of both sides by day and night and sometimes Fritz, as we call our opponent, drops a shell a little way behind your trench but while we were in he never dropped one on it. Ours [the British gunners] seemed better shots as I saw several which seemed to drop right in theirs.

You keep your head behind the parapet for the most part while sentries are on the lookout with a periscope. At night they look over the top, and if you don't look after them they want to do so in the daytime. Somehow or another you can't help jumping up and having a look over occasionally. I had several peeps over on the first day. NCOs get a good lot of duty in the trenches, going out to see how the listening post is getting on etc. The latter is a corporal and a few men who go out in front of the trench by night and listen to any sounds from the enemy. I had to go out to them the second night to see if they were all right. Also there is a good deal of digging done by night. Both sides send up rockets and use searchlights at short intervals during the night to see what the other party are about.

I was out with a digging party the first night and when I got where I had to go I found I had only 20 men instead of 40 so I wandered about looking for the remainder nearly up to Fritz's trenches, only to find after all that the beggars had not started. However, they had to go out when we came in and finish their job.

We came out last night through about a foot of mud across a mile and a half of fields in the rain. It was awful. Where there was a bit of a rise I put a foot forward but it slipped back. Then I tried the other but it was the same thing. There was I trying to get up a two-foot slope for about five minutes. At last I went round but I had lost the rest of the platoon. However, I knew which road they were going on and caught them up. When I finally got to the billet I put my waterproof sheet down, took my greatcoat out of the pack and lay straight down to sleep, muddy as I was. Then they woke us at half past five this morning to take us three miles to have a bath. We all got baths in round tubs and plenty of real hot water. Then we marched back and now I am in charge of a guard till tomorrow morning and writing under a walnut tree. I have had several of the walnuts.

I really am all right and don't mind the life, only we all wish the thing was over, and those who have been out longest wish so most of all. Love to all at home. Hoping to hear news.

I am your loving son, Bar

The novelty of war was wearing thin already. Bar wanted it to end. He had discovered it paid to keep your head down during the day while nights brought a frenzy of activity — listening patrols, squads working on the wire, digging trenches, burying or bringing in the dead and others whose job was to keep watch and guard the working parties against attack. In the Lincolns' sector, as well as the usual flares and star shells, the Germans had a particularly brilliant searchlight that threatened to expose a night patrol at any second and bring down a blizzard of machine-gun and shellfire. On 4 September, the evening before Bar and his comrades trudged back to billets for a brief spell of rest, his battalion lost four men to enemy fire. Two more were killed and another wounded during their next routine spell of a few days back in the line. It didn't take Bar long to realise the Western Front was a lethal place even when all was officially quiet.

Chris was beginning to show promising signs of progress after recovering from his bad turn. His early optimism of a leisurely but full recovery had faded as he lay paralysed but he was now able to sit up and even attend a special show the hospital laid on. Star turn was the legendary music hall entertainer Harry Lauder, who would one day describe what it meant to lose a son in the war — "It seemed for me the board of life was blank and black. For me there was no past and there would be no future."

10 September 1915
Western Gen Hosp, Manchester

The last letter was written by a Scotch girl who comes in as a visitor, most anxious to write letters so I let her. I am normal temp and mending and my appetite is returning. Starting massage again today — joints very stiff. Have been up in a chair last two afternoons, one hour first day, and went out of ward for first time yesterday to see a concert on ground floor. Harry Lauder gave us over ½hour. Other turns good.

★ ★ ★

In France, the great offensive was less than a fortnight away, but Bar still seemed oblivious to it.

15 September 1915
Sgt BR Beechey 13773
No. 6 Platoon, X Coy
2nd Battalion Lincolnshire Regiment
British Expeditionary Force, France

Dear Mother

I should think three or four letters each way must have been lost in the post, as I have written at least once a week since I have been in France. One seems to want to keep hearing from England all the time here and we all flock round when the mail comes in to see if anything is for us.

I am now in a regular battalion and have my work cut out to keep up with everything as Sergeant as discipline etc is stricter than in the 9th and also I have had all the duties etc of trench service to learn as well as carry out. In addition, I am full Sergeant and most of the old hands have only been made Acting Sergeants or Lance Sergeants (Promotion in regular battalions is naturally much slower than in the 9th where we all started as recruits together) so that I am not far from being senior Sergeant in the company.

We came into the trenches again last night, my fourth time in and I only got about an hour's sleep as I was on duty till 1am and up again at four for "stand-to" which means that we all get our equipment and rifles and wait for an hour before dawn to see if any attack is coming off. We do the same at dusk every night. This last time out we were in immediate reserve, not far behind the firing line and had to stand to in the morning as if we were in the trenches. We were only allowed to take our boots and puttees off half a company at a time for the morning or afternoon.

We get plenty of tobacco and cigarettes issued to us to go on with and we get a chance to see the Daily Mirror and Mail a day late. I should like a pair or two of socks if you have got them to spare as mine are wearing out. But we can get our clothing renewed generally. The most urgent need in the trenches is some form of vermin-killer. We are all the same from the officers downwards. Also a writing pad as writing paper is scarce and dear. We shall soon have the winter here and the nights are getting very cold already so I should be very glad of a knitted muffler. We keep fires going at the back of the trenches and generally make some coffee or cocoa once or twice a night to keep ourselves warm. I see by the papers that the Zeppelins are getting very active on the East Coast. We never see them on this side but we see plenty of aeroplanes of both sides and it is pretty to watch the shells from the anti-aircraft guns bursting around them. Is Edie going back to Bakewell this term? Please tell her to write. Her letters are generally very descriptive. I will write again soon. I think it takes four or five days for my

letters to reach Lincoln <u>when they do</u>.
    Yr loving son, Bar

Chris had unexpected news for his mother. He was leaving the 2nd Western General Hospital immediately.

                              21 September 1915
Transfer to Harefield Park Hospital, Middlesex. I travel tomorrow, Kris

Then, just as suddenly, and to joy all round, Harold turned up, in Wales.

                              5 October 1915
      3rd Western Hospital, Ninian Park, Cardiff
My dear mother
    Arrived here this afternoon from Southampton. Left Alexandria 24th September. I came over on number 1 Australian Hospital ship Karoola. Had a fairly good journey but one or two little incidents. Had a very fine view of Gibraltar by moonlight — it looked very impressive and the searchlights lit up the ship like day. Then we picked up a wireless message from the Highland Warrior — but after searching round for some hours we found her fast on the rocks near Corunna, Spain, and took off the passengers, nine of them, bound for South America. Then most of us, more or less seriously, got ptomaine poisoning from something in the food. I got off fairly light though I had some nasty spasms of pain in my little tummy the last few

days. Everybody got over it luckily. I have been sent home for a couple of months to recuperate. I'm fairly all right but pretty weak and get fagged with very little exertion. I don't know how long I shall be in this hospital but you might write straight back and I will let you know of any change of address. I expect I shall be sent to a convalescent home in a few days. Love to all and tell them to write here. I shall have at least a fortnight at home when I get fairly fit.
mLove Harold

PS I suppose you got my field service postcard telling you I was being sent back to the base sick which I sent off about the beginning of September — same trouble as before.

That "trouble" was dysentery that turned a man's guts to water. Suvla had brought only more agony for the 16th Battalion. One of Chris's 4th Field Ambulance pals, who had served in the same section and would have known "Beechey's brother", as they all called Harold, left descriptions of the men marching off to Hill 971 and of the grim aftermath. "It was a great and impressive sight to see an army marching along the beach at night, so quietly and stealthily without any undue excitement," according to Corporal E. H. Kitson, who brought up the rear with the stretcher-bearers that night of 6 August. Traipsing back two days later, he said the strain and sights along the way were enough to break the strongest of men, ". . . covered in dead and dying . . . headless bodies and stiff, cold hands."

But there was no respite for the worn-out 16th who were ordered back into the line at Anzac without a break and put to work on 9 August strengthening a hot spot known as Outpost No. 1. The next day six men were killed and an officer and fifteen others wounded. Outpost No. 1 was turning out to be almost as deadly as Quinn's, and food and water were in short supply. Morale was so low that Lt Col Pope, in charge, did the rounds of the front line trying to lift spirits. Harold's A Company commander, Major Mansbridge, was evacuated sick.

What was left of the battalion took part in another attack on 21 August, after which Harold joined the shambling line of sorry medical cases at the beach aid post. "Plight of the men most distressing," recorded a battalion medical officer. But they found the resilience to fight on. Some were so stricken by diarrhoea that they took their blankets and slept on top of the latrines, nine-foot-deep uncovered pits that spawned black clouds of flies. A pole was slung across for men to balance on "like sparrows on a perch", according to one. Some who fell in were too weak to claw their way out and drowned under a sea of excrement.

Harold, fighting his own battle against dysentery, was back in the line for another attack on 27 August, which achieved few gains and high casualties. He was reaching the limit of his endurance. One of his 16th Battalion comrades, Private Henry Daniels, totted up the number of original members left in the first four platoons —

from No. 1 platoon, two left; No. 2, none left; No. 3, four left; No. 4, four left.

An operation was launched to give the boys a morale-boosting feast of tinned fruit, chocolate and sausages, plundered from BEF stores. The provisions were hauled up to battalion HQ by a convoy of twenty-two mules with every man due to receive 20 shillings' worth and the amount deducted from his pay. As the food was being dished out, Turks on top of the infamous Hill 971 landed a 75-mm shell in the middle of men and stores, killing six and wounding twenty-two others.

Harold came through without a scratch but by September he was too ill to go on. As one of dozens of dysentery cases lying on the beach within range of enemy fire, he was given sips of water by a medic who tied the bottom of his trouser legs with string to contain the festering tide. A nurse would later have the sickening task of cutting off his clothing that was like putrid outer skin, then washing him down. "It was pitiful to see them so weak with blood and water pouring out of them," said Sister Mary Fitzgibbon, a nurse aboard one of the hospital ships, anchored off Gallipoli. It took six days for Harold to reach the sanctuary of No. 2 Australian General Hospital in Cairo, where dysentery cases were treated away from the other casualties, 200 or more to a ward.

Two nurses were left to oversee what another sister described as "great strong men looking as old as 60 . . . How they suffer. It is brutal and I have never seen anything like it. They lie there in agony night and day." All had to be kept clean and put on a strict diet, with plenty of rest and daily doses of Emetine, administered through hypodermic needles as terrifying as any Turkish bayonet. Harold could perhaps have chosen to be shipped back to Australia. His war might have ended with a hero's return and Curly waiting for him on the same wharf at Fremantle where she had waved him off a year ago. But, with Chris back in England as well, Harold could not pass up the chance of seeing his mother, brothers and sister again. It guaranteed there would be worse horrors to come, but for now he was frustrated at being stuck so far from Lincoln with few diversions.

7 October 1915

3rd Western Hospital, Ninian Park, Cardiff

My dear mother

Many thanks for your letters. It is not a bad place here, nicely treated, but I shall be glad when I get sent to a convalescent home as we are shut in here and not allowed out at all. I find it very cold after the heat over at the Peninsula. It is 18 months since I struck a winter and that was hotter than our summers. I must have passed Eric on the way from Malta as we called in there and stopped a day. I am glad Chris is getting on well. I have had so many enquiries about him from the 4th AAMC [Australian Army Medical Corps], both from the men and the doctors. He did splendid work there. I got to know a lot of his old section and was always welcomed and introduced to anyone in his section as "Beechey's brother". I had it from a pretty good source that if he had not been so unlucky as to get smacked they were thinking of recommending him for the DCM, not for any one act but for going through the work in such a fine way. He left a ripping name behind.

I am sorry they sent me to such an out of the way place as this — it is impossible to get at without a good deal of expense and inconvenience. We came from the station in motorcars and crowds of people along the streets cheered us — I never felt so bashful in my life. We have been smothered in cigarettes and things, which is a mixed blessing as my inside is not acceptable to fruit and cakes. It makes me narked to think only a few months ago I could eat anything and feel no effects, but now I have to keep to plain tucker. I am putting on weight now and feel pretty good.

Affectionately yours, Harold

A few days later Harold was writing chirpily to one of his sisters, although there is no clue as to which one, and the letter is undated.

3rd Western Hosp, Ninian Park, Cardiff
Dear Old Girl

I had just finished writing the letter to mother when in bounced the colonel, a good, jolly sort of fellow, stood just inside and said all those who were fit enough to bring their boards to him. He went round; "You feeling pretty fit now," he said to me; "Yes, not too bad." "Got any friends here, relations or anything?" "Yes, mother." "Will they have you, do you think?" "Shouldn't wonder." "Oh well, discharged" — and he scribbled on the diet sheet. So after things are fixed up in London by our own Gov, I shall be able to come home instead of going (as if I had no friends here) to the convalescent home.

We are in an elementary school, which has only just opened. We are the first patients and all the kids who used to attend here come and stare at us. We are quite a novelty and the people are making quite a fuss of us — if we could get out we would have a glorious time.

I shall be going for a motor drive round Cardiff today, I hope. A gentleman is taking us in turn.

Well good luck, Harold

For Amy, the war had been something of a blessing in bringing Chris and Harold home from Australia. Eric had reached Malta safely while Frank had been recognised as officer material and was still training in England. But every time she stepped out into the streets of Lincoln she saw women dressed in the black of the bereaved. The papers had been full of the recent big push at a place called Loos. Trainloads of casualties began arriving in Lincoln at the beginning of October and were transferred to the city's 4th Northern General Hospital by fleets of ambulances. Nothing had been heard of Bar for several weeks. Then a small, official brown War Office envelope was delivered to 14

Avondale Street. Amy Beechey would become all too familiar with Army Form B.104–82, which, contrary to the myth of legions of telegram boys roaming the land, arrived by regular post.

15 October 1915
To Mrs A. Beechey, 14 Avondale St, Lincoln:
Army Form B.104–82, No. 9521
(If replying, please quote above No.)
Infantry Record Office, Lichfield Station

Madam

It is my painful duty to inform you that a report has this day been received from the War Office notifying the death of 13773 Sergeant B. R. Beechey, Lincolnshire Regiment, which occurred at (Place not stated) on the 25th of September 1915, and I am to express to you the sympathy and regret of the Army Council at your loss. The cause of death was Killed in action.

Until her dying day, Amy kept a photo of what was said to be Bar's final resting place, showing a plain wooden cross. "Barnard's grave" is scrawled on the back. There are no other graves visible so it might have been a makeshift crucifix hurriedly erected by comrades near the spot where Bar died before war moved them on. For many of those cut down at Loos there was little hope of proper burial. One soldier described the lack of ceremony or compassion for the dead: "They lay in the trenches where they'd fallen or had been slung and earth had just been put on top of them. When the rains came, it washed most of the earth away. You'd go along the trenches and see a boot and puttee sticking out, or arm or hand or sometimes faces. Not only would you see them, but you'd be walking on them, slipping and sliding."

Today, Sgt B. R. Beechey is one of 11,368 names on the Ploegsteert Memorial, commemorating those missing men swallowed up by the mud of Flanders. Form B.104–82 provided no indication of how Amy's eldest son met his death. Newspaper reports were little better. They painted an epic picture of men going over the top kicking rugby balls, inspired onwards by the skirl of bagpipes — two pipers won the Victoria Cross on the first day of the battle. Nearer the truth were the Germans who christened it "the corpse field of Loos". With his own generals warning that an attack across such flat and exposed territory with so little cover would "cost us dearly and we shall not get very far", Kitchener merely insisted, "We must act with all our energy . . . even though by doing so we suffer very heavy casualties indeed."

The 2nd Lincolns were given only a bit part in the bloody affair. Their brigade was to act as decoy to keep German troops pinned down at Bois Grenier and distract them from the main blow further south, around Lens. They would receive only limited artillery support and no reserves could be spared to consolidate any gains. The British were using poison gas for the first time but the Bois Grenier sideshow would have to do without it, which turned out to be a blessing. "The accessory", as the chlorine was called to maintain secrecy, was mostly a curse elsewhere, choking more British troops than the enemy.

The 24th of September was damp and overcast with a hint of autumn rain in the air. At 6.25p.m. Bar and his men of X Company's No. 6 platoon fell in for the march from their billets at Bac St Maur, a hamlet beside the river Lys near Armentières. Weary, wet and muddy from negotiating the usual muddle of bodies and supplies on the move through narrow lanes and congested communication trenches, they reached their jumping-off positions at 1a.m. Across the gloom of No Man's Land lay their objective: an enemy line studded with defensive forts around a dot on the map of French Flanders called La Bridoux.

Zero hour was fixed for 4.30a.m., two hours earlier than the main advance to the south. There was a last chance to snatch some sleep or write home. Bar, as a senior NCO, had time for neither. He stayed on duty, checking sentries and lookout posts, peering over the chalky parapet for any sign of the enemy through the darkness. At 3a.m. he squelched through his platoon's zigzagging stretch of trench, stirring the men to take up their positions. Half an hour later they slipped over the top, inched through gaps left in their own wire and crept silently into No Man's Land to within 200 yards of the Germans. There, they lay down in the mud and waited for the order to attack.

At 4.25a.m. British guns opened up with a five-minute bombardment. As the barrage rumbled overhead Bar and his men rushed forward with the Lincolns through clouds of exploding smoke shells. The enemy, still cowering from the shellfire, were taken by surprise as ghostly figures leapt on them from the eerie smog. The Lincolns had bayoneted, blasted and bombed the German defenders out of Bridoux Fort by 4.31a.m. The Lozenge, Corner Fort and Angle Fort also had to be overwhelmed for the attack to succeed. Forty bombers were attached to each flank of the assaulting companies, armed with "cricket ball" grenades, a fussy, ineffective weapon. The fuse, protected by sticking plaster, had to be lit by a match struck on a special wristband worn by the bomber. The drill was: Take bomb, TEAR OFF sticking plaster, STRIKE match, LIGHT fuse, HOLD bomb for three or four seconds, then THROW. In the wet, an actual cricket ball might have been more useful.

As the Lincolns pushed on, the operation began to fall apart. Germans were counter-attacking in force and clawing back every gain. The enemy front line had turned into a noose, gradually being tightened around the neck of those who had breached it. One of the key forts remained in German hands when the central part of the British advance collapsed against uncut barbed wire and machine-gun fire. From there the defenders funnelled fresh troops into the line with better bombs. Two new companies were sent forward to bolster the faltering Lincolns but at

1p.m., after more than seven hours of hand-to-hand fighting, the enemy was back in Bridoux Fort. Men in the second line were cut off and either annihilated or taken prisoner. Surviving Lincolns, crammed into a shrinking portion of trench that was pounded with pinpoint accuracy by the German guns, withstood six ferocious counter-attacks. With dead and dying all around them, they were driven out of their position by the seventh enemy onslaught.

By 5p.m., the Lincolns had withdrawn and were back where they had started 14 hours earlier. Sergeant Beechey was not among them. Casualties were 60 dead, 229 wounded and 36 missing. Three of X Company's officers were killed. In all, the three diversionary operations cost 10,000 men for no gain. Another 50,000 were lost amid the slag heaps and mining villages around Loos itself.

Contemporary reports mentioned the heroic attack on Bridoux Fort — "The Lincolns took eighty prisoners, after killing hundreds of foes in the fighting around the stronghold," trumpeted one. "A middle-aged company cook, whose proper place was far in the rear, became so excited by the din that he left his work and ran into the captured German trench. There he seized a rifle and sniped every German who came across his line of sight, crying as he did so, 'There's another of the devils!'"

Less absurd were the casualties filling columns of newsprint. On Thursday 21 October, "Beechey 13773

Sergt. B." was listed among fifty-seven names of 2nd Lincolns killed in action. Loos had been a lamentable failure and, as well as costing Amy Beechey her eldest son, would cost Sir John French his job as commander-in-chief of the BEF.

Char was in the middle of a maths lesson at Stamford when the telegram arrived from his mother, telling him of Bar's death. He glanced at it, tucked it in his pocket and went on teaching. Only after the bell sounded the end of class did he pass the news on to his pupils before hurrying to the head's study to request time off to return to Lincoln. Edie remembered him arriving home, throwing open the front door and declaring, "Well, this is a bad business."

Pressure for him to join up, whether real or imagined, was growing. He was the only one of the pre-August 1914 Stamford masters yet to enlist. At speech day that first Christmas of the war, the head, Canon Day, had voiced his regret at losing Mr Pitt, Mr Cowie and Mr Wood to the army. But there was no doubt, he added to lusty applause, that they had gone where the need for them was greatest. He was cheered to the roof as he remarked how the many other Stamford Old Boys serving in the ranks might be trusted to maintain the honour of the old school. *The Stamfordian* listed those old boys who were paying a high price for their patriotism. Included among the roll of the wounded was Char's own brother — "C. W. R. Beechey, with the Australians, in their Army Medical Corps . . . wounded at the

Dardanelles. His letter, dated June 8, says that he is being nursed for paralysis of the hip and leg, through a fall consequent upon being hit by a bullet in the shoulder." A later bulletin reported Chris's return to Britain and steady progress in hospital.

Char, as secretary of the Old Stamfordians, announced there would be no annual cricket match that summer between the school and the Old Boys. However, he did scrape together enough players for a football match against the Essex Regiment, who were training locally before being posted overseas. The army side were two up in ten minutes when spectators spotted why they were running the school ragged — they had twelve men on the pitch. With the teams on equal terms, the rest of the match was a fairer contest and ended 4–2 to the army with Char congratulating everyone on an even game. The naturalists' club also soldiered on, but even an innocent excursion to explore the flora and fauna of nearby Ketton Pits — followed by tea at the Railway Hotel — was not without controversy. Char subsequently had to issue a school statement, insisting, "Though we received a notice soon afterwards in very large print to the effect that Ketton Pits are closed to the Public, we were not the party who set the wood on fire."

Some might have wondered what a physically fit man of military age was doing gadding about in search of buttercups and butterflies at such a time. A reminder of where one's duty lay came in a bulletin from the front line from Char's old colleague, Mr

160

Wood, now Lieutenant M. H. Wood. A few pages on from events at Ketton Pits, Wood informed readers of the summer 1915 *Stamfordian*, "There is nothing attractive, gallant or romantic about trench warfare. To wade through two feet of mud in a communication trench, to be up all night, and have but four hours' sleep in the daytime, to go without a wash or shave for four days, to know how many of your own men get hit, while you remain in complete ignorance of what damage you do to the Germans ... I have also had the experience of being shelled, and very objectionable it is too, as you feel so helpless. Fortunately, you hear the whistle of an approaching shell and at once make a dart to the nearest cover and wait for the explosion with your heart in your boots."

Harold had escaped Cardiff with its cakes, concerts and car rides, but instead of going to stay with the family in Lincoln he opted for an official spell of convalescence. If he went to his mother's he knew he would be flung back into action as soon as his furlough was over. The other attraction of opting for convalescence was that he could be with Chris. They had not seen each other for almost six months, since that shimmering evening in May when they said their farewells amid the human wreckage on the beach at Anzac. Harefield — a gift to the war effort from a wealthy, patriotic Australian — was a country house-turned-hospital set in a hundred leafy hectares a dozen miles from London. Harold's "little tummy" had yet to recover fully from the ravages of dysentery but now it was his turn to look out for the older, invalid brother who had been his friend, protector and father figure from the day he set foot in Australia.

21 October 1915
No. 6 Ward, Harefield Park Hospital,
Denham, Middlesex

My dear mother

I did not feel fit enough to come on furlough so I have gone convalescent for a bit. I asked at Headquarters to be sent to Harefield as my brother was there. We were stranded in London on Saturday so I spent the weekend with Len. I find Chris much better than I thought he would be and I give him a push round the village every day. It may be some time before I come home on furlough now. It is very pretty here and as it's nice weather and we have plenty of liberty I don't mind stopping here a bit as the sooner I get my furlough the sooner I get sent away. I find I have to undergo some treatment yet before I am right, brought on by the dysentery.

Poor old Bar had a short innings — let's hope it was a clean knockout.   Harold

The casualty forms found with Chris's war records in the National Archives of Australia refer to his arrival at Harefield in September 1915 with "B.W. [bullet wound] shoulder" and "injury to knee". He was also marked down as a "shellshock" case.* The reason it appears on his service record becomes clear from the next letter to his mother.

> 2 November 1915
> Ward 14, Harefield Park Hosp,
> Denham, Middlesex
>
> I have fairly good news to tell about my improvement. For some time I've been able to put my hands on two beds and stand up. Last Thursday I let go of the beds and stood up for a few seconds alone. I've done it several times each day since for longer times. I can walk with Harold's assistance up and down the ward. Harold is kind and attentive and is looking much better since his operation. He may have to undergo

---

* That Chris suffered from shellshock is also written across the papers for his eventual repatriation to Australia with others who would never fight again. I mentioned this in an article appealing for information about him that was published by the *Post* newspaper in Perth just after Anzac Day 2002. His grandson Nick Mayman, living in the suburb of Subiaco, was astonished to pick up his local paper one day and read about his grandfather, who had been dead for almost thirty-five years. He was dismayed by my description of Chris returning shell-shocked and "a broken man". I could not have been more wrong. Chris was no longer the tall, strong young man who had left for Australia, hacked out a living from the bush and then put his life on the line at Gallipoli. Yes, he was stooped, needed sticks for walking, then callipers and, only at the very end, had to resort to a wheelchair. But his spirit was never broken.

another slight operation. I had a letter from Eric a day or two ago and I see Len about every Sunday. I'm moved into this ward because they have collected all the spinal cord and concussion shock cases together into one medical ward under one medical officer. Love to all at home and the Snarford folk.

So Chris was bracketed with those who had lost their mind under the strain of battle. Such tortured souls might have been put in front of a firing squad for cowardice if they were in the British Army but the AIF did not shoot their own men. There was a special ward for them at 1st Australian Auxiliary Hospital, Harefield. Harold, after the boredom of Wales, was content wheeling his brother around the autumnal lanes of Denham and making the occasional sortie into London.

> 22 November 1915
>
> No. 22 Ward, Harefield

Well, I have had my second operation, for a fistula this time. I had it yesterday and am in bed and shall be for a week, I think. I hope to be on the fit list soon after that. I will manage my furlough to include Christmas as it would be nice to have a Christmas at home.

You need not send any mufflers, socks etc while I am in hospital as I can get anything I want in that line from the matron. But if you will keep the socks for me till I get out of this. It's awfully pretty

around here, beautifully wooded and nice roads —
I have been out several times since I have been
here. I went to a matinee in aid of Australian
wounded at His Majesty's Theatre, Piccadilly
Circus — it was very clever, all first-class
performances. Queen Alexandra, Princess Mary,
Prince Henry were there. I am whiling my time
away by doing a bit of fancy work. I am making a
belt — it's done on canvas with different coloured
wools. It passes a bit of time away. The stuff is
given by some ladies living near here.

Love to everybody, Harold

Chris was making preparations for himself and Harold
to have some time in Lincoln, and for his eventual
return to Western Australia.

28 November 1915
Ward 14, Harefield Park Hosp
The medical officer seems to think I'd get better
quicker in the warm climate of Australia. Harold is
nearly due for furlough. It's about a week since his
operation and he's bright and gay. So when he gets
furlough I'll apply for a special pass to come home
with him. I'm writing to the OC Military Hosp
Lincoln to ask him if I could get the massage. I
should want a bath chair — cost about 35 shillings
— but if you or I could borrow one, so much the
better. Len was here yesterday and said you could
find room for beds for us in the front room. If not
we'd take lodging in the same street. If I was there

on two Fridays I could probably see most of my friends. I can walk about 100 yards twice or thrice a day.

Love to all, Chris

As his health improved, Harold was heartened to know he would not be going back to Gallipoli. Sir Ian Hamilton had been relieved of his post and his replacement, in Winston Churchill's view, "came, saw and capitulated". Every man was to be evacuated in what turned out to be the only bloodless operation of the campaign. At Anzac and elsewhere, they stole away with sombre thoughts of mates left behind, many of whom were just heaps of sun-bleached bones by the time burial parties returned after the war. Gallipoli had claimed around 8,000 Australian lives and, even after six times as many of their countrymen died on the Western Front, it would come to define a nation.

Harold, in his cheery, uncomplaining way, was going to be fit in plenty of time for 1916. Surgeons had patched up the unsightly wounds brought on by dysentery and he was looking forward to a family Christmas. He and Chris were welcomed home as heroes. Chris was keen to give Frank his uncensored views on what Australians thought of British officers now that his brother had joined that elite class and was being trained as a signalling officer. Carrying their hatboxes into battle was the least of it. Frank retaliated by bemoaning the lack of discipline among colonials who never saluted and flagrantly failed to polish tunic buttons and cap badges. Frank had risen swiftly

166

through the ranks without getting a whiff of cordite. He had progressed from private to corporal to sergeant with the 7th Lincolnshires and was commissioned in May 1915. The house in Avondale Street was full to bursting with the girls, with Sam home from boarding school and Char back from Stamford for the holidays. Len, arriving with Annie, managed to make Char feel slightly less uncomfortable about not being in uniform. Daughter-in-law Mary was there with baby Thomas. Only Eric was missing, away on the Mediterranean island of Malta with the Royal Army Medical Corps. And Bar, of course.

Amy wanted to forget the war as she glanced around at her sons: at Chris, half crippled, at poor, brave Harold, at Frank, so smart and confident, at Char and Len, who would surely be called upon as well, and at Sam, who was desperate to reach eighteen so that he, too, could join his brothers. She kept her fears to herself as they reminisced about carefree times at Friesthorpe: their father's endearing gullibility, Harold's many scrapes, Bar's unrequited love for Miss Rawding and the delights of climbing trees and vaulting drainage ditches. It would be their last family Christmas together.

CHAPTER
SEVEN

Love to all and goodbye if I don't see you again

Len Beechey was pained to see Chris, the most formidable of his seven brothers, being wheeled around in a bath chair. Len was no coward but he had no stomach for war. It had taken him a long time to find happiness and contentment. He would not leave Annie until he had to. On 15 November 1915, the charade over his marriage had been quietly resolved. At a simple register office ceremony in Coventry, Leonard Reeve Beechey, 34-year-old railway clerk, of 24 Chester Road, Highgate, north London, wed Frances Smith, widow, aged 39, originally of 6 Cross Hill, Coventry. Neither Amy Beechey nor any of Len's brothers and sisters attended. As far as they knew, he and Annie were already married and had been for years.

Around the time Len and Annie were taking their vows, the flushing out of men who had yet to join up was under way. The glamorous view of war as a huge adventure had not survived 1915 with its near-suicidal

Gallipoli landings and the futile slaughter on the Western Front. Disillusionment was setting in and the flood of cap-waving volunteers had slowed to a trickle. Posters, most famously of a steely-eyed, finger-pointing Lord Kitchener, no longer had the desired effect. People handed out white feathers as a badge of cowardice. Men had bloodstained bandages flung at them for not being in uniform. But public humiliation was not enough.

Conscription was coming. The assurance that bachelors would be called upon first was a major incentive for Len to turn his sham marriage into reality. It was one way to delay the inevitable call-up. For Char, there was no such luxury. He was wed only to Stamford School. When conscription was introduced in January 1916 for single men and childless widowers between the ages of eighteen and forty-one, his teaching days were numbered.

The passing year had been one of brief bursts of butchery for the British army in France and Flanders. Bestriding 1916 would be a single cataclysmic event — the Battle of the Somme. On 1 July 1916 the great mass of Kitchener's volunteer army would go over the top for the first time, their bayonets glinting in the summer sun as they ambled across the wide open expanses of No Man's Land to be mown down by machine guns in front of uncut belts of barbed wire. Pals' battalions, friends from the same street, factory and football teams would be destroyed in minutes. This would go on for five grotesque months, through summer heat, lashing autumn rains and the slush and sleet of early winter, at Pozières, Serre, High Wood, Thiepval.

Three of Amy's sons would have to face the carnage of the Somme before the battle ended in the freezing mud of a bitter mid-November, but in early January of 1916 the glow of a rare Christmas at home together had yet to fade. It was as close as they could get to one of those long-ago Friesthorpe Christmases where Frances helped cook dinner and all the Beechey children would dress up to perform plays, favourite among them the gruesome story of Bluebeard, with the girls chalking up their faces and painting crimson slits across their throats. They remembered crisp Christmas morning trips to church service with the little ones dizzily riding on the shoulders of their big brothers. And when they got back there would be a big box of delights awaiting them, the annual present from another of Amy's brothers, Uncle Frank, who owned a chocolate factory.

Chris, back in hospital after the break with the family, was feeling well enough to start enjoying a social life and to accept invitations from acquaintances thrilled to have a Gallipoli veteran around for a rubber or two of bridge.

15 January 1916
Harefield Hospital

Dear Mother

Thank you very much for sending the scarf and pillow. I'm getting stronger and better I think. I'm glad Harold has another fortnight [furlough] — I reckon it'll do him a world of good. I know when I was in London a trip to Lincolnshire at any time of the year did me good. I went to Muriel Gothorp's friends for dinner and bridge last Wed. Very nice people. Old man in the Board of Trade office and well off judging by appearances.

Harold finished his two-week home leave with a visit to Stamford to stay with Char for a few days. He could expect a return to active service at any time, but he was still not fully fit. A hurried, semi-legible scrawl to his mother from his latest camp south-east of London is undated but probably written in mid-January.

> No. L3 Hut, Australian Intermediate Base
> Abbey Wood nr London

I can't say how long I shall be here — am marked "light" [lightly wounded] at present. I got to Stamford fairly well, only getting into the wrong train at Grantham threw me an hour late. Char's cough seems much better. Arrived in town 20 past 11 last night, slept Union Jack Club so did not see Len or Annie. About 50 of us came down together so they marched us from Westminster to Charing X carrying our kitbags at which three collapsed on the way.

Love, Harold . . . beastly writing!

Len's Annie had immediately taken to Harold and liked to fuss over him, cooking him big breakfasts — or as big as food shortages allowed. She was proud of the admiring glances he got when he sauntered up the road in Highgate in his slouched hat and Australian uniform. He had the same quiet, sensitive nature as her husband and, like Len, he made her laugh. He had her in fits with stories of their mother censoring the mail-order clothing catalogues that landed on the doormat at Friesthorpe with a loud thump. Betraying her Quaker roots, Amy Beechey used to seize on the books and carefully cut out any pictures of female figures modelling combinations and knickers in case they corrupted her boys. In quieter moments Annie spoke of her fear of Len being called up and how unsuited he was to the crude army life. She knew Chris expected every man and brother to do his duty, but Harold was more sympathetic.

At Harefield, Chris's life was about to take an unexpected turn. The Beechey knack of finding true love on an impulse was set to happen again. At the beginning of March, there was no trace of romance in the air when Chris gave his mother a promising update on his physical progress. Seven weeks and two days later, he would be a married man. Nor were the Beechey girls immune — Frances, at the age of thirty, certainly took Harold by surprise when she married an old workmate of his from Claytons, the Lincoln engineering firm where he was apprenticed before leaving for Australia.

Chris to his mother:

2 March 1916
1st Australian Auxiliary Hospital,
Harefield Park, Middlesex

I'm still getting stronger and am just about my proper weight but still the nerve control is a long while coming back and the involuntary movements slow in dying away. I haven't heard from Harold for a fortnight but suppose he is still in Abbey Wood. Len I haven't seen for some time. I'm enclosing a snapshot of Harold and me when he came here as one of a firing party.

Love to all, Chris

Even the briefest of notes brought some comfort for Amy. While her boys were in England, training, recovering or convalescing, they were not facing enemy bullets. Harold would be going back sooner rather than later, as his next letter indicated.

9 March 1916
Australian Base Depot, Montevideo Camp,
Weymouth, Dorset

I have been down here a fortnight and was shoved on picket duty the first night and have been on since. I do no fatigues or parades all day and am entitled to a pass from 11am to 4pm to go to Weymouth if I like. It's two and a half miles from here so don't often go in. I have marched nearly there every night, a place called Westham, where we stop to about 9.45pm and then march home. I only do about 4 hours altogether a day

— it's not excessive. I can't come home this weekend, but will have a try for next if I am not picked in a draft to go away.

I am genuinely surprised about Frances and Billy Hay but Nuph Sed. I won't comment on it. Let me know how Char's going on, whether he's going up or not.

This is not a bad camp, tucker is good, which is the main thing in a soldier's life. There is a rumour that my lot is down Khartoum way somewhere — it's some heat that way, 700 miles up the Nile. I hope they have shifted before I reach them. I have my usual cold, otherwise very good.

Your loving son, Harold

Then, uncomplaining as ever, he was off to war again with orders to join the Australian Imperial Force, not in the mud of France but back in the Egyptian desert.

24 March 1916
Australian Base Depot, Weymouth

Just a few lines to say I'm off back to Egypt tomorrow. I am rather in a hurry — we have to get up tomorrow at 3am and off at 4.30. Middle of the night I call it — I shall not get undressed! Think we shall go on to France as all the later battalions are going there now. Stayed the night at Len's, got to Weymouth in the afternoon and did not get into row for being late. Break the news all round.

Love to all, Harold

Instead of rejoining his old unit, Harold was posted to the newly formed 48th Battalion, drawn from the same areas of Western and South Australia with a core of men who had fought with the old 16th. The AIF had doubled in size since Gallipoli. Many new recruits had arrived after the evacuation and old hands like Harold were absorbed into the new units to add much-needed experience.

They were camped within a mile or two of the Suez Canal at Serapeum. Not much else had changed. There were the same daily slogs over scorching desert sands in full kit. When they weren't marching, they were digging drains, building roads or pulling punts loaded with men, camels and supplies across the canal. Harold arrived just in time for the first anniversary of the Gallipoli landing, celebrated with a swimming gala and sports. As one of the Anzac veterans, he wore a red ribbon to mark him out from the rookie recruits. His old mates from the 16th Battalion thought they were seeing a ghost when he showed up.

24 April 1916

Dear Mother

Sorry I haven't written before — pure laziness on my part. I have not much to grumble at. I can't tell you what we are doing or why and how we are doing it all. Letters are censored and I have an abhorrence to having mine mucked about so I am not putting in anything to worry the authorities. We are going to have a few sports tomorrow to commemorate the landing. It's pretty warm in the daytime but the nights are lovely and cool. I have seen a lot of the old fellows lately — they had no idea what had happened to me. Well, good luck and don't worry about me. I'm all right.

Love, Harold

Amy knew that Chris would be returning to Australia for the sake of his health. She must have been surprised to hear that he would be taking a new bride with him.

Easter Sunday 1916
Bertha and I are being married all being well tomorrow forenoon at 9 o'clock. It took me over a week at Abbey Wood to get a week's leave and through the officer being out and not signing it till Saturday, it's now only six days. The boat, I hear, is to sail about May 4th. Bertha apologises for not writing but really she didn't know anything till she saw me. I shall probably come down Wednesday to say goodbye. Bertha sends her love.

Your loving son, Chris

Bertha was thirty-three, a year older than Chris. They were married at St Stephen's Church, Paddington, west London on Easter Monday. According to family wisdom, their romance blossomed while Chris, half paralysed, was finding his feet again. Bertha was probably working as a hospital volunteer because there is no record of her as a wartime nurse. In later life she told how she helped Chris recover and how they fell in love as she wheeled him out in the early spring sunshine at Harefield. Of course, she might have been just a friend of Muriel Gothorp, one of the bridge-playing set who took the wounded Anzac hero to their heart. Bertha was as surprised as anybody at the rapid turn of events. She was suddenly the bride of an invalid soldier who would be wishing her farewell in just a few weeks to sail to the other side of the world. Chris owned the land at South Ucarty but he would never be able to farm again. Although he was going back with no prospects, no promise of work and nowhere to live, Bertha would love, honour and follow him to that particular end of the earth. Chris still held out a hope that they would be able to travel together when he wrote to his mother a fortnight later.

1 May 1916
Aust Intermediate Dept., Abbey Wood, Kent
I'm awfully ashamed of myself for not coming down or writing. Bertha and I only had such a short time together (less than a week) and we had so much to do. Trying all we could to get on same boat. We went to the Abbey on Tuesday and only had Wednesday and Thursday to go and see about her passage. I hope you won't think it unkind of me but the Commonwealth Military Regulations insist on a married soldier allotting at least 3/5ths of his pay to his wife and I've had to alter the

allotment. I feel like a traitor to stop any pay coming to you but it must be done as we are none too rich. I'm in the draft of permanently unfit to go to Weymouth tomorrow morning and will let you know my address from there.

I send you my love and duty and hope you will be well and happy. Write and let me know any news about the others. It will probably be a week at least before we sail. Love to all and goodbye if I don't see you again.

Your loving son, Chris

Frank's war had not taken him beyond home shores. He had been with the 7th Lincolns for eight months, based at Bovington and Lulworth in Dorset with occasional sorties beyond for training in his chosen speciality of signalling. The fact that he was now a staff officer would no doubt have earned more teasing reproach from Chris. If Australians regarded British officers as unworthy of respect, then the staff Poms were lower than pond life. Frank's apparent cushy number far away from the roar of the guns might also have rankled, but they never had the opportunity to discuss it. Frank was too busy to attend Chris and Bertha's wedding. His status allowed him the luxury of his own little bungalow in the small town of Withernsea, which clings to the bleak, storm-battered North Sea coast in the old East Riding of Yorkshire. From his comfy bolthole on the cliff edge, Frank wrote to tell his mother he would be seeing her soon.

4 May 1916

The Bungalow, North Cliff, Withernsea

It's ages since I wrote and I have so much to say that I shall take a day off some time this week and come and say it. 1st I am a staff officer now and am to be made Captain — am expecting to see it in orders any day now — unfortunately it will be only temporary and without extra pay. 2nd I have taken a little bungalow right on the edge of the cliff and have nearly got it furnished — mostly on hire. It is a lovely little place and is getting quite comfortable. I am living here at present all alone but another staff officer is going to join me soon and pay half the furnishing expenses. The Government, however, talk of taking it over for our officers — and in that case I shall have to live elsewhere. I have another little unfurnished house in my mind's eye. The rent of the bung. is £16 a year. I wish I could have managed to get to Kris's wedding but 'twas impossible.

I will describe my bung. when I get home — but it really is the prettiest little place you can imagine. I have got my sitting room floor polished with three Turkey rugs lying about on it — cream curtains with a rather pretty border, one set of four chairs, two armchairs and a couch (in leather) which I am buying for £6 in monthly instalments, and many other things — crockery, knives, frying pans etc which I am getting together gradually. However, I will describe it fully later.

My work is now very interesting and consists in

going round on a bike (provided by the Government) to five battalions of infantry and several artillery units to inspect and examine their signallers — to arrange big signalling schemes and generally to make myself a nuisance to battalion signalling officers, also to dine with the General on occasions.

I shall try to get home on Wed. or Thursday and stay one night.

Ever your loving son, Frank

His prediction that he might soon be an army captain would be yet another case of promise unfulfilled for Frank.

From Weymouth, Chris was sending out final farewells. The *Thermistocles*, part of the fleet that had taken the Australians to Egypt, lay at anchor off Portland in Dorset waiting to ferry him and other men whose war was over back to Fremantle. It was the same ship from which the burial at sea had taken place on that first day out of Albany seemingly a lifetime ago. Chris was unable to secure a joint passage so Bertha would have to follow on afterwards alone. There was time for one last letter home before the ship sailed.

12 May 1916
Westham Camp, Weymouth

Dear Mother

I suppose this will be the last letter I can write you from England as I expect we shall sail shortly. I shall cable to Bertha if possible at our first port of call and she has promised to let you know at once.

Write as soon and as regularly as you can giving me the news of my brothers and sisters and how you fare. I do hope the rest of us will come out of it all right and that you will be fortunate, well and happy. I have no idea what my plans out there will be, they depend so much on circumstances and my state of health. I feel so much happier in my mind through my meeting Bertha and rather precipitous marriage — luckier and happier than I really deserve. Bertha says she would rather wait to hear that I am safe before sailing but I think that she will have to wait for some time as bookings seem to be taken some time ahead.

Bertha will probably take a post until then. Give my regards to those friends I've seen again since coming to England and my farewells. I'm going out again not quite as vigorous as last time but with a doctor's opinion favourable to my recovery and a full knowledge of the conditions out there.

Love to my brothers and sisters at home and abroad when you write and dear love to yourself, Chris

Char felt the Beechey family had already given enough, but as his invalid brother was saying his emotional goodbyes to Bertha and boarding the *Thermistocles* at Portland Harbour, he was on his way to Scotland to become a Royal Fusilier.

At school, there had been further reminders of all the other masters who had left to do their duty. Mr Pitt, having tried in vain to have his dog, Henry, adopted as a regimental mascot so he could take it to war, was killed in July 1915 when the Germans used flamethrowers for the first time at Hooge, near Ypres. Mr Wood escaped the trenches he despised so much and returned to Stamford as an officer of the Army Grenade School. He gave the boys a thrilling lecture on bombs and bombing, and deposited a hand grenade with the headmaster for any pupil who cared to inspect it more closely.

Each passing Stamford Speech Day added to Char's personal turmoil. The head made much of the part being played by the school in the war, and Char would have stuck out like the point of a German pickelhaube. "Practically every able-bodied Old Boy who could possibly get away is serving in some branch of His Majesty's Forces," declared Canon Day. "Several have been killed, others wounded, and a number are reported missing or sick." He announced plans to turn the oldest part of the school into a memorial chapel to the fallen. The head, to warm applause, "could think of no more inspiring influence than for a boy to worship Almighty God in a building set apart to immortalise the memory of boys of his School who had died for their School, their friends and their country."

The *Stamfordian* of the summer of 1916 blamed the lack of Old Boys' notes on the departure of Mr Beechey, the secretary of the Old Stamfordians, "who is now training with the Royal Fusiliers in Edinburgh, and expects, at an early date, to be drafted to the front. The Rev. A. E. Burton MA took Mr Beechey's place as Mathematics Master at the end of the Spring Term when he left to join the Army."

Harold was fitter and healthier than he had been for a long time after all the mock attacks, desert manoeuvres and long marches that invariably ended with men and officers diving into the Suez Canal to cool off. Fears of a Turkish advance on Egypt sent the 48th trudging 12 miles into the desert to occupy hopeless trenches that were swept away with every sandstorm. Between the back-breaking digging, Harold wrote to his sister-in-law Mary's brother, Dick Elvidge, who had been badly wounded and gassed while serving with the Canadian infantry at Ypres. Part of the last page of Harold's letter is torn off, possibly by the army censors he was so fond of berating. There's an uncharacteristic cynicism evident, something rarely found in his letters home. For instance, he would never dream of telling his mother he would rather be killed than left a helpless cripple.

13 May 1916
Egypt

I am in the first lines of trenches defending Egypt on the Eastern Frontier and am at the moment on a bit of an outpost. It's beastly hot and the flies are very bad and the enemy refuses to attack. We hold the position as if we were in imminent danger, working hard at improving our entrenchments as well as "standing to" at an awful early hour in the morn. Personally, I am feeling much better than I have for months and taking quite an interest in the game again. The officers seem as if they are trying to do their best for us so I think this new lot I am in will put up a good show. They have not too much time for us old hands — they have an idea that because we have been to England we can't be much good. Can't quite understand their reasoning but when we have another dust-up we might be able to show up a bit again.

I sincerely hope your arm is going well this time — it's pretty rough luck for a young fellow with a useless arm. A thing like that commands a good bit of sympathy now but a fortnight after the war's finished all that will be cut out. The same people who may be making a fuss of the wounded heroes may turn a chap down for a job when it's all over and we are out of the limelight. It's a bit pessimistical [sic] but pretty near the mark. I want pretty well my whole strength or to be smacked out altogether.

I am surprised to hear about Kris's engagement. But as he is getting about on one stick pretty well I expect he will be able in a few months to do some head-work of some sort. He will get a bit of a pension I suppose, but for one of his energetic nature a sedentary life will be very trying. Charlie has been called up — his group now, I suppose. He ought to be able to get his commission easy enough, a Cambridge man of his ability. Frank will be enjoying himself as Brigade Signalling Officer, riding round inspecting the different battalion signallers — he ought to get his three stars. We have got a good record now — six brothers joined up, one killed, one practically disabled for life. Mother did not say anything about Len — I suppose he will have to come up, which will be seven of military age, seven serving.

Affectionately yours, Harold

He found time to write home too.

13 May 1916
Egypt

My dear mother

I received your letter yesterday. I was thinking it was about time I had one. I can't say I remember Kris's girl but no doubt I must have seen her. I wish him luck anyway — seems to be becoming a habit in our family. I am at present out in the first line of trenches, waiting for the Turks to come along. We have been at it pretty solid, in the trenches or outpost duty at night and consolidating our position with pick and shovel work in the day. We are a few miles from civilisation so all our tucker has to be brought by camels over some of the worst sand I have ever struck. There is not a single bit of green, only desert. The heat is pretty bad, wanders up over the hundred during the heat of the day. It takes it out of you, swinging the shovel in that. Tucker is a bit light, so is water. But we can generally manage to get enough for us to have one decent wash a day now . . . about ten of you in the same water. The luckiest are of course the first ones. I am getting very dark again. The chaps reckon I shall be getting shot for a Turk some day.

I will write and congrat. Kris. I am glad Frank has got his job. I have no doubt he can manage it. I was hoping Charlie would get out of it as there were quite sufficient of us now. What about Len? I suppose he goes up too. Give my love to everybody, sisters, Samuel, Mary and the kids and ask them to write.

This is not an entirely new battalion — there are lots of the old sixteenth in it. If you could manage to send any little things to me I should appreciate it very much. You see I only draw one shilling a day and might go a month without getting paid now when I am on active service, perhaps longer. So any little luxuries are very acceptable. If you have a few shillings to squander that would be a good way to do it, as I would take it as a loan. I could get some from the bank per reg. letter but it's not too safe. I am always shifting and it might get lost or not turn up for months after.

Every love, Harold

The flurry of letters continued with one to sister Winifrede.

14 May

My dear Winnie

How's the Yeomanry Barracks getting on? I suppose you are still running the show. Did you get away for Easter for a holiday? I have been trotting about all over Egypt since I have been back, short stay in each camp. Going farther out into the desert each time. There is not much recreation here, waiting for an enemy that won't come. It's good practice I suppose.

There seems an epidemic in our family. I was rather surprised about Chris, but still his fighting days are over and he will be able to settle down. Send a letter now and again and give my love to the others. Tell them to write as well. I could tell you a lot of news but it's not allowed so I can't write an interesting letter. We have to get up at half past three every morning — that would hurt you a bit, I think. Ask Margaret how that would suit her. I am sorry Charlie had to go. I was hoping he wouldn't.

Your affectionate brother, Harold

Chris was now en route to Australia.

15 May 1916
At sea

Dear Mother

I'm all right up to now. Let me have the latest news of Harold and the other boys. Tell Harold that I will call on the Baileys as soon as I arrive.

187

The voyage isn't doing me much good up to now on account of an attack of La Gripe. I hope Bertha has sent you my photo. I'm awfully sorry it was too late for me to sign.

Your loving son, Chris

Before May was out, Frank had been uprooted from his clifftop bungalow idyll and rushed across to France where Kitchener's New Army was massing for the attack on the Somme. He was posted to one of the Hull "Pals' battalions", who had been in France since March after an uneventful couple of months in Egypt. His first letter from overseas was simply dated "Monday", most likely 22 May 1916.

13th E Yorks Regt, 21st Inf Base Depot
APO Sect. 17, BEF, France

Have just arrived at the base and have got my things settled in a tent and am fairly comfortable. Start training work tomorrow morning and may join my unit in a few days or maybe a month. I crossed yesterday afternoon and spent one night in ————— [Frank, who would have had the task of censoring letters home from men in the ranks, was careful not to give anything away in his own correspondence]. The above address will always find me but I will let you know if I move. Notice that I have been posted to the 13th E Yorks, one of the Hull Commercial Battalions. I will write again when I have had time to look round.

Love to all, Frank

★ ★ ★

Chris sent off a postcard to his mother when the *Thermistocles* docked briefly at Durban.

30 May 1916

Off here for a few hours while we coal ship. Am feeling pretty well but cannot practise walking on account of rolling of the ship. Love to all. Shall be back in less than three weeks.

Your loving son, Chris

In Egypt, the threat from the Turks turned out to be a mirage. After two weeks in the desert on a war footing, most of it spent bailing out their sand-blown trenches, the 48th returned to their base beside the canal. Within days they were sailing for France aboard the *Caledonia* and being lectured on French habits and customs, and warned to resist the temptations of wine and women. First hint of a different kind of war came when gas masks were issued and they were shown how to fit them. The *Caledonia* docked at Marseilles on 9 June and the Aussies were packed on to cattle trucks for the slow rail journey north. It took almost three days to crawl the length of France, with hot meals dished up at occasional stops and open waggons with a scattering of sand on the floor the only toilets. When nature called, you had to stand or squat in full view of everyone as the trains trundled through towns and villages. For Harold, brought up in an environment where pictures of ladies in combinations were taboo, it was almost as embarrassing as the degradations of dysentery.

Journey's end was the town of Bailleul, a busy staging post behind the British lines between Armentières and Ypres. Although almost mid-June, the weather was raw and cold when they arrived. Setting off on the three-mile march to their billets, the rain came down in buckets and, not for the first time in his life, Harold felt like a drowned rat.

Frank, meanwhile, was settling in on the Somme, which had always been one of the quieter sectors of the line. Villages had not been reduced to brick dust and a few hardy inhabitants still remained. Trees had leaves and branches. Even the most junior officers could expect some comforts, whether it was the shelter of a dugout or a dry billet behind the lines. Frank was keen to put all that training in the arts of signalling and communications into practice. So it came as a nasty shock when he was put in charge of carrying and working parties. And the anticipated promotion had come to nothing — Frank was still the most junior of officers, a second lieutenant.

One of his men in the 13th East Yorks kept an illicit diary detailing the donkey work that was wearing them all down. "We are all as fed up as hell with this lot and fellows here are often praying for a Blighty [a wound that earned a man a ticket home and was of no immediate danger to life or limb]. On each occasion we marched all those miserable miles to the trenches, worked either carrying timber or bombs or trench-mortar shells, or digging or revetting . . . and then marched the same damnable miles back. The jobs we get are simply heartbreakingly, almost inhumanly impossible, but they have to be done somehow and I marvel daily how we stick to it. We have had a lot of casualties; some good pals have left us and we rarely return from one of our working parties without someone being hit in some way or another." Frank could at least count on having a roof over his head at the end of each day's slog.

31 May 1916
Lt FCR Beechey
A Coy, 13th E Yorks, 31st Division, BEF, France
Dearest Mother

I am having this posted in England by a fellow going home on leave so you may have a little more information than I am really allowed to give. I am at last right up at the front and on Sunday went up to the trenches to see what trench warfare was like — on Monday our battalion came out to billets two miles behind the line and on Saturday we go still further back for 10 days and then five days in trenches again and so on ad infinitum. Look for Albert on the map — almost the southern extremity of the British line — also Arras further north. We are between these two, six miles north of Albert on a comparatively quiet part of the line. I am now in a little village called Colincamps, which has been smashed to pieces by shellfire — but have found a nice little cottage not much battered to billet in. I got up here with all my kit — camp kit and blankets (in fact I gathered two more blankets on my way at Etaples where I stayed for four days). The trenches on 2/3rds of our battalion line are about 400 yards apart and the other third about 45. Last night I took a party up to the trenches for repairing work — all night at it and had to get up on the parapet to do it. Rather nervy work at first but I soon got used to it. There seems to be a sort of understanding between the Huns and us that while both parties are at work on the top there is practically no firing, but the one who finishes work first begins to strafe the other — this makes the men work harder. My lot got finished quite early.

No one can say that this life is enjoyable but I suppose one will get used to it and it can't go on for ever — four days' leave will go on fairly regularly every three or four months.

Am sending this by a fellow officer.

Ever your loving son, Frank

The men of the 48th Battalion AIF were nearly all snuffling and sneezing with head colds after their introduction to a particularly miserable early French summer. On 13 June, they were issued with tin helmets, which, as well as protecting them from flying shrapnel, would later prove useful for scooping foul water from shell holes to boil up for tea. Harold wrote a brief note to his mother the same day.

13 June 1916

Hope you haven't been worrying because I have not written for some time but I have been wandering about a bit lately and have just lobbed here in France, within sound of the guns again. Had a pretty good trip, two and a half days' journey across France — border of Belgium. It's lovely country, very similar to England.

Will write again, Harold

His battalion was still adjusting to the damp weather after the suffocating heat of Egypt and had trouble finding enough dry wood for a campfire. When the rain eased off and the sun appeared, a fine lump of willow could usually be found — "Have been playing a good deal of cricket lately, which eases the monotony," Harold told his mother. He was struck by the "practically English scenery . . . hedges, lanes, villages are all the same".

In the last week of June, 1,500 guns began pounding the enemy lines along the 15-mile front of the planned Somme offensive. Of the million and a half shells stacked up to be fired, a third were duds. They are still being ploughed up from the rolling fields of Picardy to this day. Reports that the shelling had had little impact on the enemy barbed wire were brushed aside. Harold's unit, 40 miles away to the north, could hear the boom of the bombardment as they played cricket. They were having such a cushy time that old hands pronounced the Western Front a picnic compared to Gallipoli.

On the morning the British guns opened up, Frank was still more like a navvy foreman than a junior officer. As he led his working party out from the wreckage of the village where they were based, a sudden fierce summer storm combined with the bombardment to create a dramatic Wagnerian dawn. Frank and his troops were soaked to the skin, but waterlogged pockets and boots soon dried out during another day of hard graft. At the end of it, they were desperate for food and rest, but the 13th East Yorks had moved camp while they were out. By the time the working party marched the extra 10 miles to rejoin them, everyone was drenched again, this time in sweat.

Authie, their new base, clung to a hillside overlooking the river of the same name. The smell of open cesspools rather spoilt its charm. Chickens pecked away in the muddy main street, indifferent to the mayhem going on all around. There was no shortage of smoky cafés and estaminets where the coming Big Push was the sole topic of conversation over bowls of tea or red wine and plates of egg and chips.

On 30 June, the afternoon before the attack, the 13th East Yorks were paraded in the centre of the village and told of the importance of using ammunition sparingly and conserving food and water once they went into battle. As a general addressed them, sparks flew from the grindstones where bayonets were being sharpened in readiness. Weighed down with full kit, rifles, spades, pick-axes, extra bombs and ammunition, ladders, trench periscopes and baskets of carrier pigeons, they marched off at four in the afternoon to a drumbeat of guns. Frank and his fellow officers had to keep the column together, calling frequent halts for stragglers to catch up. For men who had never faced battle before, it was a nerve-shredding journey, skirting villages ablaze from shelling by both sides and seeing row upon row of empty, freshly dug graves. "The hair-raising flashes seemed to sear one's eyebrows," recalled nineteen-year-old Private Archie Surfleet, who would come to know Second Lieutenant Beechey. "I don't know how we escaped being hit by our own guns. I could not help admiring our officers trying to lead men through that hell. As we neared the front enemy shrapnel bursts increased. Three went off right overhead — I can remember those swishing pieces plopping into the mud all around us." He recalled having to negotiate a flooded communication trench, "thigh deep in mud and water . . . staggered along with the water swirling before and behind us, in and out of the bays, to our allotted position."

At zero hour — 7.30a.m. — on 1 July, whistles trilled all along the line and Kitchener's New Army went over the top. Still burdened by huge packs on their backs, they had been instructed by generals convinced that all the enemy resistance had been blown away to amble across No Man's Land in waves at one-minute intervals and advance at a steady pace of 100 yards every two minutes. This of course gave the enemy time to scramble up from their deep concrete dugouts where they had sheltered from the bombardment. Dozens of machine guns were swiftly snapped into place ready to kill on an industrial scale. When the shooting started, most of the strolling civilian soldiers had no more chance than a condemned man facing a firing squad. Around 30,000 fell dead or wounded in the first hour. By the end of the day the losses were double that, with

20,000 dead. Three of thirteen fortified villages held by the enemy were overrun but most men died without an inch of ground being gained on that first day on the Somme. When casualties were optimistically estimated at 40,000 the following day, commander-in-chief Sir Douglas Haig was of the opinion, "This cannot be considered severe in view of the numbers engaged, and the length of the front attacked." By the time the Battle of the Somme had finished, the toll would be more like 400,000.

As zero hour passed, men of the 13th East Yorks were still in the relative safety of the trenches. They were being held back to exploit the anticipated successes of the initial advance. They peered over the parapet or through periscopes from the support lines, straining for a glimpse of battle. All they saw were ghostly figures disappearing into a haze of smoke from exploding shells. Distance and smog hid the carnage being inflicted on the other battalions of the 31st Division. These were the cheery, close-knit pals from the industrial heartlands of Accrington, Leeds, Barnsley and Sheffield who had so willingly joined up together. Only when the wounded began stumbling, staggering and crawling back to their lines was the size of the calamity apparent.

The only signalling Frank was doing was to warn his men to keep their heads down as they went back to fetch fresh water supplies. His carrying party was shelled by friend and foe alike while queuing to fill containers that stank of kerosene. Working their way back up the line, two heavy cans per man, they were soon enveloped by a mass of bandaged, broken men heading the other way. Beyond the clogged, chaotic trenches, the cries of the wounded and dying echoed across No Man's Land. One man would lie out there for ten days with a shattered leg before he was found alive.

Finally, after hours of fearful uncertainty, the 13th East Yorks received their orders to move, not forward into the sights of enemy machine-gunners, but back to camp. Frank and his comrades had been spared on 1 July, but it was a postponement. The Somme fighting would last another 139 days.

On 4 July, with the dead beginning to rot in No Man's Land, the corps commander addressed the remnants of the 31st Division and expressed his admiration for the courage, determination and discipline of everyone who took part in the attack. Archie Surfleet summed up the feelings of the men. "Our position has been one of constant anxiety," he wrote. "If any man in our battalion has awaited with relish the expected order to return and follow up the work so heroically started by our pals in the other brigades, I have yet to meet him. Every hour has been spent fearing to be sent back to that hell up by Serre." The 13th East Yorks were right to be fearful.

CHAPTER
EIGHT

Very lucky; nice round shrapnel through arm and chest

Forty miles to the north of the Somme, the Western Front still held few terrors for Harold and the boys of the 48th Battalion AIF. The youngest of the fighting Beechey boys probably had no idea as he crossed the river Lys that he was in a part of Flanders already stained with Beechey blood. A sudden burst of shrapnel forced the Australians to duck as they crossed a creaky wooden bridge and entered the village of Fleurbaix, opposite the row of German fortifications at La Bridoux. It was the same spot where Bar had charged to his death the previous September. Somewhere across No Man's Land lay the final resting place of Harold's eldest brother, under a simple wooden cross or by now unmarked and lost forever in the midst of enemy territory.

There was little trace of the bloody battle of nine months earlier. A German sniper nicknamed "Parapet Joe" turned out to be the only irritation at Fleurbaix.

For sport, tin helmets were hoisted aloft on the end of a shovel but the German was a cunning marksman and never gave away his position. The Australians found more amusement in enemy newspaper reports regretting "that the noble sons of Germany should be pitted against such filthy refuse, the descendants of convicts and blackguards who were transported to Tasmania by England".

Chris had reached Western Australia and was in hospital again after six weeks at sea, but he reassured his mother that it was more a matter of convenience than any relapse.

2 July 1916
F Ward, No. 8 Australian Gen Hosp,
Fremantle, Western Australia

You will see by the address that I am again in Hosp. I wasn't too good when I came off the boat. A bit of malaria on going on board and the cooking was bad and just enough roll on the ship to stop me walking about. So when I got here they gave me tea and next morning asked me if I had any friends to go to and I said it will probably be Mrs Boarding House (because it was no good going up country), and the major said, "You'd better go up in one of the wards and we'll give you a daily pass until 11p.m." I've improved a lot since landing and attend the Fremantle Technical School daily just across the road. I start massage again tomorrow and don't suppose they will be in any hurry to discharge me. I hope to be proficient in shorthand typing and bookkeeping soon and expect to get the promise of a job before discharge. Bertha is home at Camberley but says in her letter that she expects to sail about the end of June or beginning of July. I am anxious to have her here as soon as possible and hope to be in work and out of the army before Christmas. I ought to get full pension for 6 or 12 months at least and after that according to what change or improvement I show. Give my love to the girls and write and let me know the latest about the boys. I heard of Harold last week through Miss Boyce. Bertha's address is 16 Barossa Road, Camberley.

Ever your loving son, Chris

Australian lives had yet to be squandered on the Somme, which was being trumpeted as a magnificent feat of arms in every corner of the empire. It was hardly necessary to read between the lines of stirring newspaper reports to detect how hollow this "great victory" was. The casualties would soon be filling column after column. The *Lincolnshire Echo* of 1 July splashed a "Great British Advance — Main attack launched this morning — Enemy overwhelmed on a 20-mile front — Several villages taken". The War Office reported, "We have taken Serre and Montauban, two important tactical points south-west of Hébuterne . . . so far the day goes well for England and France." Ominously, a German communiqué spoke of "extraordinarily high bloody casualties". Serre, contrary to the official line, had not been taken. The name of this tiny French village would have meant nothing to Amy Beechey as she waited for news of her sons. It would be many weeks before she received another letter from Frank. After hard days of strenuous trench duties he could only stay awake long enough to dash off the occasional Field Service Postcard to reassure the family he was well. Harold was fighting against boredom. Apart from the distant rumble of the guns, the 48th were so far untroubled by the bloodbath going on to the south. Harold's main concern was the lack of letters heading in his direction from home.

3 July 1916
France

My dear mother

Many thanks for the parcel. I have been expecting a letter from you as I have not heard from you for some little time. We had a nice little supper out of the parcel at our last billet. Things are not too bad at present. I am very well and the weather is exceptionally good, rather hot in the middle of the day. I will send off those field service cards as often as possible. They are nearly as good as a letter because we are not allowed to put anything about what we are doing. Keep writing regularly.

Love to all. Your loving son, Harold

It was followed by a postcard two days later, after a longed-for letter from home had finally arrived.

5 July 1916

Received letter from you yesterday. Things very quiet here, the weather a bit wet lately. We have not been into the trenches yet. We have a bit of cricket and football here for relaxation, otherwise we are kept up to the mark training etc. I would like to hear from Char if you will let him have my address. Hope you and the girls will be able to get away for a little jaunt.

Harold

The war was quickly catching up with Char, who had only been in the army since May.

Wednesday, 5 July 1916
Section 13, C Coy, 28th Battalion Royal Fusiliers
Kings Park Schools, Edinburgh

My dear mother

Just a line to thank you for your letter and to say that I'm getting on all right. The Company are sending a draft on Friday of partially trained men, 55 from C Company, who are to finish their training somewhere in France. I have just missed it by a week or two, as a good many men are on it who have been here only a week or fortnight longer than I have, and one man is going who came on the same day as I did. I think there is a good chance of my getting a six-days leave pretty soon — I am entitled to it in three weeks time. I shall be glad to hear that Frank and Harold are all right after this recent attack.

Best love to all from your affectionate son, Char

Chris, on the other side of the world, picked up snippets of information about Harold from Curly, but most of it was stale news. Letters from home took weeks to arrive by steamer. By mid-July Harold had been in France for five weeks. The Somme battle was in its third week. Chris would have been relieved if he had known that the 48th Battalion had not taken part in so much as a trench raid in all that time. But he thought Harold was still in Egypt. As for himself, he was out of hospital and in a job that would last him the rest of his working life. Having escaped the tedium of all those years at the Railway Clearing House in London, Chris had once more found employment as a railway clerk. His new bride was well on her way to joining him.

16 July 1916
2 Russell Street, West Leederville
W. Australia

My dear mother

I'm back in civilian clothes and working in an office and curiously enough a railway office, to whit the accountants office of the W Aust. Gov. Rlys. at Midland Junction about 12 miles up country from Perth. I am staying with some very nice friends here until Bertha comes on the 3rd of next month and then hope to buy a suburban piece of land and get a bungalow built on it. I'm getting £3 a week and have put in for a pension and judging from what others are getting ought to come off pretty well. I stand the railway journey (14 miles) all right and the office work is fairly straightforward but requiring plenty of care. I got the latest about Char and Frank last week from Bertha but nothing about Len. I heard that Harold was still in Egypt from a young lady here. I hope to start a little home in about a month and think I am very lucky and have much to be thankful for. I'm feeling stronger and a bit steadier and though pain is still constant it's seldom acute. Give my love to the girls and Sam. I do hope that you are doing well and that you are fairly comfortable and free from worry and Zeps. I'm so pleased to have gotten a job before Bertha arrived.

PS I've had to change my handwriting to learn shorthand.

Harold had left the comfort zone on the morning of 14 July and was on his way to the Somme. The battalion was given an early breakfast but went without a scrap of food all day. By the time they reached the town of Doullens by train they were starving. But instead of being fed they were ordered to fall in and march with full packs and empty stomachs to their new, temporary billets in the village of Berteaucourt, 15 miles away. Here, to the curse of streaming colds that most of the men had was added the blight of badly blistered feet from endlessly tramping over the cobbled roads. Berteaucourt did have one blessing. There was no shortage of estaminets selling a popular local version of champagne. From there, Harold sent a postcard to his mother.

21 July 1916

Just a few lines to say I am very well and things are pretty good. Hope you have good news of the others.
Love to all, Harold

He was on the move again before July was out, with his battalion earning a sharp rebuke from on high for their conduct as they marched towards the Somme. The 12th Brigade diary described their progress as "deplorable". Seventy-five men had fallen out and held up the whole column even though conditions for marching were considered ideal under a cool grey sky. The brigadier threatened to remove some of their leaders for incompetence and the divisional commander also squawked his displeasure at such a poor show. However, the brigade war diary explains that sore feet were probably not the only reason for the dropouts: "as last night the 1st Australian Division passed through and halted at some of the billets of this brigade, and there were many meetings of old friends at estaminets etc. and a good deal of liquor consumed". Harold's head was clear enough for him to send another quick note to his mother the following day.

28 July 1916

A Coy, 48th Battalion. AIF, France

Still in good health and excellent spirit whatever that may mean, but it sounds well and fills up [space]. You might pack up a couple of decent pairs of socks and send them over if you don't mind. Hope you had a good holiday.

Your loving son, Harold

On 1 August, the 48th Battalion entered the axis of British operations on the Somme, the town of Albert with its leaning golden virgin, an immediately recognisable landmark, hanging her head in shame over so much horror. She keeled over after being hit by shellfire and now reached out at a 90-degree angle from the top of the 200-foot tower of the Basilique Notre Dame de Brebières with the infant Christ in her outstretched arms. It was said that when she fell the war would end. The Australians christened her Fanny Durack, after their gold-medal-winning swimmer of the 1912 Stockholm Olympics. Installed in bivouacs near an old brickfield outside town, they waited to learn what part they would soon play in the battle. Throughout the night Albert was battered by enemy shelling, with British artillery answering in kind. The picnic was over.

At home, the scale of the disaster on the Somme was only just becoming clear at the beginning of August. Daily casualty lists that used to take up a few inches in the newspapers stretched from top to bottom of a broadsheet page, spilling over into the next column. And that was just the dead.

In Scotland, Char had found a refuge from rough camp life. For the admission price of a penny, he could hide himself away in the reading room and library of the Edinburgh Working Men's Club and Institute, a dour Victorian building in Infirmary Street. There, he could also play chess, write his letters on the headed notepaper provided and read the newspapers sent from home. Scanning the casualty lists in the *Stamford Mercury* he would have found the name of another of his old school colleagues, Mr Cowie, who had been killed on 8 July. Arthur Cowie had arrived at Stamford as Classics master about the same time as Char and was remembered as a strict disciplinarian with the kindest of hearts. He survived two major attacks on the Somme only to be mortally wounded by a shrapnel bullet while in the reserve lines.

7 August 1916
Address as usual

My dear mother

Many thanks for sending Frank's letter and Harold's. I'll make a note of their addresses and write to them in a few days. I'm not put down to go on the next draft, which is to be a large one from A & B Companies only, so have put my name down for a course of pioneering, which sounds interesting though I don't know what it means.

I had a game of cricket on Friday, playing as a substitute for the 31st RF battalion against the

28th, as the 31st turned up three men short. I found afterwards that another substitute playing was also from Stamford, namely Lord Burleigh, though I fear I didn't recognise him as a Lord until I saw the name in the evening papers. I myself scored 29 not out and was sorry I didn't get a better chance as the bowling wasn't difficult, but I was put in last but one. I have been away from the barracks for three days on guard duty at Craigleith Hospital so didn't get your letter until this morning.

No more news at present so best love from your affectionate son, Char

Chris was at last settling down to the life of a happily married man now that Bertha had reached Western Australia. West Leederville was a picture of suburban calm with its leafy streets, neat clapperboard homes and a railway station just a minute or two from the front door. Instead of bitterness at being only half the man he was before Gallipoli, the contentment shone through in his letters home. Simply getting out of bed to go to work was painful enough. The daily train journeys must have been a trial for someone whose disabilities made even bowel control unpredictable. But Chris was eternally thankful instead of self-pitying.

9 August 1916
2 Russell Street, West Leederville

Dear Mother

Bertha arrived here last Sunday at 10 in the

forenoon after a very rough voyage from the Cape. She was very sea-sick on the voyage and looked thin and knocked up but is picking up now. Bertha likes W.A. very much and we are in a very nice house; staying with the widowed sister of a man in the artillery who came back on the same boat with me. I go off to business about 10 to 8 each morning but Bertha is taking a good rest. I've read rather disquieting reports of the Zep raids around Lincoln but trust you are all right.

Things seem to be going well with me since I married and barring occasional acute pain I'm well and extraordinary happy. Bertha will answer Winnie's letter she says when she has finished feeling the swaying of the boat.

Love, Kris

Nothing had been heard from Harold for two weeks. Then his mother received two postcards at once. He was wounded and back in England.

13 August 1916

Have lobbed here, Southampton, tonight and am at present in hospital train which will be leaving for London, I believe, not quite sure, in a few minutes. Will let you know what hospital I get to at once. Very lucky; nice round shrapnel through arm and chest but did not penetrate ribs. Arm is not out of action hardly at all — a bit clumsy.

Harold

The second was an official service postcard, designated Army Form W.3229.

> 13 August 1916
> Unit II Ward 9

I have just arrived at 5th Southern General Hospital at Portsmouth
   Name: Beechey H. R Pte.
   Regiment: 48 AIF
   Wounded slightly

Harold had been hit at Pozières, one of those villages of the damned like Passchendaele. The 48th Battalion was to take over a treacherous section of captured German trench between points defined as the Elbow and the Windmill on British maps. Today there are a few knobbly humps left to identify the site of the mill beside the road to Bapaume, just past the last house of the rebuilt village. A plaque sums up its lasting infamy: "The ruin of Pozières windmill which lies here was the centre of the struggle in this part of the Somme Battlefield in July and August 1916. It was captured on 4 August by Australian troops who fell more thickly on this ridge than on any other battlefield of the war."

The Germans had had two years of unmolested occupation in which to transform the woods and villages of the Somme into fortresses. In the attack of 1 July, eight battalions of Tyneside Scots and Tyneside Irish had set off from the romantic-sounding slopes of Tara and Usna Hills into valleys called Sausage and

Mash towards Pozières. Because of congestion and chaos ahead of them, many went over the top from rear trenches and were gunned down before reaching their own front line. A joint British and Australian attack in late July was half successful — the Australians took Pozières, winning two Victoria Crosses in the process, but their 1st Division lost more than 5,000 men. They were relieved by the 2nd Division, who pushed on up to the ruins of the windmill on the crest of the ridge at a cost of almost 7,000 casualties. In one week at Pozières, Australian deaths had almost equalled those for the entire nine months at Gallipoli. An official War Office communiqué made no mention of Australians when it announced the vital village had been taken by "the British".

Harold's 48th Battalion were part of the 4th Division, which was camped on Tara Hill waiting to be sucked into the fighting. From their vantage point, the whole of Sausage Valley was spread out beneath them, a riot of smoke, explosions and fire through which they would soon be plodding. Every now and again the air was torn by the sound of one of the mighty shells from the British artillery's monster howitzer in Albert, roaring overhead like a passing express train.

On 5 August, the 48th received their orders to take over the newly won positions and hold on to those gains at all costs. They set out in the evening in single file, platoon by platoon, across the smoky bedlam of Sausage Valley and through the desolation of Pozières, littered with dead from both sides. Their mission was to relieve troops who had captured the mound, which was all that was left of the windmill at the top of the village.

After picking their way through shellfire for three terrible hours, they found that the only troops left to relieve were either dead or wounded. Bodies lay partly buried with bloody hands and feet sticking out. The ground had been smashed by the original British bombardment and then repeatedly churned over by the enemy's guns so that it was just a wasteland of shell holes. These had to be scooped out and turned into strong points to combat the inevitable enemy counter-attack. The work could only be done under cover of darkness with moonlit skies streaked red by the incessant firing. When star shells lit up the battlefield at night with their magnesium flares, men could only hug the ground and brace themselves for the next hurricane of high explosives. They were constantly being buried alive and had to depend on mates to dig them out from under tons of earth mixed with the mangled remains of those blown apart.

Harold was spared the trench digging and given the role of a battalion runner. Communication wires did not last five minutes amid the fury of shellfire so the humble runner was often the only link between forward positions and battalion and brigade headquarters. Rifle in hand, message tucked into a tunic pocket, heart racing, he had to scramble across the cratered, featureless void to deliver new orders, pleas for support and reports of situations that were rarely anything less than desperate. Only the bravest volunteered for the task. At Pozières, the German artillery, dug in at Thiepval and Courcelette, had such command of the battlefield that they could "snipe" at individuals

212

crossing the barren moonscape. Harold had not only bullets zinging past his ears but also projectiles with pet names such as Flying Pigs, Plum Puddings and Whizz-bangs, any one of which might smash him to atoms. He saw the human debris of fatigue parties annihilated by artillery fire, and the rations and ammunition boxes that lay splintered and scattered over the broken ground. For a runner, life expectancy could be measured in seconds.

The adjutant of the 48th Battalion was Captain Ben Leane, whose fate would be inextricably bound up with Harold's. Leane was two years older than Harold and before the war had been a warehouseman in Prospect, South Australia. His brother Raymond, a lantern-jawed hulk of a man, led the battalion. He had been wounded twice as a company commander with the 11th Battalion at Gallipoli, but he later ranked Pozières as his worst experience of the whole war. Another brother and a nephew also served with the 48th, which gloried in the name of the Joan of Arc Battalion in France because it was "made of all Leanes". Compared to the rest of the fighting Leane clan, Ben looked puny and bookish in his wire-rim spectacles. His diary reveals a courageous leader amid the nightmare of Pozières. Two days before taking over the line at the windmill, he tells of reconnoitring the front: "It is HELL," he says. "The dead are lying everywhere, some of them several days old, others only today and yesterday. The stench is terrible but that is nothing. It is the sight of the poor fellows huddled up there — gruesome and bloated — that makes you realise to the full the beastly side, the awful side, of war. Went to see General Gellibrand [commander of the Australian 6th Brigade] in his HQ, a captured German dugout, a most elaborate affair where you go down two flights of stairs into a room about 30ft below ground level with two iron bedsteads and electric light laid on and a stove for warming.

"5 Aug — We are to go up this evening and take over the new ground and hold it against the counter-attack which is almost bound to come.

"6 Aug Pozières — We had a hell of a time last night. We lost a fair number of men coming up to take over. The enemy shellfire was pretty constant and the communication trenches became crowded and blocked. Ray and Major Imlay and self got tired of wriggling along the trenches so got out and scattered across the open.

"8 Aug 10p.m. — Of the 900-odd men we took into the trenches at Pozières, we brought out less than 200. The remainder are all either killed or wounded. Gallipoli was a paradise to it. Pozières is a veritable charnel house. God, the sights one sees. How any of us are alive seems a miracle. Unless one has actually been under barrage fire they could never imagine what it is like. Shells rain down like hailstones, exploding everywhere, changing regular lines of trenches into an unrecognisable chaos of craters, men are thrown bodily into the air, others are torn asunder, others again receive great gaping wounds, and scores go down with such severe shell shock that they are worse than useless for months after."

Harold was wounded on the 6th. The men of the 48th came under intense bombardment the night before and throughout most of that day. The battalion diary, written up by Raymond Leane, gives a dry, matter-of-fact summary of the action: "Relieved 27th Division under a very heavy barrage. Suffered heavy casualties in taking over — no trenches were constructed, mostly a mass of craters. No communication trenches existed. Had to go 400 yards over the open to get rations and water. All wounded had to be carried back in the same way. Very heavy casualties during the night of 5 Aug and day of 6 Aug — constant efforts were made to dig trenches but they were almost immediately blown up by enemy shellfire. This barrage continued increasingly throughout the 5th, 6th and up to 12 noon on the 7th of August."

The importance of Pozières was highlighted by an unequivocal order of the day from General von Bulow issued to German troops sent in to claw it back: "At any price, the Pozières Plateau must be recovered, for if it remained in the hands of the British, it would give them an important advantage. Attacks will be made by successive waves 80 yards apart. Troops which first reach the plateau must hold on until reinforced, whatever their losses. Any officer or man who fails to resist to the death on the ground won will be immediately court-martialled."

A continuous procession of wounded — haggard and dazed — stretched to the dressing stations behind the lines. Everywhere were the bodies of the dead, most of them grotesquely mutilated. However, the Australians in their shell holes held out. The morning of the 6th brought a brief lull. The guns fell quiet and both sides observed an unofficial truce to bring in their casualties. One German stretcher party ventured too close to the Australian line despite warnings to keep their distance. When a sergeant of the 48th Battalion shot one of the bearers, a stuffed bag made to look like a body tumbled off the stretcher.

That evening, support companies relieved what was left of the front-line defenders who had resisted so bravely. The following morning, as a group of the survivors huddled round a cooker for a warming drink of tea, a shell landed in their midst, killing twenty-six and wounding sixteen of them. According to the battalion history, "The memory of this disaster remained long with the men of the 48th. Men had survived so much only to be wiped out when away from the front line." It goes on to record how at the end of that spell of duty, "It was not a battalion that marched out of the trenches but more like a jaded, tired, worn-out working party."

Ben Leane provides a clue to how Harold might have been wounded when he tells how he sent out his battalion observer to bring back half a dozen runners. As the man was returning across open ground, he was buried by a shell blast. After being dug out, another shell exploded almost at his feet, killing three of the runners and wounding two others. Miraculously, the observer was untouched. But there was madness in his eyes when he got back. Leane, who became used to seeing grown men weeping, recalled, "Early on the morning of the 6th I heard someone come tumbling along calling out my name. He rushed up to me looking like a maniac, crying out: 'Message for Captain Leane.' I said, 'Here I am, lad, it's all right!' He looked wildly at me as I went to take the message from him, and then jumped back . . . 'No, don't take it,' he cried out; 'no one but the adjutant must take it.' I said: 'All right, old man, I'm the adjutant.' He recognised me then and collapsed on the ground crying like a child, and talked wildly about his having started off with six runners for me, and getting blown up twice and all the others killed . . . I made him lie down in a fairly sheltered place. Soon he was sleeping heavily, but several times he started up wildly, his face full of terror. In the morning he was very weak and I sent him to the rear to rest. That afternoon he was back, and, although he was still full of terror, he fought it down, and several times went out to the most advanced portion of the line under intense fire, until at last he said to me: 'It's no good, sir; I'd go out willingly but I can't face it any more.' I said: 'All right, lad, don't worry, you've done well.'"

Harold was one of the lucky ones. The "ghastly great mincing machine" that was Pozières chewed him up and spat him out almost in one piece, but he was hurt enough to get a ticket away from there. The Australian official historian tells of "wounded devils laughing with glee" as they were carried out of the holocaust on stretchers. Within days, Harold was back in a clean hospital bed in England and writing to his mother about his good fortune. He spared her the appalling truth about what he had been through.

14 August 1916
Section II Ward 9
5th Southern General Hospital, Portsmouth
My dear mother

Hope you got my p.c. which I sent off from Southampton last night. I am disappointed we were not sent to London or somewhere in the Midlands as I am so out of the way here. I am in good health — my arm does not trouble me at all. The bit of shrapnel hit me in the upper part of the left arm, went clean through the muscle — it did not touch the bone or anything like that. The same piece then hit me on the ribs in a slanting direction. It had not enough force to go through but slid along for about three inches and is still there, lying on top of the last rib. If it had gone another inch or two it would have come out again. I can feel it — could nearly take it out myself with a knife. In fact, I feel an impostor. I can hardly believe I am wounded till I see the hole through the arm. I got it at Pozières in some newly captured German trenches. The trenches were taken on the fourth and we went in to hold them on the night of the fifth. The trenches were unrecognisable as trenches, nearly all shell holes. And the Germans had been shelling all day. They simply smashed up the battalion in one night. You could not imagine what it was like, knocking us out in sections. Many chaps got buried four or five times during the night. I was lucky — I got mine running a message. I was running up in the open

218

in full view across from one position of a trench to the other. There were four of us — two of us got hit with shrapnel.

Don't suppose I shall be in this hospital long so tell all the others to write because it's rather lonely and dull in bed all day. I have not seen the doctor yet — he might allow me up.

With love, Harold

Harold also wrote to Curly, making light of his injuries and telling her of his good fortune in getting a nice, clean "Blighty". Newspaper reports of Pozières gave a conflicting picture. "The first of the wounded Anzacs have reached London," said one. "A few are gravely wounded but the majority are suffering from slight injuries inflicted by the German machine guns." Elsewhere, it was stated, "The unanimous verdict is that the battle of Pozières is the worst of the whole war." By the time letters with news of his wound reached Curly, the prospect of an imminent return to the trenches of France in the depths of a cruel winter would be preying on Harold's mind.

The Somme was insatiable in its demand for more men. From camps all over Britain came a steady flow to the ports of Folkestone and Southampton to be shipped out to fill the depleted ranks. Char received short notice and was on his way in a matter of hours. Unlike the cramped cattle waggons across the Channel, there was still enough room to swing a pencil on a troop train chugging south from Edinburgh. Within days of hearing that Harold was once more a hospital case, Amy Beechey learned that her most dependable of sons was bound for France.

                                    15 August 1916
                        Written between York and Selby
Dear Mother

Just a few lines to say I'm off to the front and am now on my way and shall pass through Lincolnshire soon. I will post this at Doncaster or Grantham. I have had a very busy afternoon as I only got warning that I was on the draft after 2 o'clock and had to get everything ready by 5.15. I am sending my bag home with a tennis racket tied on to it. I'll make Sam a present of the racket as it was his birthday on Sunday. I think I shall be sent somewhere near Harold, so may have a chance of seeing him.

I have put some pairs of socks in the bag I am sending home as they were dirty and I had no time to get them washed. Do you mind getting them washed and sending out two of the pairs when I let you know my address? I think it will be Etaples first. I myself am feeling very well and fit.

From your loving son, Char

Harold was contemplating sending his mother a souvenir of the Battle of the Somme — the "lucky" shrapnel ball that had lodged in his chest, just missing heart and lungs.

17 August 1916

Section II Ward 9, 5th Southern General Hospital,
Portsmouth

I am going on well, too well in fact — my arm is nearly healed up and I feel hardly any effect from it. The arm is a bit stiff, the pellet went clean through just below the shoulder — it is a pretty big bit of iron and I will enclose it if you promise to take care of it, as I want it again.

They took it out of my chest yesterday, put me under gas and cut it out then sewed it up and now, because I am so terribly restless in bed and always working the bandage off, they have trussed me up properly this time. I would not mind lying in bed if I felt ill but I feel tiptop and it's terribly irksome. I have to be trussed up like this for eight days without the bandage being removed and then the stitches will be taken out. I think I will keep the pellet at present. I will give you the size of it [sketch of a round shape about half-inch in diameter]. It's round except in one place where it hit the bone.

The tucker is poor here. Dinner is the best meal, the other meals being only bread and butter. We might get an egg or a kipper for breakfast but the tea they brew is hardly worth drinking. There are nine on my ward, four Australians — we are all bed patients and as the ward is rather out of the way we get poor attention from the orderlies. I don't like the RAMC — they are a poor lot taking them all round. The nearer the firing line the more conscientious and obliging they are. I think a lot of the orderlies you get here are NCC men [Note: Non-Combatant Corps was made up of more than 3,000 conscientious objectors who were given other war work] or practically so. I told one yesterday he would look better if he enlisted as they want men at the front. The operation took little effect on me — I was asking for a feed 3 hours after it. I have heard from Len and Annie. Len says he might run down some time.

Well, goodbye, your loving son, Harold

Perhaps he kept his shrapnel ball as a lucky charm after such a narrow squeak or maybe he sent it to Curly as a keepsake. "Miss Boyce" passed on any titbits to Chris from her love letters — as far as she knew Harold was still "all right in France". Bertha wrote to the mother-in-law she had never even met with "love to all . . . I expect Chris told you what an awful time I had on the voyage; however, I am all right again now. Chris is improving wonderfully. I was so surprised to find he had started work, and discharged from the army too."

Char, like Bar before him, had been seasick on the short hop across the Channel from Folkestone to Boulogne in one of the grey-painted old tubs pressed into service as troop transports. The dusty, sprawling city of tents at Etaples was his next port of call. Whenever there was a brief break in the drilling and training, he wandered the camp looking for anyone who might be from his brothers' units.

August 1916
28th Royal Fusiliers, 39 IBD, France

Dear Mother

I'm in France now and am at base camp where I have to do a bit more drill for going up to the lines. I felt very ill on the passage but recovered quickly on reaching land. Did my bag and racket arrive? I left them in the charge of the corporal of my section who only had to see that it was taken to the station. I am enclosing a small cheque for £2 as a present for yourself, though I think a good deal of it is only a repayment of money you have spent on parcels, etc. I had made up my mind to be photographed before leaving, but only had a couple of hours' notice before departure and dozens of things to do in the time.

There are a good many here of the same division as Harold but I have not met anyone of his battalion yet, nor have I found any of Frank's regiment. We are permitted to write nothing whatever about our doings here, so I must close as I can't think of anything more to say.

After shuttling from battalion to battalion and sampling the dubious delights of French troop trains, Char settled into the ranks of the 8th Royal Fusiliers, who had just been through a tough time on the Somme — at Pozières. He described some of the discomforts of army life to sister Edie.

26 August 1916

17th Battalion Royal Fusiliers attached to and in D Company of the 8th Battalion Royal Fusiliers, BEF, France

I am now within marching distance of the lines and shall be going into the trenches this evening. The railway carriages that brought us this far are just boxes and are marked "36 hommes 8 cheveaux" and there is just room for us to sit on our packs, but when it comes to lying down at night it's unpleasant. I myself managed to get to sleep and awoke with about 4 others lying on top of me, which made it impossible for me to get up and relax my joints, so I lay still and went to sleep again. On my first night in France I slept in a tent, but there were too many of us, so since then I have slept out of doors and pulled my waterproof sheet over me when it rained. I am told that I shall be in a quiet part of the lines and certainly there wasn't much doing about here last night, though the guns about 20 miles away were making a lot of noise. I hope Harold is going on all right and will soon be at home. Best love to all. I will write and tell you what I think of the trenches in a day or two.

Your loving brother, Char

Three weeks after being plucked from the inferno of Pozières, Harold was out of bed and exploring the sights of Portsmouth and Southsea with Len for company. Strolling the narrow lanes of the old town and the wide seafront promenade, Len knew it was only a matter of time before he would have to swap his bowler hat for a tin helmet. Married men were being conscripted and the Railway Clearing House could get by without him. Fewer and fewer staff were needed as the government made rail companies pull together for the national good. Patriotism had initially solved the dilemma of too many clerks and not enough tickets and paperwork for them to shuffle. Almost 400 men left the hallowed halls of Euston in the first rush to join up in 1914. Another 200 had gone by the end of the year. As work continued to shrink, hundreds more were farmed out to the Ministry of Munitions and Board of Trade. Len's days there were numbered. Harold, ten years younger, had been in uniform for almost two years but would never reproach his brother. He had hoped Char would be spared and felt the same about Len. Six fighting Beechey brothers — one killed and another crippled — was enough for one family.

27 August 1916
Section II Ward 9

5th Southern General Hospital, Portsmouth
My dear mother
    I saw Len on Wednesday and we had a stroll around the town, rather poor old town — narrow, few good buildings, the town hall the only nice one I saw. The promenades are nothing much. Since then I have been in bed, caught a delightful cold in the head, sore throat, blithering headache too. Of course my temperature went up but I feel a lot

better tonight and it's only 101 degrees so I will be getting out in a couple of days. My wound is practically healed up so after a few days' convalescence I shall get a fortnight furlough. I don't think my arm will trouble me at all.

Your loving son, Harold

By the end of August, Frank was at last employed as signalling officer. The 13th East Yorks, horrified bystanders on 1 July, escaped the continuing carnage of the Somme while other units were being pounded into oblivion. On 9 July, they were packed into cattle trucks for the rail trip north. The first stopover at Robecq was like paradise. Orchards dripping with fruit, cherries at one franc a kilo, eggs at tuppence each and a warm and friendly welcome from the locals quickly boosted sagging morale. After a blissful 48 hours they were back on the road, marching miles into the night towards the flash and thunder of fighting around the battered village of Laventie. Despite a 3a.m. welcoming fireworks party of enemy shelling, it was a live-and-let-live sector where both sides kept their heads down behind scorched sandbags. Next stop was Richebourg St Vaast, near Neuve Chapelle.

Battalion HQ was in a remarkably intact old farmhouse beside a tree-lined road which was surrounded by pock-marked fields, showing death was never far away. The 13th East Yorks signallers were sitting around a biscuit box in the farm cellar watching one of their mates dismantle the nose cap of a large enemy shell when it went off. Jagged metal flew everywhere, injuring half a dozen men, two seriously. Replacements had to be hurriedly found, with Frank providing a crash course in the mysteries of battlefield communication, which normally required anything up to fourteen months' training. Having such a novice bunch would pile pressure on him to lead from the front. It was like being back at the Choir School and cramming facts and figures into young brains for the Cambridge Locals. Because field telephones were such a liability, with wires being repeatedly blown up, the newcomers had to be instructed on how to crawl out in the heat of battle to make running repairs. Morse code was more reliable but primitive. It was transmitted by heliograph or Aldis lamp or wagged over short distances with a blue and white flag or flapped by opening and shutting two small boards hinged together and painted black on the outside and white inside. All of which made the front-line signaller a choice target. Frank had his work cut out but he was relieved to be rid of the carrying and working parties, as he told his mother.

28 August 1916
13th E York Regt, BEF

I'm just out of the trenches again and have a few days more or less rest. I have left the Sapping Coy, and have been Signalling Officer to the Battalion for a fortnight now. I jumped at the chance of getting to my own job again and am getting on well with it — in fact our Signal Office is now like a Telephone Exchange in England.

I can't tell you any news of our part in the war, which has been considerable, because it is forbidden; you will have heard from Harold (I hope he is doing well) about things down South in the big offensive. I enclose an appreciation by our late Corps Commander of our own work down there. My "leave" is more than due now but all leave is still stopped. All I can hope is that I get it as soon as it does start. A week's leave in England would be distinctly pleasant. My bungalow is still let furnished to a friend of mine in the regiment, a wounded officer and his wife and kiddie. I let them have it on condition that they pay the rent and hire of furniture so I don't have any worry with it at all.

Will you please send me out a couple of towels and a parcel of cakes and things — not that I want cakes at all, but in the mess all parcels are common property as far as eatables go and I have benefited so much from my colleagues that I feel I ought to return something. I send a cheque to cover cost with a little change left over to help out the household expenses. I hope things are not getting any dearer in England. It must be pretty bad already.

Well, mother dear, I will write again soon. Keep cheerful — the war looks like being over fairly soon now Romania has started.

Love to all, Frank

Over the weeks and months, from his bijou bungalow at Withernsea to his arrival in France and his trek from the Somme to the quieter sectors further north and back again, Frank had hardly written a line. Instead, he sent a succession of official postcards to his mother, sister Edie and sister-in-law Mary, Mrs Eric Beechey. It was an efficient way for a son worn out by fatigue duties or with responsibility for battalion signalling to reassure his family he was OK.

Harold was convalescing on the Isle of Wight and thoroughly sick of the antiseptic monotony of military hospitals. It was surely no coincidence that wounded men seemed to be sent as far away from their homes as possible. The authorities appeared to actively discourage relatives from descending on their loved ones. Whether Harold eventually got away to see his mother is not clear. His words in the weeks to come would indicate a certain frustration and desperation as he returned to the drill and drudgery of camp life.

> 2 September 1916
> Afton Lodge Hosp
> Freshwater, Isle of Wight

My dear mother,

I have been transferred today — it seems a nice place, old country house but terribly quiet, nothing to do. The tucker is pretty fair. I wish you could let me have some money by return. I am nearly stranded and cannot get any while I am in hospital, so if you could oblige as soon as you possibly can I will let you have it back as soon as I come on leave, which won't be much over a week, I expect, as my wound is healed. I am disappointed with the I.O.W. — not nearly as pretty as I thought.

Tea is ready, in haste, Harold

Char was finding lice and mud the biggest enemies in the trenches. He could do little about either. Lice began multiplying in the seams of his army shirt within 24 hours of him starting his mole-like existence in the dirt of northern France. Despite the tons of concoctions sent over by well-meaning relatives to get rid of them, they were never beaten except on the rare occasions when the troops might get a bath and change of clothes. Char would find the carbolic he asked for from home as useless as all the other supposed medications.

The 8th Royal Fusiliers had been sent to a quiet sector to regroup. They alternated between spells in the line near the village of Agny and billets at Dainville, a mile or two either side of Arras. Char marvelled at the resoluteness of local people still living in their smashed houses and packing their children off to school each morning. In Arras, the inhabitants were forbidden to leave their homes until after 9.30 in the evening, when they would pick their way through the debris under cover of darkness to do their shopping.

Despite shells and occasional machine-gun fire, the battalion suffered few casualties. Its war diary records that patrols were pushed out into No Man's Land and that German trench mortars caused the men some discomfort but few losses. The nights were mostly spent digging new trenches and improving the positions. Char was posted to keep watch while the working parties laboured through the hours of darkness. When he next wrote to his mother, he was out of the front line and bedding down on straw on the floor of a farmer's barn. The keen naturalist in him had seen little of interest and he was rather snooty about his comrades. So far, his war was a bore.

13 September 1916
D Coy, 13th Platoon 8th Battalion Royal Fusiliers,
BEF, France

We came out of the trenches yesterday and are having a fairly easy time some few miles behind the lines. I spent most of yesterday cleaning myself and the equipment and now hope to get several letters written. Our duty in the front line was chiefly sentry work, which sounds easy enough, but I myself would rather march for an hour than stand perfectly still for an hour. By the by, will you send me a cake of strong carbolic soap — men say it is useful for lice whereas they (not the men) simply fatten on Keatings. The army recommends a mixture of naphthalene, creosote and something else but don't supply it and no one knows where to get it.

We are now in a large barn. Our beds (those who were lucky enough to get them) are quite comfortable. They are just a wooden frame with chicken wire nailed across. I, of course, being new to the business was one of the last to arrive at the barn and sleep on the floor. The civilian population is still here and the children go to school with gas helmets slung in little satchels as they say the gas in a steady wind will sometimes carry several miles.

The march here was most uninteresting as it was in single file along trenches for most of the way. The country is very much like the English Midlands. With one or two exceptions, the flowers are the same. Birds are scarce, except swallows, but all I have seen are the same as the English, as are also the butterflies.

We are fortunate in having a very decent lot of NCOs, the rest of the 8th are chiefly Londoners whose language is mostly adjectival and gets very boring. A seven-penny novel or two would be welcome here — I'm tired of reading about the war. I wish my overcoat was like the one Harold has — it's all the bed clothing we have at night as it's still supposed to be summer. Last night was very cold and I couldn't get much sleep, which reminds me to ask you to send out two of my winter vests.

Last night was again very cold but today is beautifully warm and bright. I have just spent all the morning waiting in the shoemakers' room whilst my boots and about a dozen other men's were repaired. Mine took less than 5 minutes. Bath parade this afternoon, for which I shall be glad. I am told that summer in the army officially ends on

September 30th, which date is independent of latitude and longitude. Don't send any more socks at present as I've got 5 pairs in good condition.

Within days Char was writing home again with a shopping list.

> 17 September 1916 (same address)
> My last two letters were practically filled up with suggestions for a parcel, but in case they haven't arrived yet I'll make out a fresh list.
>
> writing pad and envelopes
> a packet of safety pins
> a seven-penny red book and a copy of Pickwick Papers if you have one to spare
> tinned paste (meat or fish)
>
> Please send in a tin box otherwise all I don't eat on the first day will be eaten by the rats the following evening. And please don't send anything that needs boiling water as it's very difficult to get.

The army might have been making a mess of the Battle of the Somme, but its postal system was a model of efficiency. Char received two parcels in one day and wrote a brief note of thanks to his mother. That same night his company was to carry out a trench raid, slipping over the top in darkness, crawling across No Man's Land, breaching the enemy wire and killing as many Germans as possible before bringing back information about which unit they belonged to. If he knew about the imminent operation then Char had no intention of causing his mother any anxiety by mentioning it.

> 21 September 1916 (same address)
> I've just time to write a few lines to thank you for the splendid parcel you sent me; it came yesterday and the smaller parcel and letter also. Everything in there is absolutely ripping and so well packed they were all perfectly fresh and unbroken; luckily for me I'm now in quite a small shelter in the trenches, only 2 others and a lance corporal, so that I can share with them and still have a large amount for myself.
> The comforter is grand, in fact everything is just as perfect as it could possibly be; I am indeed in luck in having had brothers out here before me as you seem to know just exactly what we want.
> Very best thanks and love, Char

He came through the raid unscathed. The men of D Company had cut through the enemy wire and got within seven yards of the German front line when the alarm was raised and star shells lit up the night. Char and his comrades had to scamper back under a fusillade of gunfire and bombs, suffering only a single casualty. Safely in his own trenches, Char was glad to tuck into what was left of the parcels from home. On 27 September, refreshed and reinforced with mostly untried recruits like Private Beechey, the

8th Royal Fusiliers left the comparative peace and quiet of Agny sector and began their journey south to the Somme.

CHAPTER
NINE

To deny a fellow a final leave seems miserable spitefulness

The army had now taken Len as well. Annie still clung to him, travelling to Winchester to be close to him at weekends while he was being trained to kill Germans. There were terrors to be faced before Len even set foot in France. The first was a doctor wielding a hypodermic. Whether inoculation was meant to combat typhoid, yellow fever or flat feet was never made clear to those lined up outside the medical hut, shirtsleeves rolled up above the elbow. Rifleman 6679 L. R. Beechey was just happy to suffer no ill effects beyond a throbbing left arm as he passed the time writing to his mother and Annie.

Friday, 22 September 1916
A Coy, Hut L3
3/18 Battalion London Irish Rifles
Morn Hill Camp, Winchester

Dear Mother
I have just been inoculated for the second time,

and as it gives me 48 hours free from parade I have a good chance of writing a few letters. I am writing this at once in case I feel bad afterwards — it seems to take some hours to work and then one feels a bit stiff and feverish after it. Annie came down last Saturday. We had about seven hours together. She had not heard from the Army people up to a day or two ago, but has now heard from the RCH [Railway Clearing House] and got her first week's allowance from there.

I wrote to Harold at Avondale St as I thought he would be there. I suppose his furlough is up this weekend. I hope they will not send him out again, or at least give him some weeks' rest first. I am getting more used to the life and the days seem to go by quickly now, one as much resembles another. We get up at six and if we have a parade before breakfast, generally finish about four, which means we finish tea about five. Two nights a week there are what we call "night ops" — our stage only go out for an hour or two, but the more advanced stages stop out most of the night.

I don't know if Annie will be able to come up tomorrow, Saturday. I am waiting to hear from her but we have orders that we are not to go out of the camp during our 48 hours off, as some of the chaps are apt to "flop out" afterwards. When the last lot were inoculated there were four or five that dropped while we were waiting for meals, but I am fortunate in not being much affected.

I have had two paydays since I have been here, the first one I got a shilling, the second 3/-. I suppose that will be the usual amount as the odd 6d is deducted for sundries, hair cutting etc. I have had two haircuts in 17 days. I used to have one about every three months.

We get good food and I eat it up without troubling much as to what it is. But have not been able to eat piccalilli for breakfast yet — they sometimes give us that.

With love to all from your affectionate son, Len

The recruiting office for the London Irish Rifles was at Scotland Yard. Whether Len marched in of his own accord or whether he was conscripted is academic. He would have been given a date to report to regimental headquarters at Chelsea Barracks. There, an elderly sergeant welcomed new men like a fussing mother hen as well as relieving them of every last farthing. He told them to make sure they put on two pairs of socks before having army boots fitted and thoughtfully provided string and brown paper for them to wrap up their civilian clothes. Few could resist his offer to send their parcels home for half a crown or the chance to buy a souvenir khaki handkerchief embroidered with a small harp. At half a crown each, the proceeds would provide comforts for the poor London Irish boys who had never recovered from being wounded at the

Battle of Loos two years earlier. When he reached Morn Hill Camp in Winchester, Len found the same regimental hankies on sale at sixpence each and was surprised to hear from Annie that his parcel had arrived home stamped, "Soldier's Civilian Clothing. Post Free". The elderly sergeant at Chelsea Barracks was reputed to have made enough on the side to buy a large hotel on the south coast after the war.

Morn Hill was a great cluster of tents and wooden huts high on the downs to the east of the old city of Winchester. Len could expect to be there for three months, learning to form fours, to drill and to keep every piece of his army kit pristine and polished. He would also be taught that the rifleman was a breed apart, marching at a quicker step than soldiers from other regiments and carrying his rifle at the trail. He had to spend hours fondling his Lee Enfield before being allowed to load it. The firing ranges were in a valley close to the camp. Recruits were marched down there, issued with live ammunition and taught to shoot while standing, kneeling and lying down. From 1,000 yards away, the bull's-eye of a six-foot-square paper target looked no bigger than a pinprick. Each rifleman had his individual ration pack with him so that at lunchtime the whole scene was said to resemble a picnic at Bisley, home of the National Rifle Association.

Annie was taking every opportunity to travel from London and be with her husband before he was posted to France. A wife would not be allowed in camp so they strolled in the countryside or walked the lanes of Winchester arm in arm.

Monday, 24 September 1916
Rfn LR Beechey 6679
A Coy, Hut L3
3/18 Battalion London Irish Rifles
Morn Hill Camp, Winchester

Dear Mother

Annie came down again yesterday. We had about seven hours together, wandering round behind the camps. She brought me a waistcoat down. I feel a little more civilised now I have got it and a little warmer in the early morning.

We have just had church parade on the south slope of the camp, and have had a fine morning for it. There were some larks singing overhead and a very pretty country scene in front of us.

Pleased to hear about Chris. From what you said about Bertha I think he will be well looked after. I haven't had any effects from the second inoculation, just a bruised feeling in the arm during the second night. I should like to come up and see you but shall not have a chance till I get a few days, and that is somewhere in the dim future I think.

I got a game of chess in the reading room the other night. They provide chess, draughts and dominoes so shall have something to fall back on during the dark and wet evenings. The evenings will start an hour earlier in a week's time so it will be dark soon after we have had tea.

Another thing I haven't got used to is the kitbag; everything I want seems to get to the bottom. I really want an opening each end. I sleep very comfortably but it gets cold in the early morning. We have nearly all the windows open. The camp is in rather an exposed position right on top of the hill. The surrounding hills are about a mile away. The position is something like the egg cup in the middle of a round pie dish.

We are just going to have dinner, with much love from your affectionate son, Len

Harold was out of hospital and back in camp on bleak, windswept Salisbury Plain.

> 28 September 1916
> Pelham Camp
> Salisbury Plain

Hope the Zeps did not trouble you last night. I shall not be here long. When I have been classified I shall be sent off to my training battalion, via that to Etaples and from there to my Batt. again, which is stationed near Ypres at present. It is not very pleasant coming back to the camp life again but I shall get used to that I suppose.

Love to everybody, Harold

Zeppelins had been spreading panic and terror since January 1915. Forty-eight people were killed and more than sixty injured when they dropped 233 bombs on

Lincolnshire, Suffolk and London on the night of 31 March/1 April 1916. The airships returned at the end of July, dropping thirty-two bombs on Lincolnshire and Norfolk, but only managed to kill a cow. A Royal Flying Corps pilot fired off two trays of ammunition into one of the lumbering beasts of the skies before his machine gun blew up and he was knocked senseless by a lump of metal casing. When he came round, his aircraft was still flying but the Zep had escaped in the dark.

Harold read about the latest raids with disquiet. Fourteen Zeppelins targeted Lincolnshire again, killing four people in the town of Boston. That same September night a 19-year-old pilot won the Victoria Cross for shooting one of the airships down in flames over Hertfordshire, witnessed by thousands watching from the ground all over north London. For Harold, there was no such excitement to enliven his miserable existence at Pelham Camp. He wrote to his mother some time around the end of September or beginning of October.

My dear mother

I am in the convalescent part of the camp but there is a weekly classification so after I have been here a week I may be transferred to A class which is the fit men.

This is a lonely sort of place. I have plenty of liberty but there is nothing to do. There are two small towns nearby — Ludgershall and Tidworth — very uninteresting places. The camp is very full. The slightly wounded from the Great Push are beginning to roll in and the tucker and sleeping arrangements are a bit disorganised. The food is good but scanty and badly served, being undercooked and cold when you get it. My hut, which is built to accommodate 30, has 41. The Hut Corporal is an old friend of Kris — he was in the same ward at Harefield and remembers me visiting him there when I was at Abbey Wood last February.

This is a dreadfully dismal place when it rains. We have a stove and good supply of fuel so it's not so bad if you have a decent book. I read a thing by B and CB Fry about a perfect youth — it's called Mother's Boy. He did everything tiptop and did not swank about it either — I wanted to kick him all the time.

I am writing this in the YMCA — there is a concert just starting. I have not much pleasure in concerts as they are all on the same line, same old items and style. I hope you have good news of the others. I think I am pretty certain of getting at least 4 days' leave before I go out again so you may expect me some time.

Your loving son, Harold

Char's unit had reached the Somme where there were no more little French children to be seen marching off to school with gas masks in satchels. The 8th Royal Fusiliers were holed up at Pommiers Redoubt, a former German stronghold that had been overrun in one of the few successes of 1 July. It was now far enough behind the lines to offer some sanctuary for troops in reserve but it was a quagmire notorious for the fattened rats that fed off the dead and brazenly gnawed at the living. One junior officer described the accommodation as consisting of "about 150 holes in the ground, none more than three or four foot deep — in fact they are glorified shell holes with a light roof of wood and sandbags over them."

On 30 September an enemy plane buzzed the camp and dropped three bombs. Next day Char was on his way up to the front at Flers, an insignificant village of a few wrecked cottages that had a special place in history. It was captured on 15 September when British tanks were seen in action for the first time. The Flers road, along which D Company trudged, was a morass littered with the remains of mules and horses. Char's battalion was part of 12th Division, whose historian tells of men found drowned in shell holes and pack mules sinking into the mire over their hocks. The trenches were no less awful and by early October Flers was an infamous hellhole. Amid the mud and mayhem and daily toll of dead and wounded, Char was anxious to reassure his mother that he had settled his affairs.

12 October 1916, France
I haven't written for some time but it has been almost impossible. Still I sent off 2 field cards to say I was still all right. I did try writing a letter about a week ago but after carrying it in my pocket for three days and getting wet through and covered with mud as many times it would have been

244

impossible for anyone to read it.

It is awfully good of you to have sent so many useful things and parcels. I have now quite as much as I can carry and am well supplied with socks, so please don't send anything more in that line until I ask.

A date at the top reminds me that it is a birthday, Winnie's I think, so will you and the family treat yourselves to a good tea at Kirke White's and I'll send a little cheque to cover expenses when I can get some ink. I have had a week of very hard work but am in the best of health though tired out and rather foot sore. I can't tell you any details but am sure things are going on well in my part of the line.

With regard to my few dividends, I have arranged that they shall be paid straight into the bank and I have also sent my will to the same bank to be kept there for me. I had it made out in a legal form by a Stamford solicitor and sent to me out here for signatures.

There are so many of us in the army now and you must not stint yourselves by sending parcels too often, postage being so dear.

I haven't had much time for reading lately but enjoy reading the Pickwick Papers when I do get some spare time and am delighted to get the Stamford Mercury each time. I see by the last that another of our Stamford old boys has been killed, one of the Glews, an aviator whom Bar saw fly at Horncastle.

* ★ *

Char had been too distracted by his first real experience of trench warfare to read much of Dickens. In their first 24 hours at Flers, the Fusiliers had lost thirty-three wounded and two killed from heavy shelling. They had to dig a new protective forward trench by joining up two strong points in front of D Company's section of the line. Two officers were evacuated with shellshock but Char had kept his nerve under fire. In the hours before dawn on 7 October, they completed the earthworks while being hammered incessantly by German guns. A junior officer and a further half a dozen men were killed and eighteen wounded, but the army had still more work for the Fusiliers that day.

At 1.45p.m., troops still numb from their exertions, from the mud and the enemy bombardment scrambled over the top behind a creeping barrage. D Company formed the supporting wave behind the initial advance. British artillery laid down a curtain of fire 150 yards ahead of the attackers who were to follow on as it edged forward at a rate of 50 yards a minute. Their objective was a section of the German line known as Bayonet Trench, 500 yards away. Only twenty or so brave souls got that far. They were either killed or driven back by counter-attacks. The Fusiliers lost nine officers and 244 men without gaining an inch of ground. The division suffered more than 1,300 casualties. The enemy had been ready and waiting, opening fire on the attackers and causing carnage as they massed in the British line even before zero hour. The Germans had occupied a line of old gun pits connected to deep dugouts, impervious to the creeping barrage. As the firestorm passed harmlessly over, machine-gunners emerged to mow down the attacking waves.

Char's unit had been relieved at 11p.m. In the morning they were lined up in camp to hear their CO read out a message from the brigadier, thanking all ranks "for the magnificent gallantry they displayed yesterday. They advanced steadily under a very heavy fire, which only the best troops could have faced. Though unfortunately unsuccessful, their gallant conduct has added to the fine reputation which you have already won for yourselves."

For the battered Fusiliers, it was back to fatigue duties, hauling trench mortar ammunition to the front, burying the dead horses on the vital route between Longueval and Flers and trying to repair the road so wheeled vehicles could use it. The lethal gun pits that had defied them were overrun in a smaller, well-executed outflanking operation a week later. A Fusilier, posted as missing presumed dead, was found alive but badly injured, sharing a hole with two wounded Germans. After his experiences, Char was remarkably cheerful when he wrote to thank his mother for more treats from home.

17 October 1916
With the BEF

It's kind of you to have sent me two more parcels. They were excellent and the cake was superb. I'm still where I was when I last wrote, a few miles behind the lines, but am feeling much more chirpy and less tired and now that I've got a new pair of boots can keep myself dryer and more comfortable. The last pair had a hole in them that I could put four fingers through at a time.

Our chief duties are carrying and trench digging, a fatigue usually lasting about seven hours and generally at night. This makes our clothes and equipment filthy so that we have to spend most of the day cleaning it.

Many thanks for the books. Here, I have no time to read so shall keep them till we get into less strenuous parts for a rest. I've had a long letter from Mr Rea [a teaching colleague] and also from Mr Day [the headmaster at Stamford]. The school is still going up in numbers (130 now) so that it's a good thing we had new classrooms made last summer. This summer the science lab has been entirely re-fitted and things at Stamford are going on well. I got a letter from Harold all right and will answer it soon.

At the end of October the Fusiliers were ferried back to Arras aboard a fleet of French motorbuses. For Char, there was the rare treat of a bath to wash off some of the filth of the trenches and a welcome change of clothing. If only the army could organise an attack with the same precision as bath times. It reminded Char of communal scrub-downs at public school. A dozen men at a time stripped off, dumped their mud-clogged clothing in numbered bins, soaked and soaped their itching bodies for five minutes in a lukewarm tub before leaving the murky water for the next naked contingent. After drying himself with a towel as rough as sandpaper, Char was handed clean underclothes and a uniform that had been brushed down and oven-baked in a bid to destroy tiny invaders. He was just as lousy again when he wrote home a couple of days later.

8th Battalion Royal Fusiliers
BEF, France

My dear mother

I am back away from the lines now and am thankful to get away from the sound of the guns; the perpetual rattle gets on my nerves a bit.

There is one more thing I must ask you to send out. It is some ointment called Harrison's Pomade. The soap did very well where we had a chance of washing our shirts but for three weeks we were unable to wash even ourselves properly, and two days ago I had my first bath for a month.

Please don't send anything more in the way of clothing as I already have to carry about a hundredweight. On our last march, for instance, we each carried an overcoat, a mackintosh, two blankets, a waterproof sheet, rifle, equipment with ammunition, underclothing, cleaning material etc.

I have got over the state of fatigue in which I was and am feeling quite well again and comfortable except for the insects.

Best love to all from your loving son, Char

★ ★ ★

Harold had been shifted to another camp in Dorset and instead of asking for little loans to tide him over he had scraped together enough cash to send sister Winifrede something for her birthday. He was also showing remarkable goodwill to a fellow soldier who had fallen foul of the military authorities, though he doesn't say what the man's misdemeanour was in a letter to Winnie in late October.

Hut G10, Bovington Camp, Nr Wareham, Dorset
Sorry I have not written sooner for your 21st. I am forwarding a 10/- note and you can do what you like with it. This is not very far from Weymouth but it's very out of the way. We only came down here today — the camp itself is better than Pelham Down, being much cleaner. The parade ground and round the huts has been paved and so when it's wet it is still quite decent outside.

I had a trip to St Albans the other day on escort duty. We should have come back on the same day but instead stayed the night in London. I went and roused Annie up about eleven o'clock. She did not seem to mind but insisted on cooking me some supper so it was one o'clock before I went to bed. I never got into any trouble for being overdue. There was only a L/Cp (an old pal of Kris) and myself. It was rather a farce of an escort — the prisoner, handed over to us at St Albans to take to Pelham Down, we let go back to his home for the night, telling him to meet us at the station in the morning. We were running a great risk but he seemed such a decent fellow that I had every confidence in his turning up.

Well, good luck and love to everybody, Harold

After being away from the fighting for almost three months, there was a certain dread creeping into his letters.

25 October 1916
Bovington Camp

Dear Mother

I have been put into A Class and going back to France on Saturday. I am going to Etaples and then to my battalion. I am going back in a hurry, same as last time, all leave is cut out. I am not looking forward to the prospect. I find difficulty in keeping warm with four blankets, I don't know what I'll do with one.

A few days later Harold gave his mother a glimmer of hope that he might yet be coming home before the army packed him off to France again.

28 October 1916
Bovington Camp

The draft has been cancelled for today — expect to go end of next week. Slight hope of leave. Have had a lot of old mail lately, some letters 14 months old. It's fall-in in a few minutes so cannot write very much.

Well, good luck, Harold

★ ★ ★

Nearly a week later, he was still stuck in Dorset, bitter and resentful at being denied leave.

3 November 1916
Bovington Camp

My dear mother

I don't know when or where we are going now. We are all ready and equipped so they may bung us off at any moment, but whether it's straight to France or through our training battalion, which would mean me going to Godford near Salisbury.

I have been fooled about since I joined the AIF but this takes the bun. We have been for hours on parade doing nothing, just hanging about and getting cold. They promised us four days' leave then now quietly tell us it can't be done, men are wanted very urgently over there, and all the time they are putting the draft off from day to day.

If I could have been sure of the draft being put off like this I would have taken leave, but I don't want to miss the draft and have it slung in your face you were afraid to go back there. I don't think there is anyone who has been through the Hell at Pozières, or any of those little places down on the Somme, who wants to go again. I know I jolly well don't but I won't shirk the thing for all that.

But to deny a fellow the right of a final leave — supposed to be given to everybody before going over — seems to me to be miserable spitefulness on their part. They won't give us a definite idea of when we are going, just to keep us from taking leave. I would be much obliged if you would send me a singlet — sox I don't want at present.

Your loving son, Harold

[Same letter continued]

Saturday

I have just heard it's very likely we may not be shifting for a fortnight so if you would like to take the trouble and write to the O/C No3 Command Depot, Bovington Camp, Wool, Dorset, and ask him to let me have a few days' leave. Give my unit and that I am on draft for France, and any little thing that might influence him, it might come off.

In Australia, the legacy of Gallipoli was still playing havoc with Chris's health. Bertha wrote to Amy to tell her of the latest setback.

6 November 1916
9 Holyrood St, West Leederville

It seems strange writing to wish you all a happy Xmas so soon and the weather so hot too. We were so sorry to hear Harold was wounded again but I hear from Miss Boyce that he has been sent back to France. Chris has been rather bad the last few days and I had a local doctor to see him — he didn't do him any good so I just took him down to the base hospital and they are keeping him there for a few days at least. I hope it won't be longer.

They tell me he had dysentery rather badly and of course it has pulled him down and he is much thinner. I went in to see him this afternoon and he says except for the weakness he thinks it has done him good. He wishes me to say he cannot write himself but I really think he is glad of an excuse for not writing. I am ashamed of never writing to Winifrede as I promised but I seem to have such a lot to do now that we have moved into our own house.

Please give my love to all at home and tell Harold if you see him we are keeping a room for him.

Yours affectionately — Bertha

Almost two years to the day since waving him off, Curly was still devoted to Harold, sharing any snippets she received from him with Chris and Bertha. Despite Western Australia's proud record for sending its sons to war — more than a quarter of the Australians who landed at Gallipoli on 25 April 1915 came from the state — men still heavily outnumbered women in Perth. Curly would have had no trouble finding other suitors but her heart remained true to Harold.

Char, with bathtime just a fond memory, was fighting a losing battle to stay dry in the waterlogged line near Arras. The battalion diary for early November tells of a constant struggle to stop the sides of the trenches caving in but Char was not unduly troubled and was more concerned with the progress of Stamford's young footballers when he wrote to Edie.

10 November 1916
8th Battalion RF

I have just had another letter from Stamford — the boys are doing very well indeed in their games this year; they were a good team last year and only wanted confidence.

Work hasn't been so hard lately and I'm keeping well and fit though not always comfortable owing to the bad weather. Have just had a leather jerkin issued so can keep myself much dryer in the daytime and still keep a dry overcoat for night covering.

Many thanks for sending the Stamford Mercury so often. I read every word of it, advertisements and all. It comes all right for the halfpenny stamp and it's a small paper so will you shove in an old Daily Mail or Mirror with it to give me something to clean out my mess tin with (paper is better than anything and requires no carrying). I am enclosing the small cheque which I wasn't able to send before owing to absence of ink. Ask mother to divide it up amongst those who are at home, including Sam.

PS Can you send me a pair of woollen gloves — quite a cheap pair will do as well as the best. I have managed to lose one of the mittens but gloves will be better.

Harold never did receive the final leave the army owed him. His mother had done as he'd asked and written a plea on his behalf, but the military would not be swayed. A brief note told Amy he was being posted overseas again.

11 November 1916
Bovington Camp

My dear mother

They would not let me off the draft so I am leaving for France tonight. By the time you get this I shall be in Etaples. If I had not been on draft they would have considered your letter — thanks for writing. Goodbye, keep on writing. I might be back again before Xmas.

Love to everybody, Harold

His hopes of being home for Christmas were wishful thinking. Before rejoining his battalion on 2 December, he would spend three cheerless weeks at Etaples, which the soldier poet Wilfred Owen called "a vast, dreadful encampment . . . a kind of paddock where the beasts were kept a few days before the shambles". While Harold was square bashing on the vast sandy training grounds of the Bull Ring at Etaples and being bawled out from dawn to dusk by sadistic NCOs, he was at least spared the last bloody convulsions of the Battle of the Somme.

As long ago as 10 September 1916, Haig had observed, "The season for fighting is nearly over." But he was unwilling to call a halt. Rain had fallen throughout October and the chalky ground of the Somme valley had been turned into a thick porridge that could swallow horses and men. Still, the offensive went on in some of the most appalling conditions of the war.

Rumours had been flying around since late September that the 13th East Yorks would be returning to the area of the 1 July fiasco. In the meantime, Frank had been working with his team of signallers and trying out one or two initiatives that were not always heartily appreciated. Private Surfleet had been transferred to the "flagwaggers" after the exploding shell-cap incident. His diary mentions some of the scrapes the men got into as a result of Frank's enthusiasm and eagerness to try anything once. "Signal officer set up a test box midway between supports and front line which attracted a lot of shellfire and gave little protection except from bullets. Signalling officer also had the bright idea of using a new Lucas Daylight Signalling Lamp at night from the test box — its beam fairly cut the blackness for some two or three hundred yards, a really glorious beam, but much too conspicuous; we had barely begun our message when a salvo of Whizz-bangs nearly blew the lamp to bits and us with it. NCO in charge of us was most profane about the exercise and we did not use it again from that test box."

For a few exquisite days in early October the East Yorks had been billeted in the small town of Merville, one of those rare places hardly touched by war. The guns were a distant, muffled memory. Men enjoyed the comfort and camaraderie of the cafés and estaminets and overcame their English modesty as they used the open-air urinals built into the side of the lovely old church. When they left, the battalion band led the way through cheering crowds of locals. Then it was back to reality as they were put on to more cattle trucks for the rail journey to the Somme.

Almost four months on from July and they were trudging towards Serre along the same road through Colincamps where they had once shuddered at the sight of rows of open graves. In summer the trenches had been bearable, despite the ever-present danger of sudden death or mutilation. Now they were a sea of mud. Frank's signallers laid down new lines from battalion headquarters at the rear to company positions in the waterlogged front trenches in preparation for an impending attack. It was a miserable task, ploughing through the mire day and night in pouring rain with reels of wire. Maintaining the link with HQ was a thankless and hopeless exercise. The telephone lines were always being blown up and having to be repaired again.

In his diary, Surfleet describes how when the line went dead to battalion HQ, "I slid out fearfully into a blackness slashed at intervals with streaks of red or yellow. God! I was frightened. It was an overland line. It left the trench immediately outside the signal office and ran over the top, back through supports to the headquarters. I gripped my pliers, got the line in my left hand . . . and ran. Shells fell more or less all round. Presently, the line finished. I marked the spot where it ended with an old rifle and went in search of the other end. Fortunately, it was near. It did not take me many seconds to join it up, insulate it and tap in with my spare phone to hear C Company getting battalion HQ. Then I ran like a hare back to the safety of the trench. No sooner had I got back than the line was broken again."

Even before the planned attack, Frank's team of signallers was being further depleted. Three were killed by a shell burst. Another was bayoneted in the backside by a soldier on a night raid while carrying out repairs in No Man's Land. To add insult to injury, the wound was deemed self-inflicted and the hapless victim had his pay stopped.

The renewed assault on Serre was originally scheduled for 25 October but rotten weather forced the first of several postponements that played on the nerves of men haunted by 1 July. Private Surfleet was disgusted to see men digging yet more graves in the back areas in full view of those storming imaginary trenches in preparation for the coming stunt. "It is a damned shame they are allowed to dig our graves before our eyes like that," he complains in his diary.

The rain finally eased off on 8 November and colder weather set in. On Saturday, 11 November, the decision was made to go ahead with the operation against the same German defences that had defied and destroyed the "Pals" battalions nineteen weeks earlier. Zero hour was fixed for 5.45a.m., an hour and a half before sunrise, on Monday, 13 November. Parts of the British line had been pushed forward since July, reducing the width of No Man's Land to be crossed, but the previously wide-open grassy slopes had been pummelled into a shell-shattered wasteland. A tank commander inspected it the day before the attack when the mud seemed stickier and thicker than ever and pronounced that his machines could not possibly operate over such conditions.

The British official history tells of the infantry's long and trying march to the front but notes "the spirit of the men was remarkable considering that they had spent weeks, generally cold and often wet to the skin, in muddy trenches or in poor billets and bivouacs behind the line with little respite from battle preparations and from such uncongenial tasks as scraping mud off the roads".

The 13th East Yorks were in their assembly positions opposite Serre soon after midnight. They were to attack in four waves and take three German lines of defence. The bitterly cold moonlit night had given way to dripping fog that shrouded the whole battlefield, reducing visibility to a few yards in the eerie darkness. As the troops sat shivering in their sodden trenches sipping tea laced with rum, the British guns opened up at 5a.m. with a preliminary bombardment along the whole front. It simply served as a calling card to the enemy deep in their dugouts. At zero hour, the artillery laid down a barrage covering the assaulting troops but many were still stranded in the deep mud of No Man's Land when the firing lifted, allowing the Germans to emerge from their dugouts and turn their machine guns on the floundering attackers.

In the fog and confusion, parties of the 13th East Yorks reached as far as the third enemy line but were cut off. The battalion on their right were stopped dead and driven back into their own trenches by 7a.m. Troops who had taken the German second line fought off a series of counter-attacks and clung on until two in the afternoon when they pulled back to the first line.

One of Frank's brother officers paints a desperate picture of events in a report attached to the battalion war diary: "Zero hour, owing to thick fog, was dark instead of dawn as it should have been. One could only control those men with whom one was in immediate contact. Men a few yards away were merely dark moving figures dimly seen by the light of barrage . . . Owing to uncut wire in front of the German 1st line it had been arranged for two platoons to go left and two to go right of it and spread out afterwards . . . No single spot of ground seemed free from shell holes and churned mud and water. We sank knee deep in places. One of our shells fell in the middle of company HQ and knocked out or disabled eight or so men near the German front line . . . fearful mud between the German 1st and 2nd line. Men sank in above their hips and their officers were endeavouring to get them out and forward.

"The ground was so churned up and light nil that you could not see the trenches until you crossed them . . . attempted to work along trench but [it was] blown to pieces by shellfire. Progress over ground was now made impossible by German machine-gun fire at close quarters — one could see a little now and we had to fight where we stood . . . I looked around for some signs of our men, left and right, but failed to find any and soon came to the conclusion we were the only party who had reached the third line ... We were getting shelling from our own guns now ... snipers tried to jump from shell hole to shell hole to get at us. These were killed." Captain R. M. Woolley, who wrote that account, was cut off and taken prisoner by the Germans with the handful of survivors from his company.

The last of the 13th East Yorks retreated from the German first line at 8.45p.m. Lieutenant Colonel K. W. Savory, their commanding officer, wrote in the war diary, "From 9.45a.m. to 6p.m. the Germans barraged all our lines and in particular Caber Trench where battalion HQ was situated. Owing to the barrage it was impossible to get either supplies or reinforcements over, though several attempts were made. The battalion took over 200 prisoners but a number of these escaped. In addition to the German artillery barrage, they employed machine guns and snipers in sweeping our trenches and No Man's Land."

The furious German shelling that had cut off supplies and reinforcements also kept stretcher-bearers and medics pinned down in their own lines unable to help the scores of wounded. Signallers still had to go out into the inferno. Linesmen working in pairs took turns at fixing broken wires. That morning, one after the other they crawled out never to be seen again. The situation was desperate from early in the day. When there were no more men to send out, Frank volunteered to go.

The attack was already doomed when he left the protection of battalion HQ, dug into the side of Caber

Trench, to thread a line through the devastation. The blinding pre-dawn smog had given way to a grim daylight haze and gunners and snipers set their sights on anything that twitched in No Man's Land. Frank armed himself with reel of wire, pliers and telephone for the forward survivors to report back to HQ. The battalion staff wished him luck as he strapped on his tin helmet and climbed from the dugout. Hauling himself over the parapet he was immediately plastered from head to toe in mud. He could only have crawled a matter of yards before a shell-burst blew his legs to pulp.

No Man's Land in front of Serre was swept by enemy fire. A medical officer risked his life to crawl out and tend to him. Captain H. E. Yorke of the Royal Army Medical Corps dressed Frank's wounds and administered morphine to deaden the pain. With shells exploding around them and sniper bullets splattering in the mud, the two officers were surprised to discover that they were both Old Johnians, ex-pupils of St John's School, Leatherhead. Captain Yorke later wrote to Amy Beechey about her son's bravery through it all.

Frank was finally brought in under cover of darkness. The call had gone out for men to help with the wounded. Archie Surfleet was one of those who volunteered. It took him and another man two and a half hours to carry a stretcher case to the aid post through the mud, falling into shell hole after shell hole, tripping over barbed wire, phone lines, dead bodies and discarded equipment. Surfleet tells how the medical officer, sleeves rolled up, looked about finished — "On all sides were bleeding men and the sickly penetrating smell of iodoform [a compound like chloroform] and iodine. Something not unlike the scene and smell of a slaughter-house."

The 8th Royal Fusiliers were still fighting the elements. "Trenches falling in everywhere owing to the very wet weather and practically the whole day and night is spent in repairing the same," records their battalion diary. Char had lost his closest comrades in the fighting at Flers but was keeping his spirits up with thoughts of toast and dripping, a kitchen fireside favourite of Friesthorpe days.

15 November 1916

My dear mother and Edie

Many thanks for your letters and the paper and magazine. I got them last night but haven't had time to read them except the account of Mr Webster's death. I'm out of the trenches now which probably means that I shall be in again by the time you receive this. I had written you a nice interesting account of existence in the trenches but it wasn't allowed to pass [the censor] so I had to tear it up and the next attempt I must have carried about for at least four days before I could get it into the hands of the post corporal.

We did get quite a good rest after the strenuous days and are well as ever again, though my three best friends didn't get back — two wounded and one missing. As for the pork pie, I should just love one — I don't think there is anything that exists that I should like so much. And if you have some at the time of sending, could you send some dripping? It would be such a change after my not having tasted it for half a year. You see, here one has exactly the same every day — bread, tea, stew, cheese, bacon, jam, butter — not always all seven but usually five or six. Just a small mustard tin-full would do splendidly and I'll be able to make some dripping toast.

We've had some dry weather the last few days and fairly warm until today, but we console ourselves with the well-known verse, "Many are cold, but few are frozen". Sorry I forgot about Edie's birthday so wish her many happy returns now.

Best love to all, Char

As he sat writing in his slimy hole in the ground, a telegram boy was weaving down Avondale Street on a cycle too big for him and counting down the house numbers until he reached number 14. Curtains twitched nervously at the knock on the door. Amy answered it and there was panic in her blue eyes as she took the buff-coloured War Office envelope with trembling hands.

15 November 1916
To Mrs Beechey, 14 Avondale St, Lincoln.
Regret to inform you that 2 Lt F. C. R. Beechey

13 East Yorks Regt admitted to 43 Casualty Clearing Station 14/11/16 shell wound, dangerously ill. Further news will be sent when received. Regret permission to visit cannot be granted.
Secretary War Office

Report of Frank's grave condition had first been telegraphed to the authorities in London from a casualty clearing station on the Somme at 5.13p.m. the previous day. At 8.12a.m. on the 15th it was received in Lincoln and despatched to Avondale Street. Amy could only wait and pray. Frank, in his officer's uniform, stared down from the mantelpiece as the Rev. Beechey's fine old clock from the rectory ticked off the minutes and hours. Some time after 2p.m., the telegram boy came once more to Avondale Street. Edie was at work and unaware of the unfolding events. Amy had sent for daughter-in-law Mary, who was with her when she read the second telegram.

15 November 1916
Deeply regret to inform you that 2 Lt F. C. R. Beechey 13th East Yorkshire Regt. died of wounds Nov 14th. The Army Council express their sympathy.
Secretary War Office

There was no chance of Char — her "rock" — rushing home to provide wisdom and comfort. The girls did what they could to console their mother but they were just as distraught. Frank had been Edie's favourite. She knew that her generous, penniless, most beloved and lovelorn of brothers had to have died a heroic death. A letter arrived from Frank's commanding officer.

16 November 1916

Dear Madam

I regret to inform you that your son 2nd Lt Beechey of this battalion was severely wounded in both legs on the 13th inst. This happened during an attack. I was for some time unable to communicate with my battalion, which was attacking, owing to the fog and smoke. I tried all ways and eventually your son volunteered to take out a telephone wire and telephone. He had not gone far in this gallant attempt before he was hit. The doctor went out to him and dressed him but owing to snipers we were not able to get him in for some hours — at dusk. He must have been suffering a good deal but he would not show it. I hope he will recover but he is very severely wounded. He was a valuable and clever officer and a most cheery friend. Any further news I get I will send on to you immediately.

Yours very faithfully, K. W. Savory, Lt. Col., Cmdg 13 E York R

Perhaps most painful of all, Amy was to receive a postcard from Frank, postmarked 16 November. Frank had always had the Field Service Postcard down to a fine art. He regularly let everyone know he was "quite well" and acknowledged letters and parcels sent from home. Every postcard, despite its banal, regimented formality, had brought relief for Amy Beechey. This postcard raised terrible hope.

It wasn't unknown for the War Office to make a mistake, particularly with men reported missing presumed killed when they had been taken prisoner. The address was in a stranger's hand — Frank must have enlisted the help of a fellow soldier or medic to let his mother know he was wounded. From the depths of despair, Amy suddenly had reason to think her son might still be alive. How could he have sent her a postcard two days after he had supposedly succumbed to his wounds? At 10.36a.m. on 20 November, the telegraph line between Lincoln and London chattered out a reply-paid plea addressed to the Secretary at the War Office:

Is report of death of 2nd Lt F. C. R. Beechey authentic, as field postcard has been received from him in hospital postmarked November 16? Please reply to Beechey 14 Avondale St, Lincoln.

As Amy awaited news of her son's fate, the Royal Family condolences she received must have seemed premature if not insensitive.

Buckingham Palace

To Mrs Beechey

The King and Queen deeply regret the loss you and the Army have sustained by the death of your son in the service of his country. Their Majesties truly sympathise with you in your sorrow.

Keeper of the Privy Purse

Then word came back from the War Office.

> Report of death of 2nd Lt F. C. R. Beechey was made by Medical Officer, 43 Casualty Clearing Station 14/11/16 as having died same date. Regret therefore there is no reason to doubt.

Frank's final postcard must have sat in a comrade's pocket before being innocently fed into the army postal system. Those four italicised, army-formatted words "*am going on well*" had brought such soaring hope that the truth was almost too much to bear. Frank's commanding officer merely confirmed the worst in another kindly letter:

> Dear Madam
>
> I have just heard with the deepest regret that your son died of wounds on the 14th inst. As soon as I can find out where he died, and where he is buried, I will inform you. Your son was a very valuable officer, and was very much liked by all ranks. Please accept the deepest sympathy of all ranks in your loss.
>
> K. W. Savory, Lt. Col., Cmdg 13 E York R

Official notification followed, telling the family where Frank was buried and where he lies to this day, the only one of the brothers with the family motto inscribed on his headstone.

6 December 1916
War Office, Winchester House,
St James's Square, London SW

To Mrs Beechey,
14 Avondale Street, Lincoln
Dear Madam

I am directed to inform you that a report has been received which states that the late Second Lieutenant FCR Beechey, East Yorkshire Regiment, is buried in Warlincourt Halte British Cemetery, Saulty. The grave has been registered in this office, and is marked by a durable wooden cross with an inscription bearing full particulars.

Yours faithfully
Director of Graves Registration

Frank had indeed died bravely. Edie could be proud of her favourite brother.

CHAPTER
TEN

Let me now hope we have had our share of the losses

Attached to the 13th East Yorks war diary are eight foolscap pages of casualties, nearly 450 names of dead, wounded and missing from that single disastrous day, 13 November. The pages and pages of carbon-copy blue type start off with a list of nineteen officer casualties, including Second Lieutenant F. C. R. Beechey, recorded as wounded with "since died of wounds" pencilled in afterwards. News of the death of another brother would take several more weeks to reach Australia where Chris had recovered from his relapse and was sending seasonal greetings to his mother with hopes that the war would soon be over.

19 November 1916
9 Holyrood St, West Leederville
It's rather late to wish you a Merry Xmas and a Happy New Year. I was too ill to write last mail as I had a bit of a breakdown. But Bertha assured me

she would write. The doctor called it dysentery but I think it was a change of medicine. I lost a lot of blood and am very weak and on light diet but I think eventually it will be better for me.

I do hope you have a happy and contented Christmas and that all are well. I thought it would be peace this year; I don't think victory is far off. I hear Harold has been home again. I wish he were safely back here. Bertha and I are getting the house and garden nice slowly.

Len, in the final phase of his training at Winchester, was the first of the serving Beechey boys to hear of Frank's death. The news arrived the day after his first wedding anniversary. He, too, was expecting to be posted abroad at any time and was anxious to see Annie once more before setting off into the unknown.

Friday, 17 November 1916

I got your letter about seven o'clock yesterday. It came as a shock to me when I read about Frank. It is very hard for you. I, like you, can't seem to realise that he has really gone. I couldn't about Bar either. I haven't written and told Annie yet.

Our lot are sending out a lot to Salonika next week. It seems quite certain that they go there so I suppose that is where I shall go. It seems a long way away. But one never knows what is going to happen in the army. They send you off almost at a moment's notice to anywhere.

We go into C stage on Monday. That is the last

stage. In it they give you some pretty severe route marching and night operations. One reads on orders that C stage will hold the trenches, which are about two miles from camp, from nine o'clock at night to five the next morning. I don't know whether it will suit my constitution, but am certain it will not my somewhat lethargic disposition.

I heard that Annie's father is not so well as he was, and I think she will have to go down and help nurse him again, but I wanted her to come down and see me on Saturday, as things are so very uncertain when one is in the last stage of training.

I have been on a fatigue today, sawing and chopping wood; the sawing wasn't so bad but I didn't get on as well with the chopping.

I hope you are quite well and the girls and Sam and Mary, Joan [Eric's baby daughter, whom her father had not yet seen] and Tommie. I know how upset you all must be.

I will write again soon, with love from your loving son, Len

Char, bogged down in disintegrating, waterlogged trenches at Agny with occasional respites in the only slightly more hospitable surroundings of Dainville, was devastated at the loss of another brother.

22 November 1916

I got your letter with the sad news last night. It comes as a terrible shock to me who am more or less accustomed to death out here and it must be still more terrible to you at home. I always considered Frank's chief characteristic and asset to be the ease with which he could keep order either among his boys, who almost worshipped him, or among men when captaining a team. And knowing him to be absolutely fearless I think he must have made one of the finest officers in the service.

I wish I could be at home for a day or two as I was after Bar's death but that's impossible. These last three years seem so awful to us after the 20 we spent in such peace and enjoyment at Friesthorpe, so let me now hope that we have had our share of the losses although we are taking more than our share of the dangers. Trusting that we shall soon all meet again to make a happy though smaller family circle.

I am your very loving son, Char

PS Gloves and handkerchiefs just arrived — many thanks

At Morn Hill Camp, Winchester, the routine went on for Len. The railway clerk was now a disciplined rifleman, an expert peeler of spuds and, perhaps to Annie's horror had she known, savagely efficient with 12 inches of cold steel. The mock butchery of bayonet practice probably never came up in conversation as they explored Winchester and took tea in one of the little restaurants close to King Alfred's statue during one of Annie's weekend visits. She could never have imagined her most unwarlike husband charging bulky, straw-filled sacks yelling like a wild animal, "In! Out! On guard!" while sergeant-majors screamed abuse and taunted, "You couldn't prick the skin off a rice pudding."

Wednesday, 22 November 1916

Dear Mother

We feel very uncertain here. I don't know how much training they are going to give us before they think we are fit. I have been having it fairly easy this week, everybody has to have a certain amount of bombing practice before they go out, about three days, so since Monday the programme has been: the usual parade and inspection, the physical "jerks" and bayonet drill, which takes about two hours, and the rest of the day lectures on bombs or throwing old ones for practice, but I think the good time ends tomorrow.

Len wrote again a few days later, still no nearer France and having been selected to help with guard duties after a growing number of men had been locked up for going absent without leave.

Sunday, 26 November 1916

I am glad to have heard some details about Frank. It does not seem as if there was much chance for him from the beginning. It must have been hard for him till they could get to him.

I have had a different job since Friday. There

have been so many who have added a little to the leave that has been given to them, or taken some when it has not been given to them, that they have an overflow in one of the huts, and they picked me out as one of the extra military police. I had to take my bed and everything into the hut, and I have practically a 24 hours guard — of course, I don't have to do any parades, but it is rather a tie, otherwise I cannot complain as I am treated quite as well as the prisoners. I am afraid as Christmas approaches the number [of absentees] will not decrease.

I don't know anything as to when we shall be going out. Of course, there are all kinds of rumours. As a matter of fact, I don't think anybody knows till you get there, and when you get there nobody expects you.

On the Western Front, winter had set in with a vengeance and a halt had finally been called to the set-piece fighting. The Somme battle had officially ended on 18 November, although men would go on dying. There had been minor excitement in Char's section of the line when two German intruders crept through the British wire at night and ambushed an officer and NCO doing the rounds of sentries. The officer shot dead one of the attackers but he and the NCO were both wounded by the other German who escaped across No Man's Land. The only identification on the dead man was a cap with a Prussian cockade.

With two sons dead and Chris damaged for life, Amy Beechey lived in fear for her other boys. The army had taken them all apart from young Sam but it had been quite unmoved when she pleaded for Harold to be allowed home on leave. There would be a similar cold lack of compassion in the year ahead. All she could do was try to make sure her sons were kept well stocked with socks, something to combat the lice and a few little luxuries. Bulging food parcels, so unstintingly sent by his mother and sister Edie despite shortages at home, helped keep Char's spirits up. He let Edie know how grateful he was for the latest pack of goodies.

30 November 1916

I got the parcel all right yesterday. It was a splendid one. The pork pie was as fresh and unbroken as if it had just been bought and the biscuits and chocolate too I've enjoyed very much, the ginger bread being still crisp as I like it. I haven't tried the dripping yet but am waiting till I can make a fire and make dripping toast.

Perhaps mother forgot to send me a copy of the Echo with the account of Frank's death. I should very much like to see it so will you send me one if it has not been sent already. How we shall miss him when we all manage to meet again. It is a miserable climate here, damp and cold with frost at intervals. I've been having a few good games of chess in the evenings lately and have been able to exchange my circulating library of two books several times, but stick to the Pickwick Papers and read them often.

Very best love to Mother and yourself and all the rest, Char

Len was spending his last weekend in Winchester before being posted to France. Annie was in south Wales with her dying father so missed the chance to say farewell. Len told his mother he hadn't given up on seeing his wife, but events would move quicker than either expected.

Saturday, 2 December 1916

They warned about a hundred of us yesterday that we were for a draft for France. They have issued our pay book so I suppose we shan't be long. I am hoping we shall be a week or two yet but of course don't know, but if we stop over next Saturday it will give Annie a chance of coming to see me. There are another 50 warned for Salonika, but I am not in that. There does not seem to be any chance of getting a leave as one man I know who was down for a weekend this week had it washed out.

I got off my military police job last Monday morning. I thought it funny their letting me miss parades. They spoilt my Saturday and Sunday because I was on duty both days. I would personally rather have spent Christmas at home, but the choice does not seem to rest with me.

Annie says she has a cold. I likewise, since I helped to hold the trenches for a night about 10

278

days ago.

We have had very cold weather the last few days with a nasty east wind, and we have felt it hanging about on the parade ground. They have issued a pair of gloves to each of us. As I was just going to buy a pair I was very pleased. I hope you and all at home are well and Mary and Joan and Tom. I will write directly I hear anything definite.

Harold was back with his battalion on the Somme and still had not heard of Frank's death when he wrote to sister Winnie.

> 2 December 1916
> Somewhere in France

Just a short note in case I don't summon up energy to write again before the 25th. I will wish you all the compliments of the season. I'm writing this under difficulties as we have a wood fire in the hut and it is smoking excessively. It is burning in an open tin with no outlet except the door and windows, so you see it is pretty smoky inside and I am weeping all the time I write. The weather is very cold and freezing hard tonight, which will be a relief in a way as it will be a treat to walk on hard ground again after wading up to your knees in mud.

My battalion has just come out after a particularly gruelling time in the line. Trenches are in awful state. We are lying just a bit back doing fatigue work. I am rather surprised I have not received any letters from the family. It is up to you all to send a good batch for Christmas. We shall, I expect, be going back some distance in a day or two so we may not have too bad a time for the 25th after all.

Your loving brother, Harold

When the post from home eventually caught up with him, he wrote to his mother with sympathy before going off on a rant about the French.

6 December 1916

France

I can't say how sorry I was to hear about Frank. I expect if it had been dry weather he might have stood a chance. Round this district, if a chap gets hit in the front line, or going over the top, and he cannot get back of his own accord, the high explosive will put him out. The country is in such an awful state and it is a heart-rending job for the stretcher-bearers, as the saps are up to your knees in water in places across the open and it is all you can do to drag yourself along. I was up the line one and a half days this time as the battalion was being relieved. I was lucky but I saw enough of the mud and got enough on me to satisfy me. Still, a high explosive shell does not do half the damage it would in dry weather as owing to the soft earth it penetrates a good distance before exploding.

We are lying some miles back at present from the line, billeted in some pretty dilapidated old buildings in a village which was just in our territory before the "shout". The place is not so very knocked about. There are not many inhabitants. What are here are on the make, all small storekeepers with the minimum of stores and the maximum of prices. They rob us right and left. We have to go without or pay up. Whether it's from experience, or their own taste in the matter, the four principal things they keep to pass on to soldiers at exorbitant prices are sardines, biscuits, chocolate and tinned fruit. They seem to have a fixed idea that those four things will bring a glad smile to the face of any poor pack-humping swaddy. Prices per example — me, "Combien tinned fruit Madame?" She, "Trois francs." Me, "What do you think I am, Rothschild or Carnegie? No bon, no bon, finis!"

Oh well, it is bitterly cold today, the lice are thriving vigorously and it's pretty cheerless altogether. We shall not be going into the line for a week or so. Let's hope the family luck will change soon.

Ever your loving son, Harold

Char came through another spell at the front unharmed and dashed off another list of little comforts the small army of parcel-makers at home might send to make his life more bearable.

I've just time to scribble a line before next parade. I haven't been able to write for the last week as I've been living in a dugout and candles have been unprocurable, whilst the weather has been too cold and rainy to allow letter writing out of doors. Tell Edie the dripping was grand and I've made myself some fine dripping toast. Will you please send me another tin of Harrison's Pomade; it certainly does do a lot of good and adds considerably to one's comfort: and will you also send me a towel, not a bath towel, but just one of the ordinary small kind, and one more thing, a watch-key — size six. There's no glass left to my watch but I keep it in a tin box and it still goes.

I'm still in a nice quiet part of the line and am comfortable when the weather is favourable or when I can get near a fire.

I'm out of the trenches at present and billeted in a broken-down old cottage. If it wasn't raining I'd go outside and draw, or I should rather say, sketch you a view of the place and you'd see whether there was sufficient shelter there to cover a rabbit. One seems to be able to look right through the building in so many places but there are two rooms left quite habitable, not to mention a cellar. No orders yet for parade — physical jerks — probably owing to the rain still falling heavily, so will continue writing and, for Edie's benefit, will expound the virtues of the only really useful thing the army send out here — viz. the sand bag.

I dare say some of you have seen them and helped to sew the edges of them at home. They are about a foot wide by two and a half feet long and their uses are innumerable. I make it my duty to steal as many as I conveniently can as soon as I get in the trenches. They are clean and dry and so are useful for cleaning purposes — rifles, boots, mess tins, etc., or we wind them round our legs and hook them across our shoulders to keep the mud off our clothes; they make an excellent foundation for a bed, especially when we have to sleep out of doors on the fire step. They do instead of brooms for sweeping out the billet; they are used for ration carrying. On cold nights I put two on each foot and pull them up to my knee. They protect one's hands and shoulders when carrying such inconvenient loads as coils of barbed wire or rough logs, etc. and of course they have their original use as a protection when filled with earth and for building purposes, so I repeat that they are the one and only really useful thing that we are supplied with out here.

No time for more now as I'm a mess orderly today and have to go now and fetch the dinner dixie.

Len immediately fell foul of the battalion censor with his first letter to his mother from France.

12 December 1916

3/18 Battalion London Irish Rifles

7th Inf Bde Depot, BEF, France

You will see by the address that I have "flitted" again. We were warned on Friday night and started about . . . [censor's thick crayon has obliterated parts] but did not get to our destination . . . [more censor's crayon]. Annie lost her father a week ago on Saturday and had to go home on the Monday. I think she was coming back on the Friday, and she might have come down to see me on Saturday, but I sent a telegram to stop her. We spent the first night here fairly comfortably, but missed the luxury of a hut. There are 12 of us in our tent and it is a case of "if one turn all turn". It is a little difficult to find a place for everything, so I expect the less useful things will have to be jettisoned.

Have you written to Annie this week? She would, I know, like to have a letter. She told me she had a very bad cold and is I think a bit run down. I expect she will stop in London till after Christmas as she has some friends coming up for Christmas.

Have you heard any more of Char or Harold? I don't think there is much chance of my running against either of them, but the unlikely sometimes happens.

We have struck a bit of bad weather. We heard it raining in the night, some felt it, and this morning found a kind of sleet falling, which was a not very encouraging start. The sun came out for a little while in the morning but it has been raining on and off all day.

Harold shrugged off his air of despondency and was once again making the most of his lot, in and out of the trenches. His mother must have been heartened to hear him sounding more like his chirpy self, even though an enemy shell seemed to have scored a direct hit on his latest box of treats from home.

14 December 1916
France

Many thanks for parcel. It was very acceptable but it was all smashed up and some of it was missing. Edie mentioned the dates were her part of it — they were conspicuous by their absence. The box had collapsed altogether and they had to bring it across in a bag. The pie was better than you would expect after seeing the wreck of the parcel, parts of it were standing but still it looked as if it had been hit by Whizz-bang. Canvas is the best, well sewn up. The weather is still pretty crook, but we have a good billet and we have a decent fire which we rigged up and plenty of coal. It's a lovely toasting fire. I don't know what we would have done without it — it's great for the chaps after the line. You can get warm and dry if you get wet through. I am keeping fairly fit at present and intend to remain so if I possibly can. Don't worry about me. I can keep pretty cheerful now under most conditions and I have a good knack of making myself comfortable.

Len had yet to experience the mud and miseries of the trenches when he sent seasonal greetings from France.

18 December 1916

Dear Mother

The country we are in reminds me a good deal of my native county. We have had no rain the last few days, and arrived at our present position on a bright sunny day, which makes a lot of difference. I am still with my camp mates. We have managed to keep together so far. I suppose you will get this about Christmas so I wish you all a nice comfortable Christmas.

For Char, four months of life at the front had taken their toll and he would spend the third Christmas of the war in a hospital bed, wearing clean, louse-free clothing and with a proper roof over his head to keep out the elements.

Monday, 18 December 1916
In hospital in France

My dear mother

Just a few lines to say that I'm getting on well and have progressed from a barley water diet to the bread and butter stage. I got the two parcels just before I went sick and wished I could have eaten some of the good things but had to content myself with a mince pie or two and the biscuits. I brought the tin box along with me to hospital and shared the other among my friends and I know they enjoyed it, especially the pork pie. Frances sent me a box of State Express cigarettes about the same time and will be wondering why I haven't written to thank her. One of the sisters said she would write you a line when I was first admitted and would not let me sit up and write myself. There is no cause for any anxiety but I hope to get to Blighty for all that.

From your loving son, Char

There is no disguising the relief when he writes again.

> 22 December 1916
> Ward 24 2nd Canadian Gen Hosp
> BEF, France

I think I'm better off in hospital in this bad weather than if I were in the trenches. My illness is just one of the ordinary ones contracted in the trenches but takes a month or so to get rid of. I expect to be in Blighty in a few days now.

With only Sam at home out of her six surviving sons it was the saddest of Christmases for Amy. But she would have been much cheered by news that Char was back in England and, in his usual, impeccably organised manner, was already making preparations for her to visit him.

27 December 1916
Ward D2, First Southern Gen Hospital
Edgbaston, Birmingham

I'm very comfortably ensconced in a converted science lab in Birmingham University. I'm sending a form which will allow two of you to come over to Birmingham some day soon and see me and as I've a note for a pound which is of no use whatever to me here, I'm enclosing that too for expenses. It took me some time to get down to the coast, being dumped at three separate hospitals for periods of four, two and four days respectively. My complaint is called nephritis — I don't know what it means but I feel pretty well and very comfortable, and hungry enough to eat anything. I managed to get a good dinner on board ship as they didn't press the point about diet there: perhaps they thought the sea would be so rough that it wouldn't matter.

With nothing else to do, Char wrote to sister Edie the same day and set her the task of mapping out his movements from the time he arrived in France the previous August to his departure by hospital ship for England.

27 December 1916

Dear Edie

Many thanks for your long and interesting letter. I wish I could think of something interesting to tell you in return, but things don't vary much here and the view from my hospital bed is very limited. One of my Stamford colleagues called to see me on Friday as he happened to be going through Birmingham on his way home to Ipswich. I think I'll try to remember the places I went to in France and then, when you've time to spare, you might look them out in Harold's atlas and draw me a map with the journey marked on it.

The spelling will be very bad, I expect, as I rely chiefly on pronunciation. Here is the list: Folkestone — Boulogne — Etaples (a large training camp on the sand dunes near the mouth of some river or estuary) — Abbeville — Bernville (near Arras), then we got into the trenches at Agny, going out to Daneville six days out of 24 for a so-called rest, which often meant navvy work on the road or unloading trucks on the railway (these two last places also near Arras). Then we went to the Somme, stopping for the first night at Warlus, then British motor vans took us to a village called Neuvillette (near some fairly large town, possibly Doulens) and French buses took us on to a camp that I don't know the name of, whence we marched next day up to the lines between the villages of Flers and Gueudecourt. We went over the top there 7 October and then back to Longueval in Bernefay Wood, where we did fatigue work for rather more than a fortnight which meant chiefly carrying rations, ammunition, barbed wire etc. up to the trenches. Next we marched to Fricourt camp (via Meaulte) near Albert. We marched next day through two or three villages that I don't remember the name of and then French buses took us back, passing within a mile or two of Amiens to the same trenches again near Agny.

When I went sick 13th December I walked to Achicourt, then by ambulance to Wanquetin, next to Frimont (I only guess the spelling of the place) then by train in a GER dining car fitted up as a Red Cross ward to Tréport near Dieppe, and by train again via Harfleur to Le Havre. It's a very bare outline I fear as I have forgotten the names of so many of the villages we passed through. Will you see how many of these places are given in Harold's gazetteer? And if there are enough, send me a rough sketch map with places marked.

I'm not sorry I'm in bed today as it's horrible outside — a very cold sleet.

Best love to all, from Char

It had taken six weeks for news about Frank to reach the other side of the world. Chris remained as steadfast as ever in his commitment to the war despite the terrible cost to himself and his brothers.

29 December 1916
9 Holyrood Street, West Leederville
My dear mother

I was very sorry to hear of Frank's death from wounds. It came as a bit of a shock. I somehow expected him to get hit but hoped it would not be too severe or fatal. I hope our luck changes and that he is the last of us to go west in this war. I should be very cut up if Harold should not come back to the West. I hope the others are well and writing frequently from the front. Bertha's sympathy is all for you but couldn't bring herself to write; she said it was my duty to write the letter. The girls are cut up a bit I suppose as they used to see him so often. I hope it hasn't upset you too much. The trial of having seven of us in the forces must be great. But we couldn't have done otherwise, you know that. I hope you have a happy and prosperous New Year and that Char, Len, Eric and Harold return safely. Somehow I think I can see peace in the near future.

For myself, I am very happy and stronger and better though I have my bad days, and though I vacillate, the tendency is towards improvement. I see Curly Boyce (Harold's girl) and her people frequently and they call for tea and we go there. Bertha complains of the heat but really she's standing it well and looks as fit as possible.

Ever your loving son, Chris

He would have been pleased to hear that Harold was bearing up well and, for once, not worrying about prying eyes scrutinising his personal mail from the front. On New Year's Eve, Harold wrote to his mother from rest camp well behind the lines. The word "uncensored" was scrawled at the top of the first page and, on the final page, he guiltily urged his mother to burn the letter once she had read it. Despite all the melodrama, there was little in its contents that would have hastened a German victory had it fallen into the wrong hands.

31 December 1916
Flesselles

My dear mother

As a pal of mine is going home on leave tonight I'm giving him this to post. Flesselles is fourteen kilometres from Amiens. We are billeted in farm buildings. I am in a shed where they keep unthrashed corn — it's pretty warm but we are very much disturbed by vermin. We have been unlucky and have not had a complete change or a bath for a long time. It's no good if you only change one garment. We are moving up the line Wednesday again but it will probably be over a week before we are actually in again. Tomorrow, New Year's Day, we are having Brigade sports. I am one of the drilling squad representing the 48th in a competition. There were five teams picked, one from each company and one from HQ. A Company's team won easy, chiefly through rifle drill, at which we are pretty smart, so tomorrow we compete against the other battalions.

I spent a very quiet Christmas but had a fairly lively evening in an estaminet. We are not doing too much work at present, a few route marches and plenty of picquets and guards. For two days I was point duty, standing at cross streets where there is a good bit of military traffic, mostly lorries and cars. My duty was to see they did not run into each other.

Our battalion is getting up to strength a bit so when we get into the line again we shall be pretty nearly sure to go over the top. It's not going over though when you lose so many men, it's holding the trenches afterwards when they get the heavy stuff on to you. I have been all round about High Wood, Delville Wood and where our front line was when I went up before. I could see about three villages in the German lines — one was Bapaume. As far as I could understand, where we were holding the line last, one of their strong points cut right into our lines and one of ours into theirs and there was a sunken road, which ran right through into the German lines. If you followed it straight through you would walk into their lines behind the front line without seeing any of our trenches at all. In fact, one of the German ration parties walked into our lines thinking they were going into their own.

Burn this letter, don't leave it lying about.
With love, Harold

PS Regarding leave, it will be about six months before my turn comes.

Amy ignored Harold's plea to destroy the letter — or, more likely, she passed it on to Edie to read and then dispose of it. But Edie had no intention of burning it.

She folded the letter, tucked it back in the envelope and kept it with all the others from her brothers, just as she kept the newspaper clippings about them. One of those cuttings from earlier in 1916 had applauded the "Fine War Record of a Lincoln Family" with pictures of six of the Beechey boys, one of whom, Barnard, was said to have made the ultimate sacrifice. It was already out of date — Len had been called to serve since it was printed and Frank lay under a wooden cross in northern France. "Their mother and sisters," says the accompanying write-up, "are following their career with pride, if with some anxiety. When the records of war service come to be duly assayed there will not be many to beat that of the family of the late Rev. P. W. T. Beechey, of Friesthorpe Rectory . . ."

CHAPTER
ELEVEN

The mud is up to our waists

1917 would be the cruellest of years for the Beechey family. That winter was the most bitter and miserable in memory. On the Western Front from the beginning of December 1916 until the end of April there were only four fine days, according to an Australian army officer who kept a record of the conditions. Char, still too sick to fight, would be spared any more of the battlefield privations of France that had wrecked his health. Harold and Len were bogged down at opposite ends of the British line, Harold on the Somme, Len near the fabled town of Ypres, which had been reduced to a bleeding corpse in a little over two years. Shelling and sniping continued to take their toll but the weather was just as much a trial for men who could hardly lift one foot in front of the other in the morass. Then came the vicious cold snap to freeze everything — men, trenches, No Man's Land — into a grotesque pale sculpture. In April, when the fighting season got back into deadly swing, fresh snow carpeting the ground would be stained red.

Amy was haunted by images of Frank lying out in No Man's Land all day, his life slipping away. Now she had to contend with his tangled financial affairs. With typical generosity, he left instructions for brothers and sisters to have a share of what little he possessed. While the War Office painstakingly calculated how to apportion accumulated back pay of £77, 14 shillings and 10 pence, Amy had to engage a solicitor to write and explain to them that her son's liabilities to tradespeople and others amounted to £90. She gave an undertaking that anything remaining from his muddled finances would be split between her children, although Private Harold Reeve Beechey and Corporal Eric Reeve Beechey wished their mother to have their share of any estate. No doubt Char provided sound advice on the matter when Amy visited him in hospital at Edgbaston. On New Year's Day he scribbled the briefest of notes to say "expecting you on Wednesday".

By the time all of Frank's assets were counted and his debts settled, there might just have been enough left to pay for a plate of egg and chips for his surviving brothers in a favourite estaminet. Not all his possessions had fallen into the hands of the pawnbroker. Amy passed on his hankies to Len while Eric, in Malta, would later be grateful for Frank's safety razor.

Len was as far away as he could be from domestic bliss with Annie and the cosy life of a railway clerk. He was stuck in the dreary wastes of Flanders, in one of the grimmest parts of the Ypres Salient where the Bluff and Canal sectors and the infamous Hill 60 stank of death, decay and desolation. He would get used to the stench over the next four months. Men skulked like rats in the steep banks of the Ypres-Comines Canal surrounded by waterlogged shell holes and mine craters. The Bluff, a mound 30 to 40 feet high made of spoil from canal excavations, was one of those pimples on the flooded, pancake-flat Flanders landscape that was constantly fought over and had to be held at all costs. If the Germans took it, which they had done briefly for seventeen days in February 1916, Ypres might be lost. Sitting in the foul trenches that zigzagged around the cratered base of the Bluff, Len was cheered by a sudden avalanche of mail that finally caught up with him.

Tuesday, 9 January 1917

My dear mother

I received my letters for the first time last Sunday, about a month after we left England. Also the parcel containing nail scissors, trimmer and two handkerchiefs of Frank's. You can guess how pleased I was to get letters after a month of waiting. I had quite a lot from Annie, who writes that she is better. We have been from one place to another since we have been over here. The longest stay at any one place was a fortnight. The conditions seem to get worse at each place but I haven't stayed at any long enough to get used to them yet. Pleased you have heard from Char and Harold. Judging by my own experience they can't be having a rosy time of it. We didn't have great things for Christmas Day, we had the day off and five dates each but the day I got the letters a pal gave me a mince pie and a piece of plum pudding so I celebrated it in the normal manner although a little late.

You can guess from my general disposition and habits how much this life suits me but I try to make the best of things. From what you say I am afraid it is not altogether well with Frank's affairs. I hope they will come out all right. I keep tolerably well but sometimes pretty well done up after a long march with my full pack. I can begin to understand now what the others have had to put up with.

The weather here has changed for the worst the last few days, mostly rain and plenty of mud. I think you would hardly recognise me when you saw me in my full war paint. I am glad Annie and I were able to come down and see you during my leave and hope that we shall be able to come down again after the war. I should like her to come and see you when she can make it as I think a change would do her good.

Please write as often as you can as you cannot imagine how we look out for letters out here. They seem to be our one connecting link with home and civilisation.

With much love to all and especially to you, my dear mother.

My address is now C Coy, 1/18 London Irish Rifles, BEF, France.

★ ★ ★

The London Irish Rifles marched back to a divisional rest camp after their first ten days in the slough that soldiers simply called the Salient. From there, Len wrote again to his mother.

Sunday, 21 January 1917

We are back for a few days to where trees have branches and houses roofs. We are in huts, there are crevices in the side it is true, but still huts instead of dugouts. The weather is very cold with the snow that fell a day or two ago still on the ground, which is now frozen hard. We had a church parade in a tent this morning, the first, with the exception of one on Christmas Day, that we have had since I came out.

My letters seem to have got hung up again, as I have not received any since the one lot I received a fortnight ago. You can imagine my disappointment as each day's post comes up and I don't get anything. There is a small addition to my address — it is now **Rfn Beechey C Coy, No. 11 platoon, 1/18 London Irish Rifles, BEF, France.**

I still manage to keep well but find life very strange and hard, but I suppose everyone does, especially at first. Sometimes one feels dead tired. The guns may be going, the rain dripping on you and round you, but presently I am soundly off, and I notice that when sleeping in most trying conditions, one has the pleasantest dreams, and the old times come up again, and things are the same as they used to be, perhaps all together in the old house. Incidents I have forgotten in any waking moments come to my mind again, and in the morning when waking up in the dark I try to recall them but find the greater part have escaped me. This is my only sheet of paper so I must finish off now.

Since returning to his battalion, Harold had earned a stripe. Lieutenant Colonel Leane, commanding officer of the 48th, had seen many of his finest officers killed or wounded on the Somme. Rather than have unknown and untested replacements forced upon him, he insisted on elevating NCOs he knew and trusted. That left gaps for experienced men like Harold, who mentions his promotion in passing to his mother.

22 January 1917

Thanks for your letters and parcels. I got all the things you enumerated. The big parcel I got the day before yesterday — the cake was very nice. We are having some pretty severe weather lately. I suppose it is the same over in England. I'm surprised you are not sure of my address — it's the same as it was before and you can put Lance Corporal if you like as I have been one for a few weeks now. Just beginning to snow properly now so we will be in for a nice time and it's a good job we are in huts for a while. Well, I have no news. I am in pretty good health and hope you are all the same at home.

Sergeant Will Blaskett, a comrade of Harold and one of the many men of the 48th Battalion who would not survive 1917, wrote home to his parents in Canterbury about the awful conditions. "I thought I had seen mud," he tells them, "but everything I'd seen previously fades into insignificance compared with what I have lived in during the last three weeks. We look like a mixture of Cromwell's Ironsides, Deal fishermen and cave dwellers. We were all wearing tin hats, long gumboots and sheepskin jackets. Also we didn't get a wash or shave for eight days and were covered in mud from head to foot." Blaskett was still a teenager when he left England in 1913 — the same year as Harold — for a new life in Australia. Like Harold, he had been wounded at Pozières, and now, at the start of 1917, he was summoned before his larger-than-life commanding officer to be told he was up for promotion.

The battalion held the line at Gueudecourt, in the same miserable sector where Char had gone over the top with the Fusiliers the previous October. The trenches there offered no protection against whatever the elements or enemy threw at them. No dugouts. No shelters. At night, Harold wrapped himself in his solitary blanket and squeezed under a dripping oil sheet. His fears about keeping warm when he got back to France were fully realised. His pack, crammed with extra little comforts and his heavy AIF greatcoat, had to be left back at base camp with those of the rest of his battalion. It was weeks before he saw it again. Life was no cosier in the reserve area with its comfortless wooden huts "like toy boats at anchor in a sea of mud". But the 48th were lucky to have a gem of a medical officer in Major A. J. Collins, who arrived at the same time as Harold returned to active service. He did everything possible to keep them fighting fit and made sure they had regular meals and hot drinks. His cocoa and hot milk laced with rum were a godsend for troops struggling to feel freezing fingers and toes. A makeshift kitchen was set up in a forward regimental aid post and one veteran soldier was given the job of cook. The stove was lit every evening, pots brought to the boil and reviving drinks dished out to every passing fatigue party. At 3a.m. each morning, steaming cocoa was poured into two-gallon kerosene cans, which were hauled up to men in the front line.

The 48th could also thank their new MO for the hot meals that reached them despite the glutinous state of all approaches to their drowned forward positions. After shifting the cooking operations up to Flers, Major Collins noted in his diary, "This should save three hours and get the food to the men reasonably warm. Two meals are despatched daily in addition to the hot cocoa and milk sent at 3a.m. . . . . Front line falling in as the rain came down, also a cold wind and the men having to set up posts in muddy shell holes. The importance of serving hot meals to those in the front line cannot be over-emphasised."

Harold's A Company were in the line when the medical officer concluded that four days was too long to be standing in a sodden, icy hole in the ground. A Poor Bloody Infantryman's feet turned a shade of blue in half that time. After their stint, there was a queue of A Company men at the regimental aid post, showing early, debilitating signs of trench foot . . . "These I have kept in various dugouts rubbing their feet every four hours with French chalk and keeping them warm," recorded Major Collins. "All these were men from the front line companies, obliged to sit in the mud all day and have no opportunity to stretch their limbs until nightfall. Supplying dry socks daily and rubbing feet with whale oil only abates the evil in such appalling conditions."

Life was no easier for Len in the Salient. Writing to his mother, he was glad of a sudden frost that turned the liquid ground rock hard.

> Tuesday, 23 January 1917
> The weather still continues cold and frosty and is much better than the wet and mud. Today has been one of those clear frosty days that reminded me of the days we used to go out skating in the Christmas holidays. I had a bath yesterday and a haircut today so I expect I begin to look a bit more presentable again.

Len was in for another treat with the arrival of a parcel from home. Having so many sons to look out for, Amy Beechey's kitchen in Avondale Street was a never-ending production line with daughter Edie in charge of the packing and Eric's wife, Mary, also helping. Biscuits, pies, cakes and chocolate were always welcome but medication for routing lice earned most gratitude from Len, despite its dubious effectiveness.

Sunday, 28 January 1917

My dear mother

I was very pleased to get the parcel. It was kind and thoughtful of you to send it, and a very nice selection too, I was just thinking of trying to obtain some of Harrison's Pomade.

You will be surprised but I did not know anything of Char being ill or wounded so you can guess my surprise when I read yours and Edie's letter saying that he was getting better. Will you let me know details when you write again? Have you seen him yet and where is he? What date was Char wounded? I don't often see a daily paper — was it very serious?

It is still freezing and a cold east wind, but it is better in a lot of ways than the wet and mud — one has one's feet dry. The other night the water froze in our water bottles and I saw some tea that had been left in a tin mug frozen. I make up my bed with another chap at night. I think that way we get a double lot of clothing above us and three times as much heat.

Len included a separate note to Edie.

I received the parcel and letter this afternoon together with Mother's and one from Annie so altogether it has been a gala afternoon. I did not know Char was either wounded or ill; which was it; where was it? And how was it? You must write by return of post and tell me, and the latest news, too. Your parcel was a surprise and a pleasant one. It was quite intact and beautifully packed. I noted the paper and admired the Wedgwood effect of blue and white. I have sampled everything except the potted meat, reserved for a special treat, and the pomade, a thing I was trying to obtain and for which I am just beginning to feel the necessity. Our enemies great and small are generally invisible and we know them only by their effect. The biscuits were in good condition and the shortbread an old favourite, the sandwich running it a good second. The chocolate is also of the best. Many thanks, and for the excellent way in which it was packed.

We have had a long spell of cold weather and East winds and there does not seem much sign of it breaking yet. The ground is getting hard as iron and there is a difficulty in getting water as small streams, shell holes etc get frozen. Have you had any skating yet? I suppose you have.

We don't seem to stay very long in one place but shoulder our packs — I feel like Atlas supporting the world when I have mine on — and march to our destination, unless it is some distance and we go part of the way by train. One of the marches we had I was more done up than when I walked from London to Lincoln, but soon felt better after I had shed my pack, and I slept like a top afterwards.

From your loving bro' Leonard Reeve Beechey

London to Lincoln is 150 miles — one can only wonder what possessed Len to make the trip home on foot. Free train travel clearly wasn't one of the perks of his previous employment at the Railway Clearing House.

Char had moved from the converted science labs in Birmingham to a picturesque spot in the Vale of Evesham, Worcestershire. He was well on the road to recovery from nephritis, which affected more than 15,000 soldiers in 1917 alone. Only frostbite, with 21,500, and venereal disease, with 48,500, accounted for more hospital admissions for sickness. In severe cases, nephritis could be fatal, causing complete kidney failure, but most sufferers got over it after prolonged rest and treatment. It crept up insidiously over a period of weeks or months, beginning with breathlessness, headaches, coughing at night, pains in the limbs and chest, and vomiting. Heavy sweats and rapid weight loss — as much as 5 pounds over 24 hours — could lead to enlargement of the heart and cerebral haemorrhage. Studies after the war pinpointed infection by body vermin as the chief cause, aggravated by the cold, exposure and fatigue of trench life or trudging miles with heavy packs.

Char was soon well enough to venture out and explore the surrounding countryside, which he describes in a letter to his mother.

29 January 1917
Abbey Manor, Evesham, Worcs.
This is a kind of intermediate stage between the

306

Birmingham hospital and a convalescent home but it's a good deal better than the Birmingham one as we're allowed out four hours of the day — 10–12 and two to 4pm. There's nothing left of the abbey here except the bell tower which about eight of us went up this afternoon and scraps of old windows and stone coffins scattered about the grounds here. We've also a monument in the grounds commemorating the battle of Evesham and a tower for the old scoundrel Simon de Montfort. I haven't examined these last two yet. We had a look in one of the churches also today to see the Pig Window. It was a very nice pink stained-glass pig. Another unusual thing was that the font had three fishes in it, not alive but made of white marble and glued on to the inside of the bowl.

There seems to be some good skating about here and the river is frozen over but there is too much current at present for it to bear. I had a walk of about six miles yesterday, including both morning and afternoon, and it's made me as stiff in the ankles and calves as if I'd been taking the most violent exercise. We are on a bit of a hill here with the river about a quarter of a mile in front and the Cotswold Hills with snow on them about six miles beyond the river. It's pretty even in this weather and in the summer time I expect it's lovely.

Edie had completed the task Char had set her of mapping out all his movements from the moment he first landed in France to his evacuation by hospital ship. Char, ever the schoolmaster, found a small error, which would have to be put right, but he was suitably diplomatic after all the work his sister had put into it. He also had some advice for Sam, who was coming up to military age and was determined to do his duty as soon as he turned eighteen, without waiting to be conscripted.

31 January 1917

Dear Edie

I haven't written yet to thank you for the map you drew for me. It was an excellent piece of cartography and will want just a slight alteration to make it perfect. One place you put in — Neuville — should have been Neuvillette, which is quite a small village and perhaps not given in the atlas. I'll then be able to keep the map for reference.

I'm having quite a good time here. We can't get very far out of Evesham as we're only allowed out two hours at a time. This afternoon I went with a pal to a village called Hampton and we were able to come back across the river by means of the ice. I expect the Witham [the river in Lincoln] will bear easily as this river has a much stronger current, which also makes the ice there too rough to skate on. We've two good-sized ponds in the grounds here, however.

I think Sam had better do the same as I did; that is, write to the Recruiting Officer of the battalion of the Artists Rifles, which he wants to join, saying that he was educated at a grammar school and that several of his friends are already in the battalion. He will have to find out from one of his friends where the reserve battalion is at present or else address the letter to the GPO.

We don't get up here till a quarter to eight, which is nearly three hours better than Birmingham. I must finish now, as it's nearly post time. I'm afraid it's a very uninteresting letter but will write again when I've found out more about the place. Glad to hear you and Daisy have got a rise in salary.

A winter paralysis gripped the Western Front as snow put a glistening white coat over the scars of war. Len Beechey was chilled to the bone, but he preferred being cold to being wet through and cold. The riflemen had a break from the front line at brigade reserve camp for a few days at the end of January. Then it was back to the trenches on the slopes of another infamous feature of the Ypres landscape, Hill 60. Like the Bluff, this was an artificial mound made of spoil from a nearby railway cutting. Unlike the Bluff, the Germans held the crest. They were blown from its heights by half a dozen British mines in April 1915 but retook it three weeks later in a deluge of poison gas and high explosives. Almost two years on, they still occupied the hill of horrors. Beneath them, British miners were preparing another lethal surprise.

The London Irish kept their heads down, ignorant of the work going on in the warren of subterranean tunnels. Temperatures sank to zero on 2 February. The ground was too hard for digging so the only job the men could do was repair and reinforce the barbed-wire defences, leaving Len plenty of spare time to write home. The family received a letter every few days. Annie was no doubt getting them on a daily basis and writing back just as regularly to lament how difficult life was without him and with the food and fuel shortages gripping London. Five quick-fire letters to Lincoln in less than a fortnight showed Len was making the best of things, reminiscing about winter strolls with Annie and the occasional joys of a soldier's life — like hot porridge for breakfast.

Monday, 5 February 1917

Dear Edie

The cold, frosty weather still continues and shows no signs of breaking yet. What you sent in the last parcel were just the things I wanted. I am afraid it is eatable things like biscuits, chocolate or cake, bull's eyes in cold weather and things like that I look for in a parcel, as sometimes there is nowhere to buy anything and at other times perhaps no money to buy them. But I am afraid it is getting difficult to get things in England. Annie tells me that she pays two shillings a hundredweight for coal and has the greatest difficulty in getting sugar. I am glad you have heard from Annie. She likes to hear from you and I want her to go to Lincoln when it gets warmer and finer, but she is afraid to move in this cold weather.

We sometimes get a fire in a brazier but have to trust to conserving our bodily heat by putting on as much clothing as possible to keep warm. The feet are the most difficult part. I think it is the cold weather that makes me always feel hungry as I have an appetite hardly equalled by a schoolboy. You must excuse the writing but we generally have to write by candle-light and in a restricted place. I suppose I shall get used to this life in time, but don't think it is exactly the best part of the year for it, though I suppose the heat is equally trying in the summer. I adapt myself to circumstances as much as I can. Oh! There is one thing that you ought to send, that is a small waistcoat pocket diary as I have not been able to get one. I got a book by Lewis Carroll the other day, called Phantasmagoria — have you read it?

Wednesday, 7 February 1917

My dear mother

I am very pleased to hear that Char is going on well and hope that he will soon be able to come home to see you. If you send me another parcel — Edie asked me what I liked, which seems to suggest one — could you put in some lime juice tablets, in a tin? I think they are good for the blood. I am using the pomade on my hair, but according to instructions on tin, it must not be used when the skin is broken.

I expect Char, when he gets home, will give you a description of the kind of life we lead out here. It wants getting used to. It is still cold and frosty here and very slippery, though it is better than the wet as when one falls one doesn't get covered in mud and one can keep one's feet dry.

I suppose the girls have had some skating by now. It must be a long time since we had such a long spell of frost. I hope when it breaks there will not be much rain or I am afraid there will be a lot of mud about.

Tuesday, 13 February 1917

My dear mother

The weather has broken, the wind changed Saturday night and yesterday it started to rain, but only a sprinkle. The ground has begun to get muddy again but I hope the rain will keep off till the snow has melted. We are having a few days' rest again, which means pay — and somewhere to spend it. I have had sausage and mash tonight, off a plate — it is a change from eating out of a mess tin. We also had fig pudding for tea.

Sunday, 18 February 1917

Dear Edie

This morning the outstanding feature was porridge, before breakfast, an unusual occurrence. Then breakfast — bread and bacon. We had a church parade then dinner at one, stew. There was a football match in the afternoon. We went up in force, pipers leading, to see it, and lost — 4–2 was the score. But hope to put it on 'em next time.

I asked Annie to send me out a pipe and shaving stick and she made up quite a big parcel which I received last Friday and which arrived in good condition. Very many thanks for getting the diary and lime juice tablets and the other things you have been kind enough to think of to put into another parcel. I think after this one I mustn't have any more as I know from Annie how dear and difficult it is to get provisions in England. I feel fearfully selfish when I am eating these good things and know what they cost.

We had some very cold weather. It is milder now, however, and of course we have the other element — mud! I find that living in the open sharpens the appetite. In fact, sometimes I feel all appetite.

Tuesday, 20 February 1917

My dear mother

I am pleased to know that you heard from Harold. Am afraid he cannot be having a good time. I don't know if we are in for a spell of wet weather but it has been raining practically all day which you can imagine means mud.

Has Sam decided what to join yet? I hope the war will be over before he finishes his training though I think he was getting unsettled.

I suppose by the time you get this it will be somewhere near the beginning of March and we will soon have spring. I have always liked the spring and can remember going over Highgate and

Hampstead Heath and noticing the different shades of green as the trees of different kinds broke from bud into leaf. My favourite view was the one looking from the side of Parliament Hill over the swimming pond to St Joseph's Retreat — perhaps you remember it? I think in autumn there are more beautiful sunsets, but I cannot rid myself of the thought that winter lurks behind them, and personally I don't care much for the winter. I can remember sometimes getting Annie out for a walk to watch the sunset but don't think she took quite such an interest in them as I did.

Today is Shrove Tuesday and I wonder if you have had pancakes. Do you remember the snow pancakes you used to make for us?

Meanwhile Char continued to recover at Evesham but he was expecting to be moved on again any day for the next stage of his convalescence.

19 February 1917
Abbey Manor, Evesham, Worcs
I know it's a long time since I wrote but all days are so much alike here that I've nothing whatever to write about. There is one thing I want and can't buy here, namely a Royal Fusiliers hat badge. It is simply a bomb and a fuse — thus [Charles supplied a sketch of the badge] with no letters: I think Lawrence's in Silver Street would have one. I was wearing my tin helmet when I went sick so lost my cap altogether.

The weather has been mild and moist here for the last few days, very misty in the mornings but bright in the afternoons. I wish they would let us out for longer at a time as I've exhausted all the walks within range. The authorities haven't said anything about moving me on yet. I expect Epsom will be my next move, but possibly Eastbourne. There's a big whist drive in the town tomorrow evening in aid of us at the Abbey Manor. I don't think we shall be allowed to take part in it. I used to spend most of my time reading at Birmingham but it's not so easy here as someone's strumming on the piano most of the time whilst two or three more are singing at the tops of their voices and perhaps one or two will be clog-dancing so that one has to read a page at least three times.

I bought a cheap pair of skates and had some skating on the pond here. We haven't had enough snow for tobogganing. I've had a cold for about a week and am just getting all right again.

In France the frozen killing fields had once again turned to strength-sapping ooze with the onset of a thaw. A more remarkable change was also taking place. The Germans were on the retreat. A chain of events had started that would rip the guts out of what at least one seasoned observer acknowledged was the finest fighting battalion in the Australian Imperial Force, Raymond Leane's 48th. Harold let his mother know that he was muddied but unbowed.

Am quite well although we have just finished a pretty gruelling time. The mud is absolutely the limit now the frost has properly broken up. It was nothing a few days ago before we came out of the line this time to go up to the waist in mud. Still it's over for a bit now. We are now engaged in trying to clean ourselves, which is no easy task. I will write more tomorrow (perhaps).

The "gruelling time" of which Harold had spoken included another spell back in the line at Gueudecourt. A new consignment of gumboots meant fewer trench foot cases this time around and the indomitable Major Collins ensured everyone got their rum issue, with or without cocoa, morning and evening. To keep the braziers burning, raiding parties were sent out to scavenge for coal among the neighbouring battalions. On the night of 22 February, the 48th launched a minor assault on the German line with no artillery support and against three belts of barbed wire. Having sat shivering for weeks, Harold and his chums were now issued with an extra blanket each to throw across the wire so they could clamber over it without being torn to shreds. Somehow, they succeeded in getting through two belts before being caught out in the open under the glare of star shells. The Australians dived for the nearest shell holes and eventually crawled back to their own lines for the loss of only three men. Everyone who took part in the debacle would remember it almost as a dress rehearsal for an assault six weeks later against

316

unbroken barbed-wire defences at a speck on the map called Bullecourt.

As the 48th Battalion were being relieved the following night their scouts reported no sign of any enemy immediately in front. With bayonets fixed, men crept out into the quagmire they had crossed 24 hours earlier and found the opposing trenches deserted. The Germans had vanished in the darkness.

CHAPTER
TWELVE

We sleep as soundly as in any featherbed

Char's anticipated switch to yet another hospital came at the end of February. Before his transfer he might have seen in the newspapers mention of a little-known sideshow being fought out in Africa. General Smuts, a South African who had taken up arms against the British during the Boer War but was now on their side, arrived in London early in 1917 proclaiming that the campaign in East Africa was over. "All that remains to be done is to sweep up the remnants of the enemy force," he declared. In fact, the Germans were far from finished and would go on resisting for almost another two years. An unfortunate few British soldiers would live to regret the general's misguided optimism.

The process of acclimatisation for a return to the rigours of army life had already begun for Char. Food, accommodation and regimen at his latest hospital all had a distinctly military flavour. He sent first impressions of his new residence and of his fellow patients to his mother and Edie.

Friday, 2 March 1917
Hut D6, Woodcote Park Hospital
Epsom, Surrey

This is the sixth hospital I've been in — they ought to manage to cure me successfully between them. We still have hospital beds but the usual Army food, the idea being to break us into barrack life again gradually. The worst is we can't make any use of our spare time, bounds extending only one mile in any direction, which puts Epsom and Leatherhead out of reach. We are free on Saturdays and Sundays from 1.30 to 9.30 but what can one do when confined in a circle of one-mile radius and chiefly occupied by tin huts? I think there are about 4000 patients here. I think I'll go and see the racecourse tomorrow though it's only really worth seeing on Derby Day. I haven't found anyone interesting here yet to make a chum of. I went to the pictures last night with a Cockney — he bored me, I bored him and the picture bored us both. I had a very nice pal at Evesham, a commercial traveller in civil life, who helped me to explore the neighbourhood and played a fair game of chess, besides being a bit of a poet. We do get paid here — four shillings a week whereas I had none from the army at Birmingham and Evesham — so that we can spend our evenings in this hut — YMCA — and get a cup of tea and buns or can go to the pictures at a cost of a penny. Expect I shall spend six weeks here and then for my ten days' leave be at home.

★ ★ ★

Len was alternating between support and front-line duties around Ypres with occasional spells in rest camp. Like Harold, he was an uncomplaining sort. His letters are self-mocking about how hard he finds it adapting to trench life, giving little indication of the dangers. Yet a glance at the registers of the war cemeteries in that area of Flanders shows fellow riflemen were dying every day, even with both sides seemingly frozen into inaction. One small graveyard near the Bluff contains nineteen of his London Irish comrades. Len had yet to go over the top or experience the kind of bombardment that shredded nerves as well as bodies and left men crying and shaking uncontrollably. Frank and Barnard had waited weeks or months for their first real baptisms of fire. Their first had also been their last.

Len, although missing Annie, had come to terms with the routine discomforts of the rifleman's existence. There was always the occasional decent meal or treat from home to break the monotony and raise the spirits. But he confided to Edie his wish that the war would soon be over.

Saturday, 10 March 1917

Char must have been very ill to have such a long spell of sickness and convalescence, but I hope he will be perfectly well by the end of the war or just after.

The contents of the parcel have gone but the memory still remains. I think a soldier is very much like a schoolboy — he has a great appetite, but it is the idea of the parcel that gives the pleasure. When I get back out of the trenches after I have been paid, or if I have any money, I have one jolly good meal at a farmhouse or estaminet, or any other place I can get it, then I don't mind a bit.

I gather Sam has not settled what he is going to join yet. I hoped he would be out of it altogether. I hope the end of the war will come soon though I cannot see any break in the war clouds yet.

It is time to blow our candles out now and get down to kip, under our blankets, a great treat, and with our ground sheet under us, to keep the draught out that comes through the cracks in the floor, but where we sleep as soundly as in any featherbed.

The arrival of another parcel was cause for rejoicing and Len wrote to thank Edie and sister-in-law Mary.

Tuesday, 13 March 1917
Very many thanks for your letter and parcel which I received this afternoon. I have already sampled it and found it very good. Your packing and Mary's pastry make a most happy combination. Each piece of pastry was snugly ensconced in its surrounding tissue paper, like a chaffinch in its nest — till my rude hands dived into the unknown and brought forward treasures as valuable in their way as those Aladdin found in the cave. Please thank Mary who must have had "two hands in it" for her pastry.

I left camp early this morning with others for another one, a mile or two away where we are undergoing a short course of instruction, but we went back this afternoon to get one or two things and I found a letter from Annie and the parcel and letter from you. So I walked back rifle on shoulder, a blanket under one arm and the parcel under the other.

You are right about my liking pastry and cakes, especially home-made ones. I am afraid I have a sweeter tooth than I ought to have these hard times.

I think in the army or navy one becomes a fatalist. You know the saying about the name on the bullet. I believe, as in Hamlet, "There is a destiny that shapes our ends, rough hew them how we will." Though in my own particular case I feel as if somebody else has been doing the rough hewing lately.

I am comfortably installed in a hut, newly whitewashed inside, and with a stove in it and a fire in the stove, which is certainly better than facing Fritz in the front line with a cold East wind making my nose red and seeming to search through my ribs in case it had left any part warm.

Char, after four months away from the front line, was finding Epsom frustratingly restrictive, as he tells his mother.

15 March 1917

It is some time since I wrote but there is so little to

do or see here that I have nothing whatever to write about. I've been put on some light drill in the mornings now with a short march or rather walk in the afternoon. There are about half a dozen men here who can play a fair game of chess so we generally meet in the tearoom in the evening and play each other.

I wish we were allowed larger bounds here; there are several places nearby I should like to visit, Leatherhead and Box Hill among others, and we have plenty of time on Saturdays and Sundays, but for some reason they won't let us go more than two miles from the camp.

Even in the bleak, brown wilderness of the Salient, Len found some solace in the first sign of winter's passing. He tells his mother, "I saw the first flower of the year today, a daisy growing. So spring is coming." For the older hands of the London Irish the first flower was a signal of battles to come. Months of inertia would soon be over as another costly campaign season began. For the British, 1917 was the year of Arras, of the third battle of Ypres — which would go down in history as Passchendaele — and of Cambrai, when church bells would ring out triumphantly and prematurely at home. Harold was about to be sucked into the Arras offensive. Len would have rifle rather than pencil in hand when he faced up to one of the most devastating onslaughts of the war in woods dripping with blood and poison gas. However, the scent of spring flowers and peaceful days at Friesthorpe were in his thoughts when he wrote to Edie after special training for what would be his first whiff of serious front-line action.

Wednesday, 28 March 1917

Dear Edie

Now it is getting near to Easter and I begin to think of daffodils, the ones on the footpath across the fields the way we used to go to church from the old house. You perhaps remember them under the apple trees in the second field between the pond and the gate leading to the road. I can see them bending in their graceful way to the wind of a bright sunny day.

Will they have Easter eggs this year? I expect not. I see the sugar allowance is reduced to half a pound a head per week.

Do you still do a lot of reading; and what are your hobbies? I suppose life is too serious for hobbies. It is all national service — they have taken the men, they have taken the money, now they are taking the labour — there isn't much left for 'em to take now, is there!

We have a wet and dry canteen in the camp and, if one gets a pass, a YMCA about 10 minutes' walk away, a new one, not much in it yet, but there is another one about 40 minutes' walk away, also a big BEF canteen where one can purchase nearly everything.

I expect Char when you see him will tell you what the individual soldier's life is like. As to the war news, I expect you, like us, get it from the papers. Such extraordinary things are happening that one can hardly be surprised at anything.

Hoping that all at home are well, with love to you all from your affectionate brother, Leonard Reeve Beechey, "Len"

Char had at last escaped the confines of Epsom and was looking forward to his first home leave since he had been posted to France. A 12-mile march around the lanes of Surrey took in Leatherhead and went past St John's, Frank's and Barnard's old school, which was closed due to a measles epidemic that cost the lives of six boys — a tragedy said to have affected it more than the growing list of casualties from the war. Char wrote to his mother in early April to say he was expecting leave any day.

Epsom

I have been waiting before writing to find out when I shall be coming home — I think it will be next Thursday — I am for medical board exam on Monday and so shall be able to tell you definitely on Monday night.

I went for a route march yesterday to Box Hill, about six miles away, had dinner there brought over from a camp, and walked back in the afternoon; it was a gloriously fine day though there was still a good deal of snow and slush about. The view southward from the top of the hill was magnificent — Dorking lying in the valley below and Leith Hill straight in front. We came back by the old Pilgrims Way and then through Leatherhead, passing St John's School. It's shut up at present owing to measles. The fire there about six years ago [1913, in fact] must have done a lot of damage as the whole front of the building appears to be new.

Four inches of snow on the ground again this morning but it has all gone now and there seems to be a fair promise of more fine weather.

Harold was feeling guilty about not keeping in touch. It was nearly five weeks since his last letter home, but a birthday parcel had arrived to prick his conscience. The failure of the "blanket raid" of the night of 22 February had been quickly forgotten in the euphoria over the German retreat. From below Arras in the north to just beyond St Quentin in the south, the enemy had pulled back to the new defensive position of the Hindenburg Line. First hint of this tactical withdrawal came at Serre, where Frank was mortally wounded and where thousands of lives were sacrificed the previous July and November. Overnight, the Germans gave it up without a fight. On the 48th Battalion front, they withdrew beyond Bapaume, laying waste to everything in their wake. Buildings were smashed, burned and booby-trapped, bridges and roads blown up and water wells poisoned. Using civilian labour and 50,000 Russian prisoners of war, a vast new system of defence had been constructed between 6 and 30 miles behind their existing front line. At the heart of it was 100 miles of the Siegfried Stellung, where the trenches were 15 feet deep and 12 feet wide with steel-reinforced concrete bunkers to shelter troops from bombardment, all protected by walls of barbed wire 60 feet wide. Lightly manned outposts were positioned to discharge crossfire. In the battle zone were machine-gun nests where enemy artillery could range to the inch on assaulting troops. At the same time the Germans had reduced their lines of communication and freed up ten divisions by cutting the length of front they held. Their new system was deemed impregnable. Harold's battalion would be one of the first to test its strength.

Harold was sickened by the trail of destruction left behind but it was no longer necessary to go plundering coal — devastated villages and towns and demolished orchards provided all the firewood they needed. Instead of pursuing a fleeing enemy, the 48th found themselves repairing shattered lines of communications. They were put to work filling in bomb craters and making roads passable again. Afterwards, they trudged exhausted back through the ruins of Albert, past "Fanny Durack" to a training camp in Hénencourt woods.

The battalion history called it "a pleasant contrast from recent labours — in the midst of peaceful, undulating country that showed none of the havoc and ruin of war". Major Collins had a different recollection, calling it, "A very poor camp with gabled huts, very draughty and cold. Huge collections of garbage and manure in the wood nearby — empty jam and bean tins containing decomposing food. I at once set to work to burn the filth." Daily routine consisted of PE before breakfast followed by military training afterwards and then games each afternoon in which all men had to participate. Army-issue footballs were given to each battalion as part of a drive to keep everyone fit and healthy in preparation for the next round of slaughter. The MO marvelled at the improvement in morale — "it is an object of great wonder to see these tired and depressed troops rendered physically fit and in good spirits."

After three weeks' rest and training they returned to country despoiled by the enemy. At Bapaume, one of the booby-traps blew up the town hall and a group of Australians resting there. They were still scraping up body parts when the men of the 48th passed through on the way to Biefvillers, where only a single house was left standing. Australia's finest fighting men were again dismayed at being employed on repairing the railway line from Albert to Bapaume, but Harold found time for that long overdue letter to his mother. It was almost Easter, which would be marked by the first British offensive of 1917 at Arras and against the Hindenburg Line. Harold, thrilled by a birthday parcel that included Easter eggs, clearly had no idea what was in store for him and his mates.

3 April 1917
France

My dear mother

I am very sorry that I have not written for some time. I have been putting it off time after time but I will get this off. I have just got my birthday parcel — it is some parcel. The pastry is particularly nice. The fruit and chocolate I'm putting away for a while if I can. But as we always seem to be shifting we generally eat things when we get them. One parcel I got right in the front line, the one with the patent heater. That night we were relieved and in handing over my post I clean forgot it and left it in the bit of a dugout. It's pretty decent country where we are. The trees have branches but Fritz has seen to it that the houses have no roofs. It makes a man sick to see the wanton damage they have done. Where we are now was at one time a typical family residence. There are a few walls standing now, one old cow stable is pretty decent, one or two odd detached rooms are still available for duty. There has been a nice little orchard, but he has put the axe into the lot. The weather is extremely cold, snow is on the ground now. We had two inches yesterday so the demolished buildings supply plenty of fuel for us poor swaddies so Fritz is unintentionally kind in that way. Wood as a rule is terribly scarce.

A funny thing about these villages is that from a distance they look fairly intact. Surrounded by trees they look quite peaceful. But directly you get into the village what looked like a solid house is merely framework, huge cracks running down the walls. He has done his job thoroughly. He must have taken house by house and blown them up or burnt them down, one by one. The only places left he had mined. Tell Edie I enjoyed the Easter eggs very much. They were jolly decent ones, not like most of them I remember — all air. I would be obliged if you would send me some more pomade, it is the best stuff I know. Well, I will shut up now. I will send another soon.

Love to all. Your loving son, Harold

Len was about to have his first taste of action in the Ypres mire. His company was one of three detailed to take part in a smash-and-grab raid on the Germans near the rat-filled Ypres-Comines Canal. Zero hour was fixed for 8p.m. on the evening of Easter Saturday, 7 April. Lieutenant Colonel D. B. Parry, commanding the London Irish, set out their objectives. They were: 1) To kill or capture as many Germans as possible; 2) To capture or destroy war material, and 3) To destroy machine-gun and trench mortar emplacements and dugouts.

Attached to the battalion war diary is the attack plan, detailing everything from ground to be covered to how to handle prisoners. It notes, "No man's land here is irregular in width varying from a possible 100 yards to a minimum of 35 yards, sloping uniformly towards the German lines. There is a double crater opposite the top of Lovers Lane, which touches both British and German front lines. Enemy wire is fairly thick in front line, weak in intermediate line and strong on support lines. Whole area of operation is under observation from Hill 60, The Caterpillar and Canal Banks. Dummy raids will be carried out at St Eloi and Hill 60 sub sector. Mine exploded Hill 60 at Zero −5 mins."

C Company was to attack between the Hedgerow and the Ravine, names of landmarks since obliterated. The Ravine was once in the middle of a wood, which had been wiped off the face of the Salient. There would be four attacking waves, with Len's 11th platoon at the forefront with large white circles pinned to their back and chest for the benefit of the following platoons and artillery spotters, not to mention German marksmen. The enemy had to be allowed to surrender as, according to the master plan, success of the raid would be judged by the number of prisoners taken. The whole operation was due to last one hour. "The word 'retire' must on no account be used," warned the London Irish CO. "Using the word is a frequent German ruse and any man doing so will be treated as an enemy." Letters, papers, identity discs and any personal effects were to be left behind in haversacks in the trenches. Len had to write his name on a piece of paper and pop it in his right breast pocket. No other written or printed matter was to be carried. And no regimental buttons or badges of any sort were to be worn.

Len, the clerk-turned-killing-machine, was hard to imagine, face smeared black, kitted out in "skeleton order drill" — rifle and bayonet, box respirator, 110 rounds of SAA in pouches, ten in his rifle magazine and two Mills bombs in his breast pockets, where he would normally carry Annie's picture. Two days before the raid, he was giving his mother a blow-by-blow account of cocoa drill.

Thursday evening, 5 April 1917

I have just made some cocoa on a little kitchen, a kind of Tommy's cooker — I had never used one before, but it didn't take long to boil about a pint and a half of water. I am beginning to feel quite well again. Life in the trenches has its advantages in some ways. Not many, but it is too cramped for the ordinary human being. That is why in the spring that I suppose one always talks of an advance. It is as if one had been hibernating all winter and wanted to stretch his legs a bit. So we may take it John Bull is going to stretch his.

As to shellfire my feelings vary inversely as to the square of the distance. That is, I view it with much greater equanimity if it is a mile or so away than if it is near enough to, say, throw dirt into your dinner or coffee. I think it is that "distance lends enchantment to the view".

"All objectives successfully gained," reports the 18th Londons' war diary after the 7 April operation. The awful state of No Man's Land meant things got sticky as the troops withdrew under a heavy enemy barrage, but eighteen prisoners were seized and marched back for interrogation. Several dugouts and a heavy machine gun were destroyed. Len returned safely only to find his haversack gone, along with his few comforts and possessions. There is no hint of the action when he writes to Edie on Easter Monday.

Monday evening, 9 April 1917

Very many thanks for your parcel and letter enclosed which I received this evening. I don't think I had ever seen such gargantuan bars of chocolate before. It was very kind of uncle Frank [Amy's brother, who owned a chocolate factory] to send them. I liked the "three-cornered things" as you called them — the jam was there but mostly settled in one corner.

I am sorry you have not heard from Harold for so long. Will you drop a line directly you do?

We have been having some cold weather. Winter, the withered hag, seems loath to leave us although Saturday and Easter Sunday were just what spring days should be. But today it has been hailing and raining and sleeting and generally nasty except for some intervals of sunshine.

I got back to camp on the morning of Easter Sunday somewhere about three. It was a lovely starlight night, nearly the full moon. I was having breakfast about four — I told you I think that this is an "Alice in Wonderlandy" kind of life — so, of course, after breakfast we went to bed and I think we woke up somewhere about 11 to find what a lovely day it was. I spent the afternoon preening myself up a bit, brushing mud off, shaving and washing. There was an informal evening service at six o'clock to which I went and a communion service after.

It is just about "lights out" now so I may add a little tomorrow.

Tuesday April 10 — a cold wind again today with snow and hail at intervals but a little warmer when the sun comes out.

After the trench raid Len's unit moved out of the front line and into billets behind the line for further training. Although careful not to alarm his mother, he does admit that it is his first time away from the sound of the guns for months.

Wednesday, 18 April 1917

Here we are in the middle of April, or past it rather, and when we woke up this morning the ground was white with snow and the snowflakes steadily falling as if it had been midwinter. Yesterday we had snow, hail and rain and the wind driving the rain into our faces gave them a kind of hot burn.

We are billeted in a barn and have been here about a week, the barn is divided into three parts. One part, divided by a brick wall about 10 feet high, is inhabited "par nos voisins, des Cochons, il y a les mères et des petits". The other two parts, divided by a wooden partition four to five feet high, we inhabit, about 70 to 80 of us. We are within fairly easy walking distance of a country town, the most prominent object being the church, the only one, but very big. There are shops and estaminets where one can get beer or coffee. We drill till one o'clock and have the rest of the day off after dinner, which is at half past one.

Have you heard anything of Harold since you last wrote, and Char, is he at home yet? I hope they will keep him in England now. We are out of the sound of gunfire about the first time for three or four months. The country around is mostly flat with one or two hills in the distance, but the country seems waterlogged. There are a good many windmills about. The people speak Flemish or French. I can generally get on very well with them. I find that my bad French is better than none at all.

Continued Thursday, 19 April — I am now having some coffee in the kitchen of a small house, for which we pay a penny a basin, and we sit around the stove while it is made. The hedges are beginning to bud and the bushes to break into leaf. There are a few primroses out against the wall of this house and if we do have a fair day, which we do occasionally, one can see the effect on the foliage the next. How is your little piece of garden? I think it is about the size I shall have if I start cultivating the earth. I shall not start with too big a piece.

Love to all, your son, Len

Still back behind the lines, he wrote again to his mother a few days later.

Saturday evening, 21 April 1917

I was very pleased to get your letter this evening and to hear that Harold was all right and had received the parcel. I am sorry he has been having such a rough time. Glad to hear Char has arrived home. I am afraid ten days will soon go. I hope he won't be sent far away afterwards. I am glad that Frank's affairs seem to be settled — it is very worrying for you.

We have had better weather the last two days, in fact quite warm when marching sometimes. The roads are cobbled and marching not easy, especially if the feet are a bit tender. Sometimes one thinks they will come to an end (the cobbles, I mean) but no — they go on interminably sometimes. There are long lines, very regular, of trees each side of the road. The country seems to be coming to life again. One sees people ploughing, harrowing, sowing, in the old-fashioned way, reminding one very much of one of Millet's etchings. I heard a lark singing this morning whilst we were drilling. I have had a bath and a change. I have had some of my little things washed — such as towels, socks, handkerchiefs — at the little place where I go for a cup of coffee. I am writing this letter at the same place, as there is a table. There are about eight or nine others seated round the stove and the coffee pot. We sleep warm and, for myself, I get into a pretty sound sleep, especially when it gets near the time to get up. We have reveille at six thirty, breakfast at seven, a march of about three or four miles afterwards and drill, then back again to dinner which is about half past one. The rest of the day off afterwards. I generally walk into the town in the evening and have a cup of coffee or two — they serve it in a glass by the bye — and I look at the news in the French papers, which are generally a day old.

It does not look as if the war can last much longer, but I have thought that all along. At first I didn't think it would last more than three months, but it seems, like the cobbled roads of France, to go on and on.

Annie tells me that Waterloo Park is divided into allotments in which to set potatoes and I think the other parks are doing the same. I had a letter from her yesterday. She not only has to pay big prices for things but they have to wait so long for them. She can sometimes wait an hour and a half to two hours to get potatoes, only to perhaps find that they have all gone. I am afraid that things will be dear for some time after the war finishes but still it will be a glorious thing to have something else to do and talk about. I lost my Harrison's Pomade when my haversack "went West". If you should be sending anything, would you send a small tin of that.

Far away from the food shortages on the home front and the deadly stalemate of the Western Front, Chris was reminded of the war by every twinge of his pain-racked body. A scar on his shoulder from the sniper's bullet that hit him almost two years earlier was the only visible sign of damage, but hidden wounds would trouble him for the rest of his life. He assured his mother he was coming to terms with his situation and the relapses that occasionally reduced him to a hospital case.

21 April 1917

Since my fortnight in Fremantle Hospital last November I've been fairly well, only off odd days now and then. I still have a lot of trouble with my innards but am steadier. I can't walk more than about half a mile but can potter about in the garden and am getting the place neat and pretty. Bertha is fairly well and stood the summer pretty good. We're getting the house furnished room by room. I hope you've got over Frank's death a bit. The girls will miss him a lot naturally. I hear of Harold through Miss Bailey.

On 25 April, Anzac Day, crowds turned out to see invalid soldiers parade through Perth in a motorcade of sixty-eight cars plastered with pleas for more recruits: "Your Mates Want You!" and "Fill Our Places!" Conscription had been put to the vote in Australia and rejected.

Back in Lincoln, there was still no word from Harold. It had been three weeks since he last wrote. In that time, Char had returned home on leave. As well as stopping with his mother and the girls, he also took the opportunity to go back to school in his army uniform. He was now the last surviving Stamford master from those who had gone away to war. Mr Skelton, a colleague for one term before he joined up in Christmas 1914, was killed around the same time as Frank. The dashing Mr Wood, who had instructed the boys in grenades and later been mentioned in despatches, was posted missing on 13 April 1917. He had recently transferred to the Royal Flying Corps and had pranged two aeroplanes without suffering a scratch before being shot down while on a photographic reconnaissance flight over enemy lines.

Discussing the terrible toll on school and family with his headmaster, Char knew he would soon be sent back to the front line. Half a dozen hospitals had cured him of nephritis and he was assigned to a Fusiliers unit made up mostly of men recovering from illness or wounds. From his new base, looking out over the English Channel across to France, he let his mother know he had returned safely from his all-too-brief leave.

24 April 1917
Hut 1, 7th Coy, 6th Battalion Royal Fusiliers
Duke of York's Military School, Dover
I've never known ten days to pass so quickly and pleasantly and yet I seemed to do very little during the time. I went on Sunday morning to Stamford and found head and family quite well. One of the old boys came into supper and he and the head and myself sat up talking till after one o'clock in the morning; however, I was up again by six thirty and got into King's Cross by eleven. I shall be going before the doctor tomorrow and shall then

be classified as A, B or C so that I shall be more able to tell whether or when I shall be going out again.

Len was enjoying a respite from the trenches deep in Belgian brewing country, although he seemed to prefer coffee to the local beer. The rest of April would be spent under canvas at a training camp before they moved forward into the reserve lines in range of the German guns. Len was preoccupied with food shortages and concerned for Annie when he wrote to sister Edie.

Thursday evening, 26 April 1917

We have trekked about eight or nine miles today. We have had some lovely weather this week, the wind rather keen perhaps when the sun went in, but everything seeming to grow very quickly. The hops are just beginning to show above the ground and what hop poles! About 30 feet high. There must be a huge mass of foliage when they reach the top.

What is it like in Lincoln? I should think it is much better with longer evenings. I think a spring evening, if it is fine, is one of the best times of the year: there seems to be such an exuberance of life in every growing thing.

We are in tents now, arrived here early this afternoon and put them up — quite close to a large YMCA canteen, reading and writing room and concert room.

I see there are still further restrictions on food. I used to get a look at the French papers at the last place. I ordered a coffee which was brought in a kind of wine glass with a long spoon to stir the sugar, and I noticed when I had gathered the papers around me that a good part of them was devoted to the restrictions that have been made or that were going to be made on food stuffs. I had a letter from Annie this evening. She said that she had been ill and was in such pain that she had to stop in bed a few days, but was up and a little better when she wrote last Monday. I hope it was nothing serious but feel a bit anxious.

From what I hear, they are turning every available space into gardens in London — is everybody gardening in Lincoln? And are they digging up the arboretum? I think if I were going to do any gardening I would sow mustards and cress as one has not so long to wait for it to come up.

Char was still awaiting his classification by doctors. An "A" rating would mean a return to the front line, "B" category men were deemed fit to serve abroad in a supporting role while a "C" would mean home service only. Each category was also graded from one to three, with C3 the weakest, A1 the fittest. But in times of crisis even a "C" class man might find himself swiftly upgraded and facing the enemy with a rifle in his hand. The only Germans Char had to contend with for the time being were those in his latest library book, which might have raised eyebrows among his comrades. It was a witty and sentimental story of family life in Pomerania by the wife of a German count. When he had finished it, Char dropped a line to his mother at the end of April.

Duke of York's Military School, Dover

I have been meaning to write all day but I had got "Elizabeth and her German Garden" out of the YMCA Library and had to finish it and it's now nearly 8 o'clock.

I haven't been classified yet. I saw the doctor on Saturday and when he heard what my illness had been he said that he would have to send to Epsom for my hospital papers before he could fix me up. I find that if I do get put on a draft for France I shall be given a six days' leave, or rather four, counting one each end for travelling.

I have been down into the town twice to have a look at the shipping, but it's been misty and the harbour is large so that the nearest vessels anchored in it are 600 yards or so from the shore. Still there were a few in the docks, including a cruiser, which we could examine more closely. There's all sorts of wire and chains lying about the harbour, which possibly are antisubmarine appliances, but I really don't know.

The guns the other night firing on Ramsgate woke me. There seemed to be almost continuous firing for about a quarter of an hour, but we weren't turned out of bed and I went to sleep again before it was over. There are three holes in the field just behind the schools where the Germans dropped shells about a fortnight ago.

Craters at the back of the military school were the result of a coastal bombardment by five enemy destroyers on the night of 20 April, when shells fell harmlessly in a ploughed field. Two of the raiders were sunk by the Dover patrol, who pulled ten officers and more than a hundred enemy sailors from the Channel. The daring strike against the south coast that woke Char happened a week later and began with two star shells bursting out of the darkness and lighting up Ramsgate before arcing inland. Then came the roar of ships' guns flashing like fork lightning out to sea. The first shell exploded only a couple of hundred yards inland, its huge splinters penetrating the roof of a sweet shop and severing 22-year-old Ivy Thorncroft's left arm as she lay in bed. She quickly bled to death. Her family had just moved to new premises after their last shop was bombed from the air. A man was killed in another part of town. A horse and a hen were the only other fatalities as thirty shells rained down, wrecking more than twenty homes, smashing the windows of an orphanage and blowing up a headstone in the cemetery. Two elderly residents dropped dead from the shock of it all.

When the dust had settled, Char wrote again. He had heard from home that youngest brother Sam — still more than three months away from his eighteenth birthday — had already applied for a commission and was intent on going to officer cadet school. His birthday was in August. His training might take a further year. By then, with any luck, the war should be over. In the meantime, his chosen path would be a drain on their mother's finances and Char was keen to do what he could to help.

1 May 1917

Dover

I wasn't a bit surprised to hear Sam's news, but I think we shall be able to find the money. I shall be able to contribute £5 and will send a cheque in my next letter.

I haven't seen anything more of Dover yet. The roads are all so dusty so I am waiting until we have a shower before I explore any further. The company I am in are all men who have been abroad and are regarded as convalescents more or less, so that we are having quite an easy time.

No further news yet so goodbye, your loving son, Char

Bar had been dead since September 1915 but the name of Barnard Reeve Beechey lived on in the bureaucratic bowels of the military machine. All the brothers who joined up from the start — Frank, Harold and Chris — had listed their eldest brother as next-of-kin rather than their widowed mother. When an official letter arrived in early May it was addressed to B. R. Beechey. It was sent to 4 Avondale Street instead of number 14 but found its way to the right house. It was from the Australian army authorities.

1 May 1917

Australian Imperial Force Administrative Headquarters

AIF, 130 Horseferry Road, London SW
To Mr B. R. Beechey,
4 Avondale Street, Lincoln
Dear Sir

It is with deepest regret that I have to convey to you the very sad intelligence that your brother, No. 200 Lance Corporal H. R. Beechey, 48th Battalion (late 16th) Australian Imperial Force, was killed in action on 10 April 1917 whilst serving with the British Expeditionary Force in France.

No further details have been received respecting the circumstances surrounding this most unfortunate happening, but in the event of any more news coming to hand, you will be communicated with immediately. I am directed to forward the enclosed message of condolence from Their Majesties the King and Queen, with sincere sympathy . . .

The signature at the end was indecipherable, and not just through a mother's tears. Harold, who had been through so much, would not be returning, either to his mother, to the girl who was waiting back in Australia or to the room that Chris and Bertha were getting ready for him.

CHAPTER
THIRTEEN

Mother dear, you will have one of us come back to you

To La Bridoux and Serre could be added Bullecourt — French place names Amy Beechey had never heard of but where three of her boys had now laid down their lives. The hopes and prayers that Harold might yet be spared had been dashed in the early hours of 10 April. It had taken three weeks for Amy to learn that her most happy-go-lucky of sons was dead.

On the other side of the world, the casualty lists in the *West Australian* made heart-stopping reading for those with menfolk fighting so far away. In late April and early May, the dead, wounded and missing filled column after column. Curly scanned the names every day until she saw No. 200 Beechey, L/Cpl H. R., 48th Battn., Killed in Action. The loving letters marked "On Active Service" would go on arriving for weeks and months afterwards, but Harold would not be coming back.

346

Bullecourt was such a fiasco that it was later used in military training as an example of how not to conduct a battle. The Australians blamed British incompetence, while the commander-in-chief, Haig, later heaped scorn on the quality of leadership in the AIF, claiming, "Some of their divisional generals are ignorant and (like many colonials) so conceited that they cannot be trusted to work out unaided the plans of attack." The recriminations were as barbed as the uncut wire the troops had to face without artillery support. "The last word must be one of regret that such dauntless courage and resolution should have been expended in vain," wrote the British official historian. Today, Bullecourt is all but forgotten except as the place where the men in slouched hats were first given the nickname "Diggers". Most of the digging that took place was to bury Australian dead. They lay so thick on the ground that there was little ceremony, even less sanctity. A shell hole or a half-dug trench provided ready-made final resting places with a few clods of earth shovelled on top of bodies and body parts. Many of those killed have no known grave. Harold is one of them.

For the 48th Battalion, the countdown to catastrophe had begun after their work as railway navvies came to an end. From the desolation of the Somme, they headed towards the front line across unbroken countryside with grassy slopes and hollows instead of rancid shell holes and a sea of mud. On the evening of 7 April, they began the final leg of the march up to Bullecourt, which bulged out from the German line like an abscess. Either side of the heavily fortified village were two horseshoe-shaped indents, known to the military strategist as re-entrants. Death traps would have been more appropriate.

Harold and his comrades left Biefvillers at 6p.m. They marched to Beugnatre, a mile or two from Bapaume, and dumped their packs in the transport lines before heading on to the Noreuil valley in front of Bullecourt. A journey of five miles took eight and a half hours as they were caught up in columns of men, horses, limbers, artillery and supplies making slow progress along single-track roads. Major Collins set up his regimental aid post in a cutting by the roadside with a canvas tarpaulin for a roof and room for three stretcher cases. Before a single Australian went over the top, enemy shelling killed one man and wounded eight more from the 48th. A victim of gas was brought in gasping for air, drowning in his own fluids — "the only man I ever evacuated for gas poisoning," recorded the MO. "I sent him away on a stretcher. He died a few days later — phosgene poisoning."

The 8th of April was Easter Sunday, a time of miracles. Those on sentry duty for the 48th Battalion were about to witness a minor one as they peered over No Man's Land through their periscopes. Out of the haze, from the direction of the German lines, appeared three scarecrow-like figures in tattered scraps of British uniforms. They were privates of the Dorsetshire Regiment who were captured in January on the Somme and had somehow escaped from an enemy prisoner-of-war compound. Half starved, they stumbled into the Australian lines to a hero's welcome of steaming hot tea and whatever treats could be dredged from the deepest recesses of kitbags.

On Easter Monday, 9 April, the British attacked over a 15-mile front from Vimy Ridge to south of Arras. The operation was a prelude to a French onslaught planned for the Chemin des Dames a week later. Its aim was to divert enemy troops away from where the French hammer blow would fall and to try to break through to Cambrai. The Canadians stormed the heights of Vimy and the British made a dent three and a half miles deep in the German lines in front of Arras. The subsidiary attack on Bullecourt was scheduled for the following day. Here, the new "impregnable" German defences were not yet finished but they would still present a formidable barrier. Lieutenant Colonel Leane, who had established battalion HQ in a railway embankment, sent out scouting patrols that reported very strong wire entanglements extending right up to the German parapet. Artillery had slashed some gaps but the wire was mostly intact. The enemy trenches also appeared to be held in strength, although the high command preferred to believe their own intelligence — and the word of the escaped PoWs — that the front was only lightly manned.

The Australians had nearly 1,000 yards of bullet-swept ground to cross so new trenches, a couple of feet deep and more like the possy holes of Gallipoli, were dug in No Man's Land under cover of darkness. The attack was scheduled to take place at 4.30a.m. on 10 April, an hour and 48 minutes before sunrise. There would be no artillery support, no creeping barrage that had brought early success at Arras. Instead, a captain of the Tank Regiment had put forward a daring proposal that was supposed to give the attackers the vital element of surprise. His machines would trundle ahead of the assaulting battalions, flattening the wire and striking terror in German hearts. The plan was accepted despite the misgivings of Raymond Leane and his brother Ben, now promoted to major and second-in-command of the 48th Battalion.

At 1a.m. the Bullecourt salient was drenched with poison gas. By 2.30, the men of the 48th were crawling out into No Man's Land following tapes that guided them to the assembly positions. There, with a dusting of snow on the ground, they crouched in their shallow jumping-off trenches, expecting to hear the rumble of approaching tanks at any second. But the tanks never made it. Zero hour was postponed until 5a.m. Then news came through that the lumbering monsters were still two miles from Noreuil. It would take another hour and a half for them to reach the front line, by which time the troops would be going over the top in daylight. The Australian 4th Division chief, without referring to his British commanders, decided to call it off, telling his staff, "I think there is just time to get the boys back."

At 5a.m. the telegraph operator at 48th Battalion HQ handed Raymond Leane an urgent message from Division: "The Stunt is off. Disposition as yesterday. Move." The postponement was relayed to the troops just in time. They started to withdraw just before sunrise and were caught in a sudden snowstorm, which is credited with saving them from certain slaughter. They got up "stiff and cold and cramped, damning the tanks and the stupidity of the higher command that backed the tanks". In the gloom before dawn, they walked back to their own lines like a crowd from a football match. As the swirling snow eased off, the Germans realised a surprise attack had been abandoned and opened up with a heavy bombardment.

The Australians came out of it with astonishingly light casualties. However, one shell blew up a party of men close to battalion HQ in the railway bank. Bodies and bits of bodies were flung everywhere. The direct hit killed Major Ben Leane and one of his most trusted and experienced men, Lance Corporal Harold Reeve Beechey.

On hearing of the major's death, Lieutenant Colonel Leane left the shelter of his headquarters to go to the spot where the shell had struck. He picked up his brother's body and carried it to a quiet spot where he dug the grave himself and erected a makeshift cross over it. Whatever was left of Harold was buried close by but his final resting place is lost forever. He had made it clear he would prefer a "clean knockout" to being left a cripple. He got his wish.

His mother received news of his last moments from Vera Deakin, the daughter of a former Australian prime minister, who worked tirelessly for the Red Cross to inform relatives of the fate of so many men. Deakin ran a busy operations room close to Buckingham Palace, where she sifted information from comrades in arms, hospital staff, army chaplains and any other source that might shed light on the dead or missing. In 1917, she was receiving 4,000 inquiries a month from families and processing thousands of eyewitness reports. One of these was from Corporal S. C. Smith, of the 48th Battalion, who was in the same company as Harold and was with him when he died.

Corporal Smith was recovering from his Bullecourt wounds at 3rd Australian Auxiliary Hospital in Dartford, Kent. He told one of Deakin's researchers how on the night of 10 April, he and Harold were constructing a dugout on the railway line between Lagnicourt and Bullecourt when the Germans sent a couple of shells over. Harold was severely wounded about the body and legs. "He died two hours afterwards and was unconscious most of the time," according to Corporal Smith. "He was a L/Cpl at the time and very popular amongst the men. I knew him well. I did not see the grave but was told he was buried about 50 yards away from the place he was killed. I saw him before he died and also after death. Pte Martin 48th Battn. A Coy, who was a runner, told me he saw him buried near Major Leane's grave, same shell killed both men. No other of the same name. He was previously wounded. Grave marked with cross, name and number of battalion."

From her Australian Red Cross Society bolthole, Vera Deakin sent two more eyewitness reports to Amy.

Dear Madam
We have now received unofficial details of the death of 200 Lance Corporal H. R. Beechey, 48th

Battalion, AIF, and we hope that it will be some consolation to you to know that his death was almost instantaneous. Number 592 Private F. J. Betts of the same unit, when interviewed in the Grove Road Hospital, Richmond, reported that he was next to Lance Corporal Beechey in the trench about eight miles beyond Bapaume when about 2a.m. a shell exploded killing several men and wounding the Lance Corporal so severely that he died almost immediately from shock. He says that he was clean-shaven, thin, 5 foot 9 inches in height with rather a large nose.

Number 1906 Private Thomas Durbridge, who was in the Old Hastings House Hospital, Hastings, gave similar information. While they were waiting in no man's land at Bullecourt on the night of 10 April, before attacking the German trenches, a high explosive shell burst close to them, wounding Lance Corporal Beechey in the leg and he died almost immediately afterwards. Later on that night he was buried near the front line in front of Bullecourt. Private Durbridge describes him as 22 years of age, 5 foot 11 inches in height, slight and upright in figure with dark hair and fair complexion. He had a very small mouth with slightly projecting upper teeth.

Should further information be received we will send it to you at once as we realise how anxious you must be for details. Assuring you of our sincere sympathy in your great loss.

Yours faithfully
Vera Deakin, Secretary

* ★ ★

Amy sent off a grateful reply. It is her only surviving response to the tragedy engulfing her family. In it, she remembers her fine, upstanding son as being almost 6 feet tall but her memory was playing tricks — Harold's army records show he was in fact only 5 feet 8¾ inches.

To the Secretary
Australian Red Cross Society
Dear Madam

Thank you very much for your kindness in sending me details of the death of my son No. 200 L/Cpl H. R. Beechey 48 Batt. I am thankful that he did not suffer long and am obliged to you for telling me where he is buried. This is the 3rd of my eight sons (all in the army) who has lost his life in France. I should like to write to No. 592 Pte F. J. Betts if he is still in Richmond, also to No. 1991 Cpl S. C. Smith if I can. The other description hardly seems to apply. My son was 26, about 5ft 11in, brown hair, pale but not fair, also broad shouldered — rather large mouth — and good even teeth, poor boy. He had been invalided twice and wounded once and we hoped he would come through all right.

With kind regards and thanks, I am yours very sincerely

A. Beechey

The abortive attack on Bullecourt was rescheduled for the same time the following day, 11 April. It was a disaster. "In the whole course of the war," proclaimed the British official historian, "few attacks were ever carried out in such disadvantageous circumstances, against such defences." Once more, the Australian troops crawled out into the snow of No Man's Land and waited for the tanks. Only four out of twelve allotted to the attack were in position by 4.30a.m. Not only did they fail to sweep away the barbed-wire barriers but they also drew enemy fire from all around. Some of the 48th Battalion heroically smashed through to the second Hindenburg Line and begged for artillery support. It was denied them. General Hubert Gough, the army commander, deluded by reports of success, sent in the cavalry instead. Enemy machine guns made horsemeat of them.

The 48th Battalion survivors were back in their own lines that night. Also among the dead was 2nd Lieutenant Will Blaskett, aged twenty-one — his parents would later name their house "Bullecourt" in memory of him. Two brothers called Watson fought side by side until they were both hit. One was killed instantly. The other, partly paralysed, used his brother's body for cover as he continued firing. Out of ammunition, he dragged himself back across the snow to die of wounds a fortnight later. In the months to come, Vera Deakin would have her work cut out with frantic appeals for information from families of the dead and missing of Bullecourt. Char, waiting for his turn to go back and fight, took Harold's death badly.

Saturday, 5 May 1917
Dover

My dear mother

It was good of you to write and let me know the sad news so quickly. It seems so dreadful and impossible to realise, and has come just when he was at the very prime of his life. I would have written yesterday but was on fatigue duty up to nearly 9 o'clock. Will write again tomorrow when I shall have more time.

With best love to all, Char

He kept his word to write again the following day.

Sunday evening, 6 May 1917

I know you must be feeling very despondent over the news of Harold's death. I am feeling the same myself. I think that after being wounded at Pozières, he never ought to have been sent out to the line again and that others should have done their share of the fighting before he was called on again.

We have been very busy yesterday and today moving into new barracks, or rather cells in a prison, two of us to a cell; we are just on the top of the cliffs facing France and my cell faces the sea, but still it's a depressing place and I shall not be in it more than I can help. I haven't heard anything more yet about the medical exam but shall be sure to hear something this week, and think that I shall be given at least three months in this country, so that would give you plenty of time to write to headquarters, if you think it is any use, trying to obtain my release, and even if that were unsuccessful they might be persuaded to put me on home defence, for I do not think many families have done more for the country than we have. The man who shares a cell with me is from a bank in Wokingham, and asked me when he heard my name whether I was related to the little old lady there. [Char had several maiden aunts, his father's elderly sisters, living together in Wokingham, Surrey.] There has been a very cold wind blowing here all day and as we were turned out of our hut at 9 this morning and have been out in it all day nearly, we're very glad the day's finished.

Have you heard anything further about Harold? He was such a splendid fellow and would have made the very best kind of colonist. I do hope this summer is going to see the end of the war, and I really think it will do, but it is a very anxious time for everybody at home and it is dreadful to see the train-loads of wounded that leave Dover almost daily. I hope you have settled to let Sam go on with the cadet course as he seems so keen on it; at any rate they cannot send him out of the country for more than a year.

Very best love to you all and if there is anything you need, be sure and let me know, your affectionate son, Char

The news had yet to reach Len, who had been away from the firing line but not away from danger. A tit-for-tat artillery duel was going on and the divisional reserve area at Reningelst, a couple of miles behind the Ypres front line, was in the thick of it. The 18th Londons were part of the 47th Division, whose historian tells how the whole area was shelled intermittently from the end of April . . . "strain on the troops was proportionately increased, no one being able to count on uninterrupted rest when out of the line. The constant whistle of our shells going over and the enemy's retaliation proved most trying even to those whose nerves were the strongest." Len showed signs of being worn down by it all when he wrote to Edie.

Sunday evening, 6 May 1917

I received both the parcels you were kind enough to send me. It was a very nice cake you made and as it came just before tea, we had it as a Sunday treat.

We have moved again and are now in trenches. I have been digging for the last ten days or so and feel horribly stiff today. I do like honey and it was a very agreeable surprise to find it at the bottom of the parcel. It doesn't seem much like a Sunday — we worked until about 12 and had the rest of the day off.

Annie is better. She says it was an attack of rheumatism. I will try to write a longer letter next time, but feel a bit "done up" tonight.

★ ★ ★

At thirty-five, Len was almost twice as old as some of his comrades. Years of sitting at a desk had not prepared him for life in trenches. Only one of his letters to Annie has survived. She would have been relieved to hear that he was safely tucked up in hospital with all the symptoms of trench fever.

Wednesday, 9 May 1917

Dear Annie

I have been suffering from a kind of rheumatism the last few days and the doctor today decided to send me to hospital so I have been driven off a few miles, had a bath and am now in one of those blue uniforms you have seen so much of. I think you have to address the letters in the ordinary way and they will be forwarded on, so don't be surprised if I don't get them as quickly as I used to. I will write as often as I can but feel as if I want to just lay still and sleep, but at night it seems to get one in the joints, legs and arms. I expect it will have to run its course. Please excuse the short letter this time. Will you drop a line to mother to tell her?

With fondest love to all.

From your loving husband, Leonard Reeve Beechey, "Len"

With three of his brothers dead, Char was still wondering if the powers that be might exercise some compassion in his case.

Sunday, 13 May

7th Coy, 6th Battalion Royal Fusiliers, Dover

Just a line to hope you are well and the girls also. I see on today's notice board that I am to be transferred to a training camp in a day or two, and I expect that means that I shall have to go out again soon. I do not know whether it will do any good for you to ask for me to be put on home service in consideration of the losses the family has suffered, but if you think it might it would be best to address your letter to the CO 6th Battalion, Royal Fusiliers, Dover.

I am sending a cheque for £5 towards Sam's expenses. There is a young officer here who looks barely nineteen years of age. We had quite a firework display a few nights ago. The guns woke me up and as my cell faces the sea I could see that the forts were firing on moving targets out at sea which they had to find and keep in sight with a searchlight. Each shell as it exploded raised a column of water 50ft high so one could see easily where they dropped. It was so clear this afternoon that I could see the white cliffs quite distinctly across the Channel.

While his brothers were fighting and dying on the Western Front, Eric remained on dental duty on the island of Malta. Mary kept him up to date with everything but her efforts to soften the blow about Harold backfired and led to him discovering the truth from one of his close friends. On receiving the news, he wrote to his mother from Malta. The letter ended mysteriously because he knew he was about to be transferred to Salonika and that German U-boats were playing havoc with the passage of troops and supplies in the Mediterranean. One of the Allied ships to be sunk was the *Californian*, which had carried Chris's 4th Field Ambulance from Alexandria two years earlier. She had been torpedoed on 11 November 1915, and lay off the Greek coast near Cape Matapan. Fearing he might not make it to Greece, Eric had sent another letter to his mother enclosing a copy of his will and a loving farewell note to Mary and the children, to be opened in event of his death.

Monday, 28 May

Dear Mother

I have been wishing to write to you since I heard the news that Harold has followed Bar and Frank into the Unknown. I have had no particulars of how it happened, but I knew that he had been hit. Mary did not tell me he had gone under, but that he had been very badly hurt. In the next letter she told me she had "nothing further to tell me of Harold, but I wasn't to hope". Even then I did not realise the truth. But after "lights out" on Tuesday, Booth came round and told me. Mary had evidently written to me to tell me and wrote to him by the same mail, asking him to help me out a bit. I have not had that letter yet but I think the mail boat will be in today.

And now, Mother dear, I do not know what to

write. We all know what Harold was, and the awful sadness is that we have to realise that his wonderful personality is lost to us. He was a man without a single stain on his character, true to himself and to others. I really cannot write much as I cannot realise that when I do get home I shall not find any of the three of us who have paid the last tribute possible to the old country, have sacrificed their lives. We can only pay them the honour due to them, and reverence them forever in our memories.

I have not time to write more just now, and it will be quite a long time before you hear from me again. If you have received a certain letter from me you will know why. [Eric is being deliberately vague because of censorship.]

Bear up, Mother, we may, those who are left, be home before so very long. Write if you feel up to it, and keep as well as you can. All we can do is carry on to the best of our ability and pray that the worst has happened to us.

Best love to you and the girls from your truly sympathetic son, Eric

Len's transfer to hospital meant the post from home had yet to catch up with him so he was still unaware of Harold's death when he wrote to tell his mother he was sick.

Monday, 14 May 1917

I came into hospital last Wednesday. I had been

having pains, which I took to be rheumatic, in my legs and arms, which prevented me getting any sleep. The pain seems a lot worse in the night than in the day. I suppose it is because there is less to take your attention off it.

There were three things that made me know I was queer — first, I didn't want to eat, second, I didn't want to smoke, and thirdly, I didn't feel like reading.

I sometimes get a little sleep just before the orderlies start bringing the water round to wash with. It seems funny that after most restless nights if one does drop off to sleep in the morning it is generally just before one is woken up.

I hope you have good news of Harold and that Char is still in England. We have had a lot of rain during the night but it is still hot and it has made everything green as emeralds.

Char was about to go home on leave, a sure sign that it would not be long before he returned to active service. He told his mother to expect him.

16 May 1917

I have just been told that I have six days' leave from Friday morning to Wednesday night so expect to be home by Friday evening. I expect that means that I shall be for France again soon afterwards but I suppose it can't be helped so we'll have to make ourselves as cheerful as possible under the circumstances and it won't be so bad now as it was in the winter.

Len, meanwhile, had received the news about Harold.

Wednesday, 16 May 1917

My poor mother

I was so sorry to hear about poor Harold's death. I got your letter yesterday. I knew the Australians were engaged but thought Harold had been through so much that he was bound to come out of it all right. Annie will have been cut up about it when she heard as she was very fond of him, though she used to scold him for not announcing his coming — what times he laughed at her. I hope he did not suffer (as we used to march past a small shrine in a street of a certain town round here I used to notice an inscription over it to "Joseph, patron de la bonne mort, protégez nous". It didn't strike me at first what it meant then I suddenly tumbled to it). I should like to know if you hear any more details but I rather doubt if you will. I know you must be very much upset and I hope it will not make you ill.

I have pains in my legs and back and don't get much sleep at nights, but my temperature has dropped to normal and I eat the meals I am given. I don't seem to get any letters sent on; the only one I've had is yours. I know how cut up you must all be about Harold. He always used to turn up unexpectedly with such an air of insouciance.

★ ★ ★

A brief note from Len to sister Edie followed.

Saturday, 19 May 1917
D Ward, 8th Stationary Hospital, Boulogne

You can imagine how grieved I was to hear about Harold's death. I had been in hospital for about a week and had been wishing for a letter. Sometimes our wishes are fulfilled but not quite in the manner we expect. It seems hard after the rough time he had of it for over two years that he should be taken now.

I am about the same, my worst time is at night. I am in a proper hospital bed now, and sleeping, that is when I can sleep, between sheets. Have they classified Char yet? I hope he will be kept in England.

Len sent regular bulletins to his mother from hospital in Boulogne.

Wednesday, 23 May 1917

I am still in hospital as you see and still in bed. I don't feel any better than when I first came in. My legs still ache and I sometimes have a "done-up" kind of feeling, as if I had reached the "ultima thule" of endurance — I suppose it is part of the disease.

It is a lovely day today. Out through the windows opposite I can see the blue sky and at the end of the ward to the right the double doors are open and I can see a landscape of brown and green and yellow, though I don't know what the yellow can be. The green looks beautifully fresh from here.

There is a Scots man next to me, and he is rather quaint. He is about 43, hair going grey, has been out to Gallipoli before he came here. I have some difficulty in understanding what he says. The sister asked him one morning how he liked his porridge; he answered "I've noo tasted it yet." When he buys a paper he insists on having a "picter" one.

Monday, 28 May 1917

I am feeling a good deal better. I had a good night's sleep and am beginning to recover my old appetite. I am still in bed but expect I shall be up soon now. It is a fine day again though windy. It was misty first thing this morning but soon cleared up. There are about a dozen books in the ward — I have read them all now. We get the daily papers in the afternoon or evening and sometimes have a gramophone on the go.

Char was back in barracks after his spell of leave, during which he stopped off at Stamford to play cricket for the school.

28 May 1917
6th Battalion Royal Fusiliers
Northfall Meadows, Dover

I got back to Dover all right though I missed the

train at Stamford through staying on the cricket field too long. Still there was a train from Cannon St station at 10 o'clock, which owing to Zep raid and all lights being put out reached Dover about 4.15 a.m. and I got to barracks only in time for reveille.

I told the doctor I didn't regard myself as fit yet and am not being sent out on the next draft, which goes in a day or two. There seems to be a great hurry to get men across the water, so that a number who commenced their final leave this morning are only to have four days, including two for travelling, instead of six. If I were one of them I'd take the six and chance the result.

Len must have hoped his illness would take him back to "Blighty" so Annie could visit him. But the army had other ideas. A comfortable period of recovery in the Home Counties with perhaps a spell of leave thrown in was not on the agenda. Len would be stuck in France until he was fit enough to go back into the front line.

Thursday, 31 May 1917
M Coy, Number 1 Convalescent Camp, Boulogne
You will see that I have been transferred to a convalescent camp, not in England — how I wish it was! We were brought over in a motor car this afternoon. I am not having so much pain, I get it intermittently but not continuously like it was, so I can get to sleep now. Annie went to the park Sunday and listened to the band for about two

hours and then went over the heath on Monday.

It is fine and a nice breeze blowing. I see we have got beds but no sheets. I don't feel up to much yet. I expect I shall feel better as I get stronger.

He wrote to Edie again the next day.

> Friday, 1 June 1917
> M Coy, Number 1 Convalescent Camp, Boulogne
> I have discarded my blue suit and red tie and donned khaki again. I haven't been down to the city yet but we can get a pass any evening. My rate of walking is at present about one and a half miles an hour and that makes me tired. We can see the cathedral from the camp, something after the style of St Paul's. They seem to have a lot of concerts here — there are two tonight.
>
> It's Chris's birthday today — have you heard from him or Bertha lately?

Char, lazing in the sunshine of the south coast of England, had yet to learn of his next posting when he wrote to his mother in pencil.

> Saturday, 2 June 1917
> Northfall Meadows, Dover
> It is too hot this afternoon for me to go out and find ink, so I am writing this lying on a bank under a hawthorn bush and overlooking the Channel, which is looking beautifully blue and smooth. I am

glad to hear the girls are having their holidays soon and hope you yourself will do the same — you could manage to go to Skegness. I don't think it would cost very much and I should be able and pleased to send you a cheque for two pounds towards the expenses. There's a hospital ship just coming to harbour as I'm writing and another one about half a mile out just coming in. They are all painted grey like the destroyers that accompany them but fly the Red Cross flag.

There is a draft being sent from this battalion to East Africa but they haven't warned me for it. They are fitted out with sun helmets and a thin sandy-coloured khaki; still, I'm not sorry I wasn't picked for it as I don't love intense heat any more than I love cold, and I believe in Africa you get both within the 24 hours.

There was a Zep alarm here last night and we had to get up about two o'clock and dress but it was all over in half an hour or so. We often hear guns out to sea but whether it's Dunkirk or the Ypres district, I don't know.

Far across the oceans, Chris scanned the daily casualty lists in the newspapers before hobbling on sticks to the station to catch his train for work in the railway town of Midland Junction, north of Perth. His overwhelming sadness on seeing Harold's name was made worse by the guilt he felt at not being there to protect his younger brother. The messages of sorrow Chris immediately wrote to his mother never reached her —

369

the mail ships carrying them were sent to the bottom by U-boats. By the time one of his letters evaded the German submarine menace and reached Avondale Street, the war seemed a world away.

> 4 June 1917
> 9 Holyrood St, West Leederville
> I wrote you last mail about Harold. I hope you got the letter. I am enclosing some snapshots of the front and back of our house. It's of jarrah weatherboard on studs painted outside and lined with matchboard inside — the best house really in this climate and on sand. The sand is very clean and with manure and a garden hose grows grass and all the English flowers. You will see the hose on the path in the snapshot of the back. Bertha and I are pretty well and you can see I keep the outside neat, tidy and cultivated and Bertha does the same inside. I'm still holding down my job and don't miss nearly so much time at the office as at first.
> Love from us both, Chris

There was no possible doubt about Harold's fate. At least the family and Curly could get on and grieve while the loved ones of many other young men were caught in a twilight world of not knowing if their boys were dead or alive. For some, the anguish went on for years, as was the case with one of Harold's old 16th Battalion chums, Tom Farrell. As the Bullecourt dead, wounded and missing were being listed in the Perth newspapers of April, May and June 1917, Farrell's family issued a moving public plea. They had last heard from him the day before the landing at Gallipoli on 25 April 1915 — "Since then, not one relation or friend has received a single word from him. Last seen by a brother-in-law on 28 April and others remember seeing him on 2 May, but since then no trace can be found. Inquiries made at Base Records Office in Melbourne elicited the statement that he was well and with his unit and an officer promised to send a cable and communicate the result. That was 12 months ago, but he still is silent. A relative made inquiries in Egypt where the result was a blank. Another relative made inquiries in England with similar results and the discovery that his account had not been drawn upon since he left Egypt for the Dardanelles. Letters written to him early in the war were returned some months ago and during the last few months 50 have come back through the 'dead letter office', some dated as far back as May 1915. Most marked 'not known' or 'Deceased or missing'. Authorities have had no report of him being a casualty. Meanwhile, those dependent upon him cannot obtain their allowance, nor can they learn whether he is officially alive, dead or missing." A couple of weeks later, among the newspaper lists of those officially posted missing was the name T. L. Farrell.

From France, Len continued to keep the family informed of his progress and how a painful toenail had landed him back in hospital.

Thursday, 7 June 1917

Number 1 Convalescent Camp, Boulogne

Dear Edie

I hope Char will not be coming out again but it rather looks like it. I am glad you are learning to swim. It is a nice camp here, well on the top of a hill. There is physical drill in the morning — I do what I can of that — and a route march in the afternoon, which I have not been on yet. I still feel rocky on my legs and I suppose my pace is about two miles an hour. I was going to try and get down to the town after tea last night but it started to rain a little and looked thundery so waited for a big black cloud to pass over, which it didn't; and presently we had a real good thunder storm. So I sat in the CWL [Catholic Women's League] hut and wrote letters and then started reading an old Family Herald I found. It was dated 1889, but I think I prefer reading pre-war literature.

Saturday, 16 June 1917

Number 2 Ward, Number 2 General Hospital, Hotel Des Emigrants, Le Havre

You will be surprised to see I am in hospital again but I had to come in for a slight operation. I had a double nail growing on my left big toe and it started hurting about last March. I found when I came from Boulogne and started marching that it was more painful than ever, with the result that I came here last Thursday, had a little gas and the nail off yesterday and am still here today.

We heard on Thursday about the dreadful raid on London and yesterday heard there was another one. From what I read in the papers the first one was over the East End and city — but I am afraid Annie will have been upset.

The Zeppelin terror over Britain, that shattered buildings and civilian nerves, had been successfully countered by fighter aircraft capable of bringing down the airships with incendiary bullets. Now there was a new horror — German Gotha bombers. They killed ninety-five people in Folkestone on 25 May and thirteen more in Sheerness, Kent, and Shoeburyness, across the Thames estuary in Essex, on 5 June. They struck London in broad daylight on Wednesday 13 June, leaving 162 dead and injuring 432. The writer and war poet Siegfried Sassoon was waiting for a train at Liverpool Street station when "an invisible enemy sent destruction spinning down from a fine weather sky". One of the massive 110-pound bombs killed forty-five infants at a school in Poplar. The Gothas would return to kill and maim hundreds more. Len was well aware that on top of the fuel and food shortages, Annie would be terrified by the new threat.

In Lincoln, there had been occasional "Zep" scares but they were a safe distance from the devastating bombing raids. Amy was preparing for a short holiday with her daughters and Char was happy to contribute something towards the cost.

19 June

Northfall Meadows, Dover

I was pleased to get your letter saying you were going away for a holiday and am sending you a couple of £1 notes to help you to have an enjoyable time.

I went before the doctor again yesterday and was marked fit again so expect to be going abroad in a week or two. There is a draft going soon to West Africa so I may be put on that. At any rate it will be a change from France and I think it would suit me better than another winter in France.

I wrote to Len a day or two ago to the address you gave me in Boulogne. If I'm sent to France I shall probably cross from Folkestone to Boulogne and might get to go to his hospital and see him.

Then came word from Char that he would not be going back to France after all, to his obvious relief. He almost made it sound as if he was off on holiday as well.

28 June

Northfall Meadows, Dover

My dear mother

I have some fresh news for you though whether it will please you or not, I don't quite know, but I'm very satisfied with it.

It is that I'm on a draft for East Africa, which will probably sail in about three weeks' time. We shall have a month or so's training at Cape Town to become used to the climate and the rest I should think will be chiefly garrison work as there doesn't seem to be much fighting going on out there, and I think the hot climate there will suit me better than another cold and wet autumn in the French trenches. And I expect I shall enjoy the voyage if there are not tin fish swimming too near. I don't even know whether we go by the Mediterranean or right round West Africa.

We're having a game of General Post here today. My company is being disbanded and split up among the other three, and we are all meandering about with beds, equipment etc. on our backs like snails and not knowing where to dump them.

We had a fire out to sea a night or two ago — it looked about halfway across to Calais and must have been a ship on fire. I saw it about 9.30p.m. and was told it was still burning brightly at midnight. I'm walking over to St Margaret's Bay tomorrow afternoon if the weather's suitable and I can get a pass signed; shall have tea there and walk back when it's cool.

Len's prolific pencil was working overtime while he continued to recuperate. He was still at Le Havre when Edith next heard from him.

Sunday, 1 July 1917

I hope the forecast you give of the duration of the war is considerably exaggerated — try another paper! I was sorry to hear Eric had gone to Salonika. It is a pity he did not come this way and

I expect he would then have got leave. It must be two years since he went out.

There was a holiday air about Len's next couple of letters to Edie from a new base beside the seaside, one of the tented cities for the sick and wounded that straggled the French coast from Calais into Normandy.

> Tuesday, 3 July 1917
> No 4 Convalescent Camp, BEF, France
>
> We had a bathing parade this afternoon. We marched down to the beach — it was hot but we found the water cool enough. It was a gradually sloping beach with shingle at the top and then sand, but there was a pathway of sand and boards down so we missed that very tender feeling it gives to the feet when you come out of the sea and endeavour to walk on the shingle. I had a nice swim and should have liked to have had a longer one but I knew I couldn't be very strong so came out directly I began to feel tired, and then dressed and lay on the beach and gradually got warm in the hot sunshine.
>
> Last night we had a lecture on Longfellow at the YMCA and tonight a cinema show, one piece of which concerned the adventures of the immortal Charlie Chaplin, who does not seem to have lost his popularity.
>
> It is raining hard now and there has been some thunder and lightning . . .

Saturday, 7 July 1917

No 4 Convalescent Camp

I went for another swim yesterday. We marched down behind the band — it was very warm so I had a pleasant swim and then read a book lying on the beach.

I had two letters from Annie yesterday. She and Maud were going to a garden party this week in Regent's Park — it should have been very nice I should imagine if the weather was fine. It used to be a fine place though they may have altered it a bit now as they have substituted vegetables for flowers.

Len dropped a line to his mother from his army "holiday camp".

Monday, 9 July 1917

No 4 Convalescent Camp

I see by the papers there was another raid on London on Saturday. I hope you had a nice holiday. Annie tells me that Sam is training for a commission. Have you heard anything more about Harold? I made enquiries and was promised if anything was known it would be sent to you.

Annie said that you had heard from Chris — does he say how he likes the work? His usual way of working in England was to work very hard for three days and slack for three but I expect it would average out about the same in the end.

Char had scribbled a quick note from Devonport where he was awaiting embarkation on the troopship *Corinthic*. He promised to write before the boat sailed if at all possible, but he was already on his way by the time his mother heard from him again. There is no date but it must have been mid-July.

> Somewhere in the Atlantic
> (I hope this won't give the
> position away — if it does, the
> censor may tear this corner off)

My dear mother

My writing paper is now reduced to a few sheets and there's none to be had. There's one thing to say in favour of this trip — it's the most economical excursion I've ever been on. The canteen never did have much, but it's now reduced to cheese and baccy and a fruit I don't care for called mango. I have just managed to borrow another of Robert Service's books — Songs of a Red Cross Man — so I expect to enjoy myself reading it. I think I've read more books of absolute rubbish since I came on board than I had done in years before. The athletic sports and boxing competitions continue on the fine afternoons — at present, a large meshed net is being fixed up in front of me like a large hammock, which I believe is to form one of the conveniences of an obstacle race. Perhaps I'll be able to tell you more about it when the competitors come along.

Wireless news just up reports big Canadian success again in France — I think that colony has done some wonderfully good fighting during the year. Let's hope the advance continues.

It seems strange to have to go for such a long time without news from home and it will probably be a long time yet before I can get a letter. As for the Stamford Mercury, I doubt whether many will even reach me in Africa until I can give a more exact address.

Best love to all at home, Char

Char was not the only one who would be experiencing an altogether different kind of war to that being fought on the Western Front. Despite his fears, Eric had reached the little-publicised Balkan outpost of Salonika in one piece. It was less than a day by sea from Malta but the Aegean in particular was a graveyard for Allied shipping. Much of the journey was spent practising lifeboat drill and looking out for torpedoes. When they finally anchored off Salonika, the city was a stunning sight with its gleaming white buildings and skyline of spires, domes and minarets. The reality ashore was rather less enchanting. New arrivals told of marching through sordid streets, with no welcome from the locals. Spies were reputed to be everywhere and the men were discouraged even from buying fruit in case it had been injected with poison.

At the end of April and in early May, the British had launched two daring night attacks against a stubborn Bulgarian enemy dug in on the side of mountains overlooking the city. The result was 5,000 casualties for no gain. Eric's arrival coincided with a scaling down of operations. Two of six divisions based there were being shipped out and he would end up serving with Serbian forces who had been routed from their own homeland. He was anxious that his mother should destroy the earlier message to be given to Mary in the event of his death. Squeezed into the only free space available at the top of his letter home was a PS: "Please send me Frank's safety razor, please do not send any eatables, and tell the Officer in charge of parcels, Edie, that papers and other reading matter would be welcomed."

15 July 1917

Dear Mother

I wrote to you not long ago telling you that I was likely to be soon on the way to Salonika, and now I have the pleasure of writing to tell you of my safe arrival. My address is 63rd General Hospital, Salonika. In regard to the letter I enclosed to Mary, to be given to her in case my luck was out, please burn it. It was just a short will and a farewell letter, and I will make other arrangements regarding the former matter.

So, mother dear, I am safe and sound in wind and limb. You will have one of us come back to you, and you will be well looked after when this war is up. I know how you feel losing three such fine boys as my brothers, and continually wondering if the same fate is for any more of us. Yet they died men and your name is firmly fixed amongst the roll of brave mothers who have given their sons to the nation.

If you have any more particulars about how Harold went under, pass them on to me. I shall miss him when I come home and will fully feel the loss then. I had hoped that we were to have him left to us, as he had so many narrow escapes, but it was not to be.

Mary keeps me informed so just write and let me know how you are and the little things you do. I expect my babes are flourishing.

Best love to the girls, and to yourself, from your ever affectionate son, Eric

The latest air raid on London, in which 250 people were killed or injured, had been too close for comfort for Len's wife. Highgate, where they lived, was untouched by the Gotha bombers but the mere sight of them droning overhead on their way to blitz the docks of the East End had given Annie a nasty turn. She made up her mind to escape to the country, Len told his mother.

19 July
No 4 Convalescent Camp

Annie had a shock the Sunday before last — she was out shopping when she saw the aeroplanes above her. At first, she was too frightened to run, but when she managed to come round she collapsed in the hall and it was some time before she could get up. She was going down to her sister last Monday, at Daventry and I think intends staying a month. It will give her nerves a rest and give time to think what to do in the future.

The sedentary life gave Len plenty of time to muse on matters far removed from the trials and tribulations of the trenches that awaited him when he returned to active service.

Sunday, 22 July 1917
No 4 Convalescent Camp

Dear Mother

We are having fine weather again. There has been a very heavy dew which glistens on the cabbage leaves. The sky is clear of clouds, hardly any wind and every sign that it is going to keep fine and very hot.

I have had a nice lot of swimming and the water is getting nice and warm. In the evening there is generally something on at the YMCA, concerts, pictures, lectures etc. We had a lecture on Tennyson the night before last but the lecturer did not mention one incident which I remember reading in a biography by his son — and that was that Alfred Tennyson was fond of sitting in a large bath, smoking a long churchwarden pipe and reading big books about little birds. And very nice too, I thought as I read it — "et moi aussi".

The gardens in the camp, both flower and vegetable, are doing well. The sunflowers are beginning to show their large staring faces and there is an abundance of sweet peas and nasturtium now growing over the borders like a weed.

Edith says that Char is expecting to go to East Africa. If I am still down this way he might come through here on his way out.

By the following day, the "holiday" was over and bathing in the Channel would soon be a distant memory. Len was already pining for convalescent camp when he wrote again to his mother.

Monday, 23 July 1917

15 Camp, 8th Infantry Base Depot, Le Havre

I am glad you have heard from the War Office about Harold but sorry you have had no details. I have been trying to find anyone who knew him but have not succeeded so far. Annie is still at Daventry and does not quite know what to do as she does not want to live in London — I think she was very shaken. I have suggested she stays with her sister. I should like to have got home and talked it over with her but I have come to the conclusion that these things are in higher hands.

I miss my daily swim and should like to have continued them until it was time to get on a boat for those chalky cliffs t'other side of the water. We had a storm yesterday, which freshened things up and made the camp very muddy for a few hours.

The beach weather that made Len long for his daily dip was about to come to an abrupt end just as the British were launching their three-month slog from Ypres to Passchendaele. His old London Irish comrades would soon be wading and dying in an ocean of slime. However, it would be many more weeks before Len was pronounced well enough to risk dying for his country.

25 July 1917

15 Camp, 8th Infantry Base Depot, Le Havre

Dear Edie

You will see that I have flitted again. I miss the Con camp with its daily swim and nasturtium-bordered pavements. I feel a lot better for the time I had there. I have heard from Annie since she arrived at Daventry and she too is feeling better since she has been in the quiet of a country town. It has been very hot the last day or two — I should like a nice long swim now to get cool for the night.

The summer will soon be gone — it's curious how quickly it seems to go and when you get to the winter what a long time that seems to be. But it has been a fine summer this year — some years you could count the fine days on your fingers.

CHAPTER
FOURTEEN

The butterflies here are most beautiful

The war was now three years old. Amid the patriotic fervour and stampede to the recruiting stations in the summer of 1914, a rousing call to arms had appeared in Sheffield newspapers. It declared with panache that, "Mr Fred Banning, the well-known local sportsman, has been authorised by Lt-Col D. P. Driscoll DSO to gather together a few young men for service with the Legion of Frontiersmen. The Corps will be under personal command of the famous scout and will shortly leave England for active work in a distant part of the empire. Such celebrated hunters as F. C. Selous, Cherry Kearton, Outram and Rainey will accompany the corps as guides and scouts. Any young and fit men who would like to participate in what undoubtedly will be a great trip, chock full of glorious incident and adventure, are advised to immediately communicate with Mr Banning at 39 Bannerdale Road, Sheffield."

That small advertisement gave birth to the 25th (Service) Battalion Royal Fusiliers. Stockbrokers, bankers, public schoolboys, artists and sportsmen all had their own battalions in the Royal Fusiliers. None was as colourful as the 25th, the Legion of Frontiersmen, who became the only British unit to be posted overseas without undergoing the usual preliminary military training. The top brass apparently saw them as a bunch of dangerously ill-disciplined cowboys — which some indeed were, having galloped straight out of the American Wild West to join up. Dismissed as an army of adventurers, they could not be sent to France for fear of unsettling other regiments. Instead, Colonel Dan Driscoll, Boer War veteran, led them off on a gung-ho expedition to German East Africa. They set sail from England on 10 April 1915 with a force of 1,166 men, many of them ageing, stout-hearted veterans of long-forgotten skirmishes in Queen Victoria's colonial outposts.

They included William Northrup MacMillan, an American millionaire of impressive bulk as well as wealth, who relied upon a 64-inch belt to keep his trousers up. He would fight alongside 64-year-old Frederick Courtney Selous, big-game hunter, explorer, writer on African flora and fauna and bosom friend of one-time US president, Teddy Roosevelt. After thirteen months in East Africa, the Frontiersmen's ranks were reduced to just 170, mostly through sickness. For every one casualty suffered through enemy action, thirty-one were struck down by sickness and fever. Colonel Driscoll wrote of "a vast and impenetrable forest . . . wild animals as well as wild devils to fight; the sun burning your very flesh; the flies intolerable. Imagine a camp at night under these conditions. Round about the lions are roaring with hunger. Hyenas prowl in the hope of snapping up a sentry or leaping in and carrying off a wounded man."

General Smuts' blithe assertion early in 1917 that the campaign in East Africa was over meant it was now regarded as a cushy posting, a place for a spot of hunting combined with undemanding garrison duties. One of Char's new comrades-in-arms came closer to the truth when he admitted, "I wish I was in France. There, one lives like a gentleman and dies like a man. Here, one lives like a pig and dies like a dog."

The latest draft to bolster the battalion's diseased and depleted ranks would not reach them until September 1917. Char was one of two hundred fresh troops being sent from England to reinforce companies reduced to twenty or so fit men by dysentery and malaria. As the *Corinthic* steamed into tropical southern waters, there was little to do but read and take turns scanning the ocean for U-boats. Dress was more in keeping with a cruise than a military expedition. Instead of rough khaki that crawled with tiny, blood-sucking intruders, Char now wore a light uniform of shorts, shirt or long-sleeved vest open at the neck with sleeves rolled up and sun helmet. Boots could be cast off, though anyone stepping barefoot on to the unshaded decks in the heat of the midday sun was soon tap-dancing in pain. Weeks at sea left Char desperate for news of the war. Scraps of information came via wireless but it was only the bland and unreliable official communiqués. Char clearly lost track of time — there was no date on his next letter home, just a vague "end of July 1917".

No. 58708, 25th Battalion Royal Fusiliers
British Expeditionary Force,
Army Post Office, East Africa

My dear mother

I am well on my way to the South now. Last night was cloudy but I had a look the night before at the old Pole Star, and was surprised to find how depressed he appeared — I expect I must soon be looking out for the Southern Cross instead. We've had very good weather all the way so far, especially yesterday when the sea was almost like a lake. I felt rather ill for the first two days but now am as hearty as ever and am enjoying the trip immensely. They inoculated me again today, but I am well used to that now and it has no more effect on me than a bee sting on an old beekeeper. My duty on board is very light and consists of keeping a lookout for submarines every third day. So far I've seen a few of the creatures one sees at home only in museums — two whales spouting up water (that's how I recognised them), a shoal of sharks ("school" I believe I ought to say), some flying fish — they skim along just above the surface of the water, often for 20 to 30 yards, but seldom rise more than a foot above the waves — and some black-winged birds about the size of thrushes that I think must be storm petrels.

I spend most of my time on board reading: I

brought two novels with me and exchange with someone else as soon as I finish either. I'm reading rather a good one by Jack London called "Adventure". There's a library on board and I will go and see what that contains this afternoon.

I was surprised to find how comfortable a ship's hammock is, and we're now allowed to sleep on deck, which is infinitely preferable to the stuffy room we had below. I spend a really open-air life here, at least 23 hours out of the 24 above deck, and it's really quite a holiday.

Best love to yourself and all . . .

If Len was a touch envious that Char was heading for the seemingly cushier and certainly warmer climes of Africa, he does not let it show in his letters. He was preoccupied with the wet weather when he wrote to Edie, but his discomfort was minor compared to the suffering of the troops now floundering in the quagmire of the Third Battle of Ypres, which had started so promisingly on 31 July with the greatest advance yet of any Western Front offensive. The four-and-a-half-mile struggle through the mud to Passchendaele would take more than four months and cost at least 60,000 British lives with another 160,000 wounded.

Wednesday, 1 August 1917
15 Camp, 8th Infantry Base Depot, Le Havre
From what you say, Char will have started [his journey to Africa]. I am afraid it will be a long voyage if he goes via the Cape, but perhaps that

will be all the better, though I imagine it will get tedious.

I should like to see a photograph of Chris's house. I have just noticed in the Continental Mail that they have had 15 inches of rain in Perth since 1 July so I don't think they will claim it as a dry country just now. It has been raining a good deal here for the last three days. I woke up three or four times last night and heard it beating steadily on the tent, and one of my boots must have been too near to the side as I emptied about half a pint of water from it before I put it on.

I expect Chris would have seen Harold's name in the Australian casualty lists and would have been upset.

Chris had Harold in his thoughts when he wrote to his mother with some joyful news for a change.

5 August 1917
9 Holyrood St, West Leederville

I wrote twice since I heard that Harold was killed. I don't know whether you got them as several mails have been sunk. I am sending you some photos taken by Miss D. Boyce (or Bailey — her mother married twice), Harold's girl, of Bertha and myself, and also some of her and her sister taken by me. I never seem even now to think of Harold as dead. I don't know why.

I have more news. Bertha and I expect a little Beechey about the first week in November. We both hope for a boy to call him Harold Reeve. I shall be very happy and pleased if it is. I still take most of my exercise gardening and am very successful having had several salads and those kinds of vegetables and French beans and have peas and potatoes nearly ready and some nice flower plants ready to bloom as soon as the heavy rains and cold weather are over.

All throughout August, one of the wettest on record, Len remained at base camp in France while the slugging match went on in the mud of Flanders. Sister Edie, now aged twenty, was working in a munitions factory in Lincoln and Annie was planning to leave London with its bombing raids and food shortages for the tranquillity of south Wales. The letters continued to fly from 8th Infantry Base Depot, Le Havre.

Sunday, 5 August 1917

My dear mother

I am glad you heard about Harold as we now know he suffered no pain — though I can understand your feeling heart-sick. I am glad that Sam is at home — I hope it will be finished before his training.

Monday, 20 August 1917

Dear Mother

I am still in this backwater but don't expect this quiet existence will last for the "duration". But I am very thankful for the rest that I have had, that is to say comparative rest.

I treated myself to a tomato today, the first I have had since last summer. We have good food here, generally have tea and dinner together, which makes a very good meal but seems to leave the rest of the day rather bare.

I hear occasionally from men at the office and have run across one or two out here who have been there recently. It seems to have changed a lot. It would seem strange to be sitting down to office work again, but I think a tranquil life suits me best.

Monday, 27 August 1917

Dear Edie

Very many thanks for your letter and the books and chocolate. It was very kind of you not only to find them but to buy and send them as a chocolate sandwich. It makes a very nice birthday present. I have brought one of the books, Dostoyevsky's The Idiot, with me under my tunic to keep him from getting wet. It has been raining now for about 36 hours.

I expect you will find it different as a munitions girl. I suppose you will find some queer characters there. I don't think you will notice the getting up early bit until the dark mornings come and that will be put off for a bit when the clock is altered.

I suppose you will wear overalls for work. I shall like to hear what kind of work you start with and your feelings towards it. Yes, I suppose it is necessary that you go munitioning — this maelstrom of a war is dragging everything into it. One feels that everything is tending to one certain end and it can't be finished until that end is reached — something like a fever, where there is a fight between the different microbes, which reaches a maximum intensity and then things gradually become normal again, but not quite the same as before.

I had a parcel from Annie today. I asked her to send me a waistcoat. Mine was held together by safety pins mostly, but I like a waistcoat as it gives me a watch pocket. So in with it she put some plums, pears, apples and chocolate. The fruit we have eaten and some of the chocolate, but I have kept part of the chocolate as lunch in the mornings.

August 1917

Dear Mother

I started reading The Idiot first so did not discover until I got through it and started the other that there were letters from you and Edie in the second book.

Annie is going down to a place near Newport — Magor — on Monday and will stop for a week or two. She sent me a ten-shilling note for my birthday. She said I was to treat myself with the money — I have got a pipe and tobacco pouch and a soap tin.

There have been very heavy dews the last few

mornings which will soon be making it cold when it is time to get up. We get up "au point du jour" and I have seen more beautiful sunrises since I have been in the army than during the whole of my life before.

With love etc . . . Len

Char was seeing the world and not being shelled or shot at. The thrill of it all was evident in a long letter to his mother and sisters from Durban. Cape Town had mostly been a blur but Char had gone ashore briefly to discover British troops were royally received in the city's cafés and bars. Six-course dinner at the Grand Hotel cost seven shillings for two. Those with a little more time to spare went on an excursion around Table Mountain. From Marine Drive, the Indian Ocean glistened on one side while the Atlantic shimmered on the other. Soldiers were granted free admission to the Kenilworth racecourse as well as to the pier and bathing pavilions. "Apart from the presence of the coloured people," wrote one, "there is not a lot to remind you that you are not in England." Back on board ship by evening it was warm enough for Char to bed down on deck beneath the stars with views of the whole of Cape Town brilliantly lit up.

Durban, their final port of call, was even more impressive. Char sent a flurry of postcards with images of Zulu rickshaw drivers — he calls it a "ricksha" — and wide thoroughfares lined with prosperous buildings, such as the imposing town hall. He was fascinated by the Zulus who worked their taxi trade along the elegant sweep of Marine Parade wearing headdresses fashioned from bullock horns and bird's feathers.

4 September 1917
Dover draft to the 25th Battalion Royal Fusiliers
East Africa

My dear mother and sisters

Here I am in Africa at last and I've enjoyed my sea trip immensely. We left Dover on 27 July and England on the following Wednesday so we've taken about five weeks. We were a big convoy with an armoured cruiser and several destroyers to look after us, and sailed well out into the Atlantic so that we saw no land till we reached Sierra Leone. The destroyers left us after a few days but the cruiser stuck to her post till we reached harbour. Here our escort was replaced by a small battleship and our numbers were increased by two, one of which was a slow old boat that was just in front of mine and rocked like a barrel and kept running out of steam. However, we found one morning we could see and easily recognise Table Mountain — it stands only a mile or two behind Cape Town. I should judge it about 3000ft high and the ascent is pretty steep. I remember Harold saying that he climbed to the top. A few of us, of whom I was one, were sent on shore here to act as a police piquet but we had three hours to ourselves and I was able to see a good deal of the town. It was much bigger and altogether finer than I had expected. The streets are all so broad and well lighted and the buildings look so clean and show a much more decorated style of architecture than ours. All in uniform who landed were welcomed most hospitably and entertained with tea, cakes, oranges and smokes. Next morning we upped anchor once more, on our own this time, and consequently at nearly double our late speed, and keeping the coast just in sight all the while, sailed round the Cape, where I had imagined the waves to be never less than 10ft high, but where the sea was actually as smooth as the Round Pond in Kensington, without a ripple on it, and reached here, Durban, in about three days.

Our actual distances were: England to Sierra Leone 3,059 miles; Sierra Leone to Cape Town 3,292 miles and Cape Town to Durban 682 miles, totalling over 7,000. There were very few incidents to break the monotony of the unbroken horizon. We were able to rescue two sailors who were found in a boat several hundred miles out in the broad Atlantic.

Now we're under canvas a mile or two out of Durban and are having the time of our life — at any rate of our Army life — food plentiful and very cheap, especially fruit; tangerines, oranges four a penny, pineapples 3d each, and we were actually paid a sovereign — one whole pound — each when we landed. Baccy here is dirt-cheap — 6d a quarter of a pound instead of 9d an ounce in England. All I've said about Cape Town applies even more so to Durban. The town lies all along one side of the harbour, which is a large bay about two miles long with only a narrow outlet. The main street therefore lies parallel with that side of the bay and about two hundred yards away and has shops in it that would rival Bond Street. At the head of the bay, the ground rises for about one and a half miles and the side of that hill is the residential part. Everything gives one the impression of "plenty of elbow room". Main streets and side streets are all so wide — quite double the width of Broad Street, Lincoln.

Electric trams run everywhere and we in khaki go on them free. Yesterday I went with a chum to the zoo. This is at the top of the hill mentioned and at one end: we went by tram, stayed most of the afternoon and then continued the circular route along the crest of the ridge where we could get a fine view of the town and harbour below and the open sea beyond. The climate here is beautiful, especially in the evenings, and at this time of the year isn't unpleasantly hot even at midday. They call it winter here now. The most striking feature of the place is the ricksha and ricksha-boy — I have posted a picture postcard showing some, but it doesn't show their brilliant colours of feathers and dress. They seem very strong and one is often seen trotting along at a good pace with three men seated behind him.

Yesterday I went to church in the evening and as we came out Mrs Vicar drove us all into her drawing room for tea and cakes. I didn't get a chance of speaking to the vicar as he'd a meeting on after service but he was probably connected with Lincoln as he had a large photo of the cathedral in a prominent position. I've lots more to say and will continue in a day or two.

Best love to all, from Char

He was to spend ten blissful days in Durban where the food and accommodation must have been beyond the humble Tommy's wildest dreams. Huts were comfortable and there were plenty of recreation rooms and canteens where a feast of eggs, bread and butter, tea, cakes and fruit salad cost sixpence. There was also a merciful lack of drill. Char told Edie how he had taken the opportunity to indulge his passion for natural history.

5 September 1917
Durban

I am sending you a small present from Durban. I remember approximately your average rate of losing brooches, so am sending one to replace the last. The stone in it is called verdite — one could almost guess that name, and they say it's only found in one particular district, though I forget where that is. Am still having a good time and doing almost no drill — no doubt the hard work will come but what matter so long as we are happy now. Today I went for a train ride four miles out into the country where we were quite in the uncultivated wilds — every tree and bird and butterfly almost was strange and unknown. We saw oranges and bananas growing and a fruit I didn't know, green and oval and varying in size from a large orange to a small melon; anyhow I was told on inquiry it was a poo-poo, or perhaps the man was pooh-poohing my ignorant question. I'll find out. There is a fine free library here. Must finish up now and get back to camp.

Best love to all, from Char

In early September, the Gothas came back to terrorise London. They had switched strategy from daytime bombing to night attacks. The naval base at Chatham in Kent was blitzed on the night of 3 September and 132 young recruits were killed while asleep in their hammocks. The following night bombs rained down on the heart of the capital. Strand and Charing Cross were badly damaged and a tramcar suffered a direct hit on the Victoria Embankment just yards from Cleopatra's Needle, which was peppered with shrapnel but unmoved by the blast. The toll of nineteen dead and seventy-one injured was low, but Londoners were gripped by fear and Len was delighted that Annie would soon be getting out of the city. There is no record of who the "Maud and Joan" mentioned in Len's next letter to Edie might be, although they were clearly close to Annie. From earlier correspondence it seems Joan was Maud's daughter. As Annie had by then turned forty, and was already a widow once over, it is possible that Maud might have been her daughter from her first marriage, although there is never mention of her having children.

Sunday, 9 September 1917
15 Camp, 8th Infantry Base Depot, Le Havre
I had a letter from Annie with yours. She, Maud and Joan were alone the night of the air raid as the landlord and his lady had not returned from their holidays. Annie says that they adjourned into the next house for company, that the shrapnel sounded like the howling of a dog and the aeroplanes made a noise like humming tops. I think she was upset and would have been more so but she had Maud and Joan to look after. I am glad they are going out of London for a bit as it makes me anxious till I hear that all's well.

Char was on the final leg of his voyage to East Africa. While in Durban, most troops had made a beeline for the beaches to swim in special cages that protected from man-eating sharks. Char, still the schoolmaster at heart, went on a tour of one of Durban's most select educational establishments. He might have felt a pang of envy as he compared notes with fellow masters who did not have to fear being suddenly uprooted from the classroom to fight a war.

Sunday, 16 September
No. 58708, 25th Battalion Royal Fusiliers
East Africa
My dear mother
I'm nearing the end of my sea journey on a smaller boat with a perpetual roll, which brings port and starboard portholes alternately down to

the water's edge. We've no idea what part of the country we shall be sent to but it's possible that it may be right into the wilds, so that if you don't get any letters from me for some months at a time you needn't consider it a cause for anxiety.

We had about ten days in Durban and it was one of the pleasantest holidays I've ever spent; but I've already told you a good deal about that. A chum and I spent one afternoon in a large technical school in Durban. The caretaker took us round — a Northamptonshire man who'd been in South Africa about sixteen years. I had a chance of speaking to some of the masters, who were all English mostly with Manchester or Birmingham degrees. The building was a huge place, five storeys, with a lift for us and the lecturers but not for the pupils. The suburban part of Durban is a splendid place to live — it's on the side of a hill facing the sea. The houses are often bungalow style, verandah in front and often on one side also. All have large, well-shaded gardens and as their servants are black and a bit of a nuisance they manage with as few as possible.

I told you about the ricksha boys. They're Zulus. Zululand is not many miles up the coast, across the Tugela [river]. I asked how they spent their money as they evidently made a good deal and are only charged 2 shillings a day by the ricksha owner. Most of them only spend six months working in Durban and then go back to their wives and kraals in Zululand, where they have a good time for the next half-year, drinking Cape beer. The thrifty ones, however, buy cattle, average £6 per head; then with ten cattle they buy a wife, and so on, the more wives the better, so that when the daughters grow up (sons are no use to them) they can sell them at ten cattle each and so live in comfort in their old age.

I had to buy myself a new watch in Durban; that ten-shilling one I got at Lidgett's ["finest stock of reliable MILITARY and FANCY bracelet watches — guaranteed," according to their adverts in the Lincoln newspapers] in April didn't last ten weeks, and I also bought myself a magnetic compass (2/6) which will probably be useful. Most things in Natal are about 25 to 50 per cent dearer than during normal times in England, but I bought myself the cheapest book I ever bought in my life. It is a guide to South and East Africa, contains 15 good maps, has 770 pages, and is very interesting, and all for 1/6. So many men borrow it that I scarcely get a chance of reading it myself. It's too heavy to carry on the march so that I shall have to leave it behind but shall keep the maps with me; there's an interesting account in it of the war in German East Africa up to November last, so I will send those pages on to you.

My job on board this trip is a permanent one, namely to wash the stairs and a passage each morning. It sounds easy and should take about half an hour, instead of which under our Army-cum-Navy system on board, which is even worse than the Army separately, one has to spend the first three-quarters of an hour begging for a pail, broom and mop or cloth: no matter, I've the rest of the day to myself and it isn't mid-day yet: and a lovely hot day too, just a few white clouds on a blue sky and I'm on deck basking and too lazy to think of anything interesting to write, besides which we're not travelling so fast today so that the old tub doesn't roll so much. I'll finish my letter now or I shall have the censor saying I write too much. Shall be glad when I get your letters and to hear news of Len and Eric, and that Sam is progressing in the honourable profession.

With love to all at home, Char

PS To Edith — don't try to send parcels to me out here. The chances of their reaching me will be very slight. I hope you got the little brooch I sent you. What I called poo-poo in a previous letter should be paw-paw — I wish I was a better botanist. It seems so absurd not to know the name of more than one tree out of thirty and the same applies to flowers. Goodbye again — must write to Stamford now. Char

To Len's relief, Annie had moved to Wales and was settling in well. Len himself had been away from the fighting for more than four months, stuck in his various French hospitals and camps. The cliffs of England must have been visible on clear days but he never moaned about being cooped up on the wrong side of the

Channel with no visitors from home and without even a hint of leave. His next letter to his mother was his last from the camp at Le Havre. By October he would be back in the front line.

> Thursday, 20 September 1917
> 15 Camp, 8th Infantry Base Depot, Le Havre
> Annie is safely down in Monmouthshire with some friends on a farm and likes it very well. She was very much upset again by the last air raid so I hope she will stop down there — though I don't know if she will care for it so much in the winter.
> I can buy fruit here — the apples seem hardly ripe but I have had some nice pears, those big Williams. They are about 2d each, but worth it — the tomatoes are good, too, and work out about the same price when you buy a big one.
> I have been playing chess a good deal lately and am playing in a competition tonight — the YMCA hut in our camp against the one in the next. We lost last time.

Eric, who had been away more than twice as long as Len, took comfort from the family snaps his wife sent to him. He had sailed from England for Malta on 25 September 1915, the day Bar was killed, and was thoroughly homesick. But writing to his mother from Salonika he does not dwell on the pain of being separated for so long from Mary and the children, including the daughter he has never seen. Instead, Eric marvels at the Serbs whose lives have been destroyed by the war.

Sunday, 23 September 1917
38th General Hospital, Salonika

It is two years from next Tuesday since I left Blighty and I am getting fed up with foreign scenery. Mary's camera is a great source of pleasure to me as I have views galore of the babes and others. I had a sweet one of herself by the last mail, and a nice one of Winnie. I have a nice little picture gallery now.

These Serbs are interesting chaps — compared with what they have undergone, the troubles of people at home are little. They have lost everything and few have any idea where their wives and children are. I have heard awful stories of how the enemy beat the latter, and a woman of presentable appearance would be better dead. England should have it continually drummed into her the suffering of these invaded countries. These stories are shocking but the people should be shocked so that this talk of peace now should be stopped. The Serb we have as interpreter himself lived for five days on grass and very little water.

The Dover draft to the 25th Battalion Royal Fusiliers had come to the end of their epic journey. Char had reached East Africa where a guerrilla war had been raging since 1914. He must have been shocked by the sorry state of the sickly outfit he was joining. Those remaining from the original 1,166 Frontiersmen who had set sail for Africa more than two years earlier were laid low by bouts of fever. The legendary F. C. Selous had died in battle early in 1917, shot through the mouth at the age of sixty-six, having been invalided home once and having insisted on returning — not for nothing was the 25th known as "the Old and the Bold" But they were up against a brilliantly led adversary.

Even before the assassination of the heir to the Austrian throne in Sarajevo in 1914, Lieutenant Colonel Paul von Lettow-Vorbeck had envisaged the impending conflict in a memorandum to the colony's governor. Conceding that the war in East Africa would be "nothing more than an incident", he concluded, however, that "we have it in our power to hinder the enemy . . . by keeping as many troops as possible pinned down in Africa".

More than 130,000 British soldiers were drawn into the campaign. Almost 50,000 died from disease. The army shipped 60,000 horses and ponies out to Africa, in some cases painting white stripes on them as camouflage to make them look like zebras. More than 59,000 of the horses died from tsetse-fly bites, thirst or exhaustion.

Lettow-Vorbeck's tactics were to hit vital targets like the rail line between Nairobi and Mombasa and then run. The British in pursuit were picked off in the jungles, swamps and bush country. Selous had noted, "This dense tropical bush lends itself at every yard to ambushes, and is everywhere in favour of the defending forces." It was a far cry from the war Char had known in France. He arrived just as Lettow-Vorbeck was preparing a new blow, which would have all the bloody hallmarks of a trench battle on the Western Front.

At the end of September Char wrote to his mother about his new surroundings. The depleted 25th Royal Fusiliers were by then a tiny part of a force of mostly black troops — the British had learned something from their ill-starred exploits in East Africa — which had set out inland from Lindi to try to winkle out the enemy and goad him into fighting.

> C Coy, 25th Battalion Royal Fusiliers
> East Africa
>
> This is a pioneer battalion I am in out here who have been in the country since the beginning of the war. We're right in the bush now, no sign of cultivation within sight, in wooded country with native paths through it, trees about the height of those in Wickenby Wood [a favourite old haunt of the Beechey children close to Friesthorpe] but well separated from one another, but undergrowth pretty thick and some of it prickly. The butterflies here are most beautiful and varied. I hope I shall be able to bring a few of the best home to show you, but that will be after we've finished the war out here. The bush itself seems practically all green with very few flowers so that I'm wondering where all these butterflies feed — perhaps they're bread and butterflies. At present, I'm in a leafy shelter erected for two with a thick roof for protection against the sun and am sucking sugar cane, which

I bought from a native for a cigarette. We passed through various plantations on the way up, some of which I could recognise — banana, coconut and sugar. I've seen no animals here yet except tame ones though I believe this is supposed to be a good hunting district.

The most odd-looking tree I've seen — it was plentiful near the coast — was the baobab. Its trunk is such enormous thickness — over 8ft diameter — for quite a small tree. It's leafless just at present but the stem and all the branches are of a silver grey colour and look almost white in the sun.

We are each allowed to have a boy — that is a native — to "do-for" us, whom we have to supply with food per day and a few rupees per month — or two or three can share in a "boy". I haven't one at present but they seem useful and trustworthy so I think I will get one — the climate here soon makes one lazy. We sit or lie in our shady cubby-houses during the heat of the day and lie in state under mosquito nets at night.

I'm enclosing a short account of the war out here from A Tourist's Guide to South and East Africa. The book's too heavy to carry any further so I'm keeping the maps and throwing the rest away after reading it.

Last night the boys were doing a war dance, plenty noise and vigour, but I believe the real thing comes off at the full moon with tom-toms complete. And then I'll tell you all about it.

We wear boots, puttees, shorts, shirt and helmet here and a pad on our back for protection against the sun.

Food good and plentiful so that I remain your affectionate and cheerful son, Char

Too far away for parcels from home, he would soon learn the art of keeping a "scoff box" in which everything from cocoa to curry powder was hoarded. The contents would then be shared out among friends around the evening campfire where charging rhino were regarded as more of a threat than the enemy. Zebra, wildebeest, Thompson's gazelle, impala and ostrich all made it into the supper pot, but the abundant giraffe were usually left alone. Apart from its meat tasting like old rope, few had the heart to shoot such inoffensive creatures. Clean drinking water was always scarce and when boiled up for tea or coffee it left a green scum, which Char was taught to skim off. Run-ins with the enemy were usually swift and brutal. "Our poor fellows were practically cut to pieces," wrote a fellow Fusilier, Private Turner, "all their clothes taken off them . . . we were all very much upset and swore afterwards we would take no prisoners." But there were lighter moments. A soldier escorting a naked native woman into camp, thinking she might provide intelligence on the elusive enemy, blushed with embarrassment as his mates burst into a chorus of, "Hello, Hello, Who's Your Lady Friend?" It was said that the fewer clothes an African wore the more moral they appeared to be — Private Turner recalled "one big fellow walking the streets of Kisumu wearing a tall silk hat and carrying an umbrella — that's all. He was very swanky about it all."

Lettow-Vorbeck had no compunction about stripping the wounded of their weapons, putting a bullet through their head and leaving them to the vultures. Yet he would allow captured enemy natives to go free if they swore not to take up arms against him again. He commanded around 8,000 men, mostly African Askaris. A considerably larger British force was on his trail and edging closer for the major confrontation of the whole wretched campaign. When the Fusiliers next pitched camp Char wrote home again, but he was anxious to conserve his meagre supply of paper.

> 4 October 1917
> 12 platoon C Coy
> Same address

Dear Mother

I'm a little further up into the bush; scenery much the same; and in a camp now well up on a hill but have been lower down near the water for the last two days, which had its advantages during the day — sufficient water supply — and disadvantages at night — over-sufficient mosquito supply.

We'd a bad night our first night here, a heavy storm coming in just after our arrival at about four o'clock and lasting over an hour and leaving us soaking and our blankets, so that we had to get through the night as best we could and get dry next morning. Still, it didn't affect me except in temper and I'm still in the pink of condition. Two days ago I had to go back to a camp about four miles off for a party of eight native porters and a headman. I managed to get a transport car to take me most of the way there, got the boys from an English lieutenant in charge and as I couldn't speak a word of the language I gave them a cigarette each and the headman two extra and then shepherded them back most happily, all with their loads on their head and in single file and I at the back with my rifle.

I'm getting quite an efficient cook — today I made coffee and mealie (maize) for breakfast for myself and chum, yesterday rice and fried bacon; I keep a supply of rice by exchanging with the native soldiers for bully-beef.

We heard last night of the success in Mesopotamia and the increase in soldier's pay and we've an impression that the war out here is going on very satisfactorily though I haven't seen a paper since leaving Durban.

I've just drawn my meat ration for today, about one and a half pounds of native bullock for myself and chum, which I'll attempt to cook this afternoon. At present it looks like soft India rubber. This will be a new culinary feat for me — if successful. I'm cook — carte blanche — for the two of us today as my pal's an orderly for the day and can't get away so I feed him at intervals. I still have one chess opponent; my others on the boat belonging to a different branch of the service and disappearing after we left the Cape. We play when it's cool enough i.e. when it's cloudy or from four to seven in the evening. I mustn't use any more paper at present as it's almost impossible to get a fresh supply out here and it's no use your sending a parcel as I'm told they never arrive; still, it would be useful if you would enclose an envelope and sheet of note paper in each of your letters — that would get through all right. Hoping you are all well and that you've good news from Len and Eric.

With best love from your affectionate son, Char

Chris was awaiting the birth of his first child but had little to add when he wrote from Australia.

> 15 October 1917
> 9 Holyrood St

The war seems to be growing more gigantic than anyone would have been foolish enough to imagine at the beginning, but I think we are driving the wedge into them now and hope that our victory will put all wars beyond the realms of possibility for hundreds of years. I think it too. The news here is of very meagre character and to all intents and purposes, as father used to say, there isn't any war on as far as we are concerned.

Len had returned to active service with the same platoon he had left in May, though many of the old familiar faces had been swallowed by Flanders mud.

The London Irish left the Ypres sector at the end of September and took over a part of the line near Arras. They welcomed Rifleman Beechey back on 10 October and carried out their first organised "hate" against the enemy at 3a.m. the following morning, lobbing 710 gas-filled projectiles into the German-held village of Oppy directly in front of them. Remembering how Harold had been sent back to his doom, Amy once more had much to fear. Char and Len, both out of harm's way for so long, were in the firing line again, but Len remained philosophical.

Tuesday, 16 October 1917
C Coy, 11 Platoon, 1/18 Royal Irish Rifles, BEF, France

I have not much chance of reading now and carrying any literature also presents some difficulty. I am, as you termed it, having a more active life. One tries to make things as comfortable as possible. It is necessary to divide difficulties into two lots — those that can't be helped and those that can, and confine one's attention to the latter. As the old sailor said:

For every difficulty under the sun,
There is a remedy or there is none;
If there is one, try and find it,
If there isn't, never mind it.

CHAPTER
FIFTEEN

It seems more terrible each time

Deep in the African bush lay the cluster of straw huts and grubby tents that made up Mtama Field Hospital Clearing Station. Medics, more used to disease cases and themselves stricken by jungle fever, had a sudden influx of battle casualties on their hands. The wounded and dying lay like giant chrysalises, cocooned under mosquito nets on stretchers stained with sweat and blood. Among them, weakened and delirious from sickness and morphine with a machine-gun bullet in his chest, was Private Charles Reeve Beechey.

> 20 October 1917
> Mtama Field Hospital Clearing Station

Dear Mrs Peechey [sic]

I am taking the liberty of writing you a few lines at the request of your son who is lying here at present with a very serious wound received in action. I am very sorry to say that the doctor can give little hope of his recovery and I think your son himself realises this — he is bearing himself up very bravely and facing the situation like a true Britisher.

There has been very heavy fighting here and many good men have gone under but in doing so have most nobly kept up the tradition of the British Army. I have arranged for a Church of England minister to go round to see your son today — everything that is possible to do has been done to make his end more comfortable. The writer of this is an old Fusiliers officer and so sorry that he should have such bad news to send you.

Yours very truly and sincerely, H. M. Peacock (Lt.), Staff Office, Forces Reserve, Mtama

Char, his breathing laboured, his lungs filling with blood, was dead before the day was out.

Instead of the usual enemy ambush-and-run tactics, Lettow-Vorbeck had decided to stand and fight under the tropical sun. The village of Mahiwa, 45 miles up the Lukuledi river from Lindi, lends its name to the battle that turned out to be the 25th Royal Fusiliers last hurrah. Fewer than fifty were left standing afterwards — the proud Legion of Frontiersmen would fight no more. Char's best pal, the one he cooked for and played chess against, the one who referred to him as Beechey in public-school manner of surnames only, was with him almost to the last. From his hospital bed in England, the comrade Char called Heath provided a detailed account of his dear friend's final days for

Canon Day. The Stamford School headmaster had now lost all his August 1914 staff.

From Ward M4, Moss Side Military Hospital,
Maghull, nr Liverpool

Dear Sir

In reply to yours of the 19 inst. respecting the death of Pte C. R. Beechey, C Coy, 25th Batt. R.F., who served with me during the time I was in East Africa, and whose friendship I valued so much.

We became fast friends during the time we were on board the Corinthic, which left Plymouth on July 25th of last year, arriving at Durban, Aug. 29th, where we disembarked and proceeded to Congella Camp, where we stayed until Sept. 11th, and then went aboard the steamer Princess, bound for E. Africa, arriving at mid-day, Sept. 18th, and landing at Lindi to camp for the night. The following day was spent preparing to move again, which we did at midnight, going aboard some barges which were towed by a small steamer to Mingora, where we landed at daybreak and marched to camp C23, arriving at noon after a very stiff march in a terrible heat, many of us falling out on the way. We were now attached to the Lindi column, who were waiting for us to assist in the advance starting Sept. 23rd. Nothing of importance took place until Sept. 26th when the Germans made an attack about 3.30p.m., but were beaten off by our black troops after a sharp engagement.

The following day, we were shelled by the enemy for a short time, but nothing occurred to check our advance until Wednesday, Sept. 28th, when a heavy downpour soaked us to the skin just as we were preparing to dig ourselves in for the night, which we always did in case of attack. We had got about 10 inches deep when suddenly the enemy opened fire on us with machine guns from the cover of thick bush, the engagement lasting for two hours, the enemy finally retiring without doing much damage to our white troops; the black troops were not so fortunate, the K.A.R. [King's African Rifles] suffering severely. From this time onwards we were trekking and occasionally getting in touch with the rear of the enemy, whose method was to hide in the bush and snipe at us in order to check our advance and relieve the pressure on their main body.

I will now come to the events closely leading up to the sad end of Pte. C. R. Beechey, which occurred on October 18th at Kovenge (I am a little uncertain about this being the correct name but I think you will find it on the map of E. Africa, it is about 4 miles from Mtama). I was on picket duty with Pte. Beechey during the afternoon of Oct. 16th, while our column passed and entered Mtama. We then formed a rearguard with other pickets and followed in shortly afterwards; the whole of us were more or less exhausted after a week's hard trekking in an intense heat. It was then that I noticed a change in my friend's condition, who had attacks of sickness. I tried to get him to report sick, but he said, "No, I shall be better after a rest." He appeared to be slightly better the next morning, but was not really fit to go on trek, and when we marched out of Mtama, I could see it was an effort for him to keep up with the column. I again tried to persuade him to fall out and report sick — he replied, "Don't worry about me, Heath, I shall be quite all right presently." It was shortly after this that we were separated for the first time, to be attached to different Lewis Gun sections, owing to so much sickness amongst the sections causing them to be depleted. I was indeed sorry to be parted after being together so long and at such an anxious time, but I had the pleasure of a few moments' conversation with him while we were being held in reserve to our black troops, who were heavily engaged with the enemy. I was pleased to notice that his condition had improved, and when we parted he said he felt better and would be able to carry on as the sickness had ceased. We then wished each other good luck as we moved off into action. I was unfortunately put out of action very soon after, several shells bursting close to me, which resulted in my getting a severe concussion. I was sent to the dressing station where I stopped for a few days, developing malaria during that time. It was then that I got news of my friend's unfortunate end. It appears that the 25th Batt. R.F. were hard pressed by the enemy, causing many casualties amongst them, and as Pte Beechey was sixth man on the Lewis Gun it was found necessary for him to go back for more ammunition, which was some distance in the rear. It was then he received a gunshot wound in the chest, which proved fatal before he reached the dressing station, his burial taking place close to the scene of action.

These are the facts as far as I am able to give them, and I feel sure they will be of interest to you and his many friends. I have no doubt you were aware of Pte Beechey's fondness for draughts and chess, and that he carried a miniature board with him which often helped to pass away the weary hours on board ship and in the trenches. He also carried a small compass and the map of E. Africa so that he could locate our position after each day's trekking, the boys often crowding around him in their desire for information, which he was always so willing to give, and I am sure his death was a sad loss to the "Boys", who had a great respect for his brave and generous nature.

I am unfortunately still a patient under treatment for shell-shock, but am pleased to say my progress towards recovery since arriving here is most rapid, and if all goes well I hope to be fit again in a few more weeks.

I must now close, hoping I have made the circumstances leading up to the death of my faithful friend quite clear to you. Should you wish to ask me anything else respecting him I shall be only too pleased to answer to the best of my knowledge.

Yours sincerely, P. Heath

Some of Heath's moving account was not entirely accurate, but then the British officer given the task of compiling an official record of the campaign for the War Office found no two reports of actions in East Africa ever quite the same. Dates, times, place names were often contradictory and Mahiwa was more confused than most of the battles.

For this great showdown, Lettow-Vorbeck cast off his normal jungle outfit of cotton shirt and trousers and hippopotamus-hide shoes to dress the part of distinguished German officer. He donned full, high-collared regimental uniform jangling with campaign medals and topped with spiked helmet. He knew the British commander, Brigadier General Gordon Beves, from the Battle of Reata in March 1916 where Beves had squandered the lives of his men on foolhardy frontal attacks. Lettow-Vorbeck suspected his opponent might have learned nothing.

Lindi force, with its smattering of Frontiersmen, was to link up with another column and finally swat an enemy which had buzzed around the bush like a bloodthirsty tsetse fly for three years. The Germans were outnumbered more than three to one. Fighting raged from the morning of 17 October to late the following day and by the end of it the British had suffered 2,700 casualties from a total of 4,900 engaged. Enemy losses were 517 out of 1,500. A captain of the

King's African Rifles, who saw his black troops shelled to bits, reported, "The trees above the trench were dripping blood for two days afterwards from limbs and trunks of men that had been blown up and been wedged between the branches." Another regiment passing through the area several weeks later reported, "Bodies must still be lying about in the bush. Smell very bad." Colonel Driscoll, though too sick to lead the remnants of his gallant 25th into battle, asserted afterwards, "Every man present must have fought like a hero." There were heroes on both sides. A British officer had to take his hat off to one German "who rode a horse at the head of his company in an assault before he disappeared, never, I should think, to lead his troops on earth again. For not less than two machine guns and two score of rifles were aimed at him."

Corporal Roland Mountfort told how his company of the 25th Royal Fusiliers got back to Lindi just seventeen strong out of two hundred, half of whom had been in the country for less than three months, ". . . so you may judge for yourself what a pestilential, fever-stricken, Godforsaken hole it was our luck to strike." Char, contrary to Heath's description, had been carried alive to Mtama Field Hospital, but was beyond medical help. The agony of his fatal chest wound evaporated in a dreamlike haze of morphine, which, according to Fusilier Mountfort, induced "an unearthly feeling of peace, stealing gently through every vein and all the fatigue, the pain and the tiredness of life just faded away like breath from a mirror".

Army Form B.104–82, with which Amy was so terribly familiar, brought news of Char's death to Avondale Street. It was less callous in 1917 than when Bar was killed. In those earlier days, it went abruptly from expressions of "sympathy and regret of the Army Council at your loss" to a coldly formal pronouncement that, "If any articles of private property left by the deceased are found, they will be forwarded to this Office, but some time will probably elapse before their receipt, and when received they cannot be disposed of until authority is received from the War Office." After stating Char had "died of wounds received in action", it now adopted a softer tone. "By His Majesty's command," it went on, "I am to forward the enclosed message of sympathy from Their Gracious Majesties the King and Queen. I am at the same time to express the regret of the Army Council at the soldier's death in his country's service. I am to add that any information that may be received as to the soldier's burial will be communicated to you in due course." Whatever words were used, they were hardly enough for a mother who had lost four sons.

When it was all over, survivors of the fighting in East Africa were often congratulated on having missed the war. Char, who had been so confident of returning with his collection of beautiful butterfly specimens and glorious tales of African flora and fauna that knocked Ketton Pits into a cocked hat, would not be one of them.

In France, Len's unit was looking forward to a peaceful winter in a less strenuous part of the line. The nearest town was Arras, badly battered by war but not entirely blasted to ruins like Ypres. There was a morbid fascination in seeing rows of houses with their fronts peeled away, exposing a chaos of unmade beds and cluttered dining tables left by fleeing inhabitants. Surrounding villages, though deserted, still bore some resemblance to normal civilisation. Len wrote often to his mother and Edie, always asking after Char. He was sure his brother was well away from danger.

Wednesday, 24 October 1917
C Coy, 11 Platoon, 1/18 Royal Irish Rifles, BEF, France

Dear Mother

Annie is still at Magor but will have to run up to London at the beginning of next month as she is thinking of giving up the rooms and will have to store the furniture somewhere.

Have you heard any more from Char yet? He must have reached his destination by now I should think. We have been having a good lot of rain the last few days, and nights, and it has been a good deal colder. I won't write any more now as I am expecting a letter from you every day.

Thursday, 25 October 1917

My dear Edie

I was glad to get mother's letter today as I hadn't had one for over a month. I am glad Sam is going into the artillery — I expect it will mean a fairly long training.

We had a concert last Monday by the "Shamrocks" — members of our own battalion. I thought it was very good . . .

Thursday, 25 October 1917

My dear mother

I am restored to my normal condition again, which is more than I can say of the weather, which seems to be getting worse. Very glad that you have heard from Char and hope he will find Africa better than France, though it will take a long while to get an answer to a letter.

Sunday, 28 October 1917

Dear Edie

We have not been having such a bad time though the rain and mud do not add to the comfort. It is kind of you to ask what I should like in a parcel . . . if you could put in a pot of honey and an apple or two, and anything else eatable.

I am pleased you heard from Char and that he had a good time — I hope he will have a better time altogether than he had out here.

Friday, 2 November 1917

My dear mother

I hope you will hear from Char soon. I suppose you have not received any replies to your letters yet. I am glad he had a good voyage and hope he will get to a nice place now that he is out there. Hope you are having a quiet time and no alarms and that you are all well.

    With love etc . . . Len

Len sounded genuinely pleased that Char was safe from the terrors of the trenches. News of his death must have been all the more shocking when it reached him. But he was used to it, surrounded every day by sights that turned a man's stomach. Writing to Edie, Len swiftly moved on to other matters.

> Saturday, 3 November 1917
> 18th Battalion London Irish Rifles,
> C Coy, 11th Platoon

You know how cut up I was to hear that Char had died of wounds. I have not long got your letter saying he had a good time at Durban when I got this one. It seems so sudden, though perhaps a good time may have elapsed between the two. It does seem hard luck. I am afraid it will upset you all. Poor mother, it does seem hard on her. I wish he could have come safely through. It seems more terrible each time.

    I am glad you like the work at Clayton and Shuttleworth's and expect you will get used to turning out early. I hope you manage to get a nice hot cup of tea or coffee or something before you start.

    It is very kind of you to send me a parcel and I will let you know directly I get it — I am afraid though it puts you to a lot of expense. Things here are about as usual, still rather muddy.

★ ★ ★

Len sent a short letter to his mother. He hardly knew what to say.

Saturday, 3 November 1917

I got Edie's letter last night telling me of poor Char's death. I know how terribly upset you must be and how you must have missed him. It seems such a great pity that he should have to go. I was hoping he would have a good time out there and it would be pretty quiet. I will write in a day or two but know how you must feel.

From Australia came word of a new addition to the Beechey family. It wasn't the boy Chris was hoping to name after Harold, but his brother would not be forgotten.

6 November 1917

9 Holyrood St, West Leederville

Bertha had a little girl, born last Saturday afternoon the 3rd Nov. She had a rather bad time, nearly 2 days' labour, but everything righted and went splendidly at the last and both are doing well. She's quite dark with a lot of hair. Curly Boyce, poor old Harold's girl, was staying with us for a fortnight right up to yesterday but has gone home because her mother was ill. She wants to come and stay with us again when Bertha gets up. She was awfully good during the trying time and did all the housework and ran to the phone several times and ran about and was a great help.

426

She says the baby is like Harold and we both with bon accord asked her to be godmother. It was to be Harold Reeve if a boy and Bertha was to choose if it was a girl. Bertha chose Kathleen Mary and I was allowed to add Reeve so the full name will be Kathleen Mary Reeve Beechey. The nurse tells me she is perfect in every way and she has such a clear skin though dark and will have the Beechey bump on her nose in three or four years.

Dear love from both, Chris

All was quiet on Len's part of the Western Front, giving him time to brood over his dead brother. The 18th Londons' war diary records little incident apart from the occasional discharge of gas. On 1 November a man in the ranks was accidentally killed but no details are given. The riflemen were eagerly anticipating Christmas. Pigs and geese were bought for fattening up far behind the lines and were being guarded from predators in other units as if they were captured German generals. Amid the bustle of the back area a small sodawater factory was also set up. At Mareouil, a village that played host to the battalion during spells in reserve, there were no fewer than sixty-five estaminets. Len had no problem finding a quiet corner in one of them to sip his glass of coffee, read the French newspapers and write his letters.

Wednesday, 7 November 1917

Dear Mother

I expect you have had a lot of letters to write

427

concerning Char. I am afraid it must have been a terrible shock to you. He was always so good and reliable and it is very difficult for me to realise that he is gone — each one seems a harder blow than the previous one. I wish I could see you.

I got Edith's parcel yesterday. It is very good of you all to send me one again and they are something to look forward to. We are not having very nice weather again, too much wet and mud today. Please write as soon as you feel up to it as I feel I should like a letter from you. Thanking you all for your very nice parcel.

With fondest love, Len

Thursday, 8 November 1917

My dear Edith

... All that I have left of the parcel is the covering — which I use for my mess tin — the tin box and the ointment. One has a little feast when a parcel arrives, like we used to at school, and I am afraid I have an ultra schoolboy appetite now. Yes I got your letter about Char — it is a great shock and I cannot yet realise it. I wish he could have been spared. I wish I could get home to see you all. It will soon be a year now since I came out.

Friday, 16 November 1917

My dear Edith

I am afraid it will be a sad Christmas for most

people this year, but it seems to be a case of endurance and the one who can stand it longest wins. So it is a case of "sticking it".

I have just had a nice cup of tea here. My money chiefly goes on tea, coffee, cocoa or biscuits, which are about half a franc a quarter of a pound packet.

It was like Char to leave everything in order — I am afraid he was the only one with any idea of business amongst the boys of the family. I am glad he left a cup for Stamford School as he was connected with it for such a long time. I think he went there when we first got to Friesthorpe, which is about 28 years ago.

Sunday, 25 November 1917

My dear mother

Very many thanks for your letter with Char's enclosed. I shall be glad of a copy of Char's other letters. I hope you will hear from the Red Cross some particulars of Char, though I suppose it will be some time before you do.

Annie was very ill after she came back from London. She had to stand all the way on the train and couldn't sleep.

Tell Edith I am writing to her at the first opportunity. How do you think her new work suits her? I suppose if one starts on munitions then he or she is bound to carry on with it unless for reasons of ill health.

I started this letter this morning and am

finishing it this evening about eight. It has been very cold, at least there has been a cold wind blowing. I don't think there is any other news I can give you.

With dear love to you and all at home, from your loving son, Len

Pigs and geese were not the only candidates for slaughter. On 19 November all plans for Christmas were put on hold. The 18th London Irish Rifles were on the march with their 47th (London) Division comrades. Rumours of a transfer to Italy sparked excitement in the ranks but they turned out to be unfounded. The riflemen were heading a few miles south-east towards Cambrai, where the final eruption of 1917 was taking place. Attacking at 6.20 a.m. on 20 November, six British divisions smashed a six-mile hole in the Hindenburg Line between the Canal du Nord and the St Quentin Canal. It was a triumph for the tanks, which had been such a failure at Bullecourt seven months earlier. Instead of a dozen hopelessly inadequate machines, this time hundreds bulldozed through the German defences. News of unprecedented early success was greeted with the ringing of church bells throughout England on 23 November.

The gains were of little strategic importance and by the time the cavalry went galloping in with darkness falling the advance had run out of steam and German machine-gunners were waiting. Instead of calling it off after 48 hours, as he had promised if there was no break-through, Sir Douglas Haig ploughed on, sending in more divisions. All he did was create a salient where men and artillery were sitting ducks. Into this unlucky horseshoe, fired on from all sides, marched the men of the 18th London Irish Rifles.

The news from Australia at this time was mostly about Kathleen Mary Reeve Beechey. Chris and Bertha had also almost adopted Harold's girl. Treating Curly as part of the family and giving her a special place in baby Kathleen's life was helping all of them to come to terms with the loss.

27 November 1917
9 Holyrood St

The baby sleeps most of the morning and all night but sometimes insists on crying in the afternoons or evenings. When good she lies and stretches and looks about. Bertha says she takes after me and glares. The nurse has gone and Curly Boyce is staying with us for a few days and then we are going to have a little maid just left school for a few weeks until Bertha is really strong.

I am going to try to have her christened on Advent Sunday if both are well. Curly is to be our Godmother. She is making its christening robe now. I can't get any particulars of pay due to Harold yet but have put it in the hands of a young solicitor, a returned man from the original 1st Aust. Force to take out letters of administration in my name.

* * *

From Salonika, Eric wrote home recalling happier family times. He was still unaware that yet another of his brothers would not be returning from the war.

1 December 1917

Dear Mother

Somehow the usual Christmas wishes seem out of place. Your heart will be full of the old Friesthorpe Christmases when not one was missing, except Maudie, whom I never knew, when the Putney parcel regularly arrived and the box of sweets from Uncle Frank also. When I think of all this I cannot realise that three of the boys have left us. Whatever comfort there is in the season, and from the season, be yours. May the rest of your days be free from pain and more sorrow. May we who are left to you help to lessen the grief for those who are, for a time, lost to you. I am enclosing a P.O. for 10/-. It is but a small sum, I wish it were more.

Amy was touched by Eric's sentiments. The piles of war letters from her lost sons included several that were enough to break any mother's heart. But the most poignant of all arrived at Avondale Street in the second week of December. The tiny envelope resembled one of those from a children's toy post office set. Amy did not recognise the strange handwriting on the front — a nurse or chaplain had addressed it — but it was flagged

432

"On Active Service" so it had to be from Len or Eric. Inside was a scrap of paper with just a few feeble lines:

> No.9 General Hospital, 16 Ward,
> Rouen
> Fri Dec 7, 1917
>
> My darling Mother, don't feel like doing much yet, hope you got my postcards, with lots of love, Len

A similar pitiful message would have reached Annie in south Wales. Within days, Amy received another letter from a hospital chaplain, offering a glimmer of hope.

> 10 December 1917
> Number 9 General Hospital, Rouen
>
> Dear Mrs Beechey
>
> Your son Rifleman L. Beechey, who is now in Ward 16 of this hospital, has asked me to write to you. He is rather severely wounded and had a poor day yesterday, but is much better today. He sends his love and hopes to be in England soon. I gave him Holy Communion this morning.
>
> Yours very truly, Stanley Hide
> Church of England Chaplain

In the days after being uprooted from their comfortable berth near Arras, the London Irish had marched until their feet were raw. Before setting out, they had been ordered to dump all unnecessary baggage so each man carried no more than 35 pounds. They were glad not to be weighed down for the marches that lay ahead. For ten days, Len's battalion and the rest of their division slowly tramped towards the new battlefront.

Other divisions were converging on the same crowded area with column after column of troops and convoys of wheeled and horse-drawn transport. The London Irish swept around Arras in a wide arc, crossing the Bapaume-Peronne road on 25 November as biting wind and sleet battered them from the south-west. Progress was slow but the weather cleared and the sun started to poke through leaden skies as they swung due east towards their objective. Bapaume itself was a mass of guns, lorries, horses and men pouring towards Cambrai. The 47th was to be the ninth division thrown into the new salient.

Len and his fellow riflemen hitched a ride part of the way in a procession of old London buses and charabancs. But the motor vehicles could only progress so far over roads filled with traffic and chewed up by tanks. Next came a wearying plod through liquid mud over unstable tracks and a restless night under bivouac sheets staked out along roadside banks or in the ruins of neighbouring farms — anywhere that provided some shelter from the bitter wind. There was little chance of sleep amid the incessant flash and thunder of their own artillery and the crash of enemy shelling.

Skies cleared the following morning and as the sun came out, the London Irish found a patch of dry, relatively flat ground and summoned the energy to play an impromptu game of football. Bourlon Wood glowered down at them in the distance, its stout trees standing tall and tightly packed together on the eastern horizon. In the coming days Len and his comrades would be sent into the dark woods with rifles, picks and shovels to consolidate the crest line which had been only partly seized in the initial attack at Cambrai on 20 November. A haphazardly organised follow-up assault on 27 November was repulsed with massive casualties to crack Guards regiments. On the night of the 28th, the 47th Division was ordered into the line. Their commanding officer protested that crowding seven of his battalions and forty-seven machine guns into the wood was madness. He argued that it could be defended just as adequately and fewer lives put at risk with a series of well-armed forward outposts covered by machine guns sited in depth outside the wood. He was overruled.

A Rifleman Bunnett, of the London Irish, recalled the eerie march up to Bourlon Wood and the ghastliness awaiting them there: "We almost had to feel our way across the country in the darkness. There were no flares lighting the sky. Shells were falling somewhere a few miles ahead. Came to a halt after walking up a slight rise in the shelter of a spinney of trees and bushes while officer was finding his bearings . . . we had arrived in hell."

Len and his comrades occupied the far side of the wood where it sloped down towards the full strength of the German army, which was hurling everything it could at them. In the misty dawn, they cowered behind broken tree stumps as shells fell all around. Most seemed to be duds and produced only muted explosions. As eyes, lips and tongues began to burn, men fumbled frantically for their masks — the "duds" were spewing out poison gas. Bunnett, a battalion signaller, clattered down the concrete shaft of a deep shelter housing signals HQ — "Everywhere and everything reeked of mustard . . . tea, water, food," he recalled. "Had to remove masks to eat and drink. After the first day everyone was affected. Phosgene gas as well. Company runners bringing up casualty lists were half blinded. Men were so parched with thirst they removed masks to drink gas-saturated water from shell holes. Phosgene was filling their lungs unnoticed. Whine of shells coming into the wood was continuous."

The London Irish had become mixed up in a confused mass of units struggling in dense undergrowth. In the darkness, men in clumsy respirators gulped to breathe as they dug themselves in while high explosive rained down and gas shells poured out poison. The trenches, where they existed at all, were four feet deep with no barbed wire to protect them. After that first awful night when the battalion suffered many casualties, control of the wood passed to Division and its commander immediately thinned out his troops. Three battalions were pulled back to provide defence in depth where they could cover both flanks. The London Irish remained in the firing line.

The bombardment increased in intensity on the morning of 29 November when the shallow, thinly held defences took a further pummelling from gas and explosive shells. London Irish HQ put up an urgent SOS signal in the early dawn light, which brought a reply from the British guns. Despite lack of cover, they kept the enemy pinned down with rifles and Lewis guns.

The 30th of November dawned gloriously sunny, the kind of crisp winter's day on which Len would have loved to stroll across Hampstead Heath with Annie. Instead, his battalion was on the receiving end of another bombardment followed by swarms of German troops pouring over the bare crest line to the west of the wood. As they advanced down the grassy slopes, the wall of field grey provided a target for riflemen and machine-gunners arranged in batteries of four. Two more massed attacks fell on the 47th Division later in the day, driving in the left flank but failing to break the line. When the ground on the left was recaptured German dead lay so thick that the bodies of many men from the London battalions could not be found among them. The London Irish had taken a battering and they would have to cling on for two more days before being relieved.

Len was one of scores of gassed and wounded. Evacuation was an excruciating process in the pandemonium that brought medical services as well as the fighting men to their knees. So many doctors tore off their respirators to treat casualties that they became victims themselves. Motor and horse-drawn ambulances had such trouble reaching the dressing stations amid the congestion that every available vehicle, including water carts, was pressed into service. Walking wounded, temporarily blinded by gas, were a pathetic sight as they shuffled through the wood in single file, up to sixty at a time, each man holding on to the one in front with a Royal Army Medical Corps orderly guiding them. The route for evacuating the wounded was heavily shelled and many were killed before they made it to aid posts. The mounting casualties included seventy members of the RAMC.

Bunnett, Len's signaller comrade, was assigned to deliver despatches between battalion and brigade, reporting on the desperate situation on the far side of the wood — "All the documents I carried were in sealed envelopes so I was unaware of casualties and how serious the crisis had become. The message I now had to transmit in Morse code by Aldis Lamp was clear — managed to establish contact with other lamp two or three miles away and across the void sent message something along the lines of 'Unless reinforcements arrive immediately, must evacuate position'."

Given the order to retreat, the remnants of the London Irish escaped Bourlon Wood along the dry bottom of the Havrincourt Canal with its brick walls, sloping up some 20 feet, providing welcome protection. The battalion, which had marched into the battle nearly a thousand strong, staggered away with fewer than two hundred left to answer roll call.

Bunnett was among the casualties but remained lucid enough to remember the tortuous evacuation process that Len and so many others had to endure. First stop was the Field Dressing Station to await an ambulance. "When it was my turn," Bunnett recalled, "I had two stretcher cases with me. I was a sitting case, planted on a little seat with my back to the driver. It was dark and rain was falling as we drove into the dressing station entirely under canvas at Achiet le Grand. Ambulance stopped inside the camp and the stretchers were carried to a huge, crowded marquee — MOs examining the sick and wounded, orderlies rushing around, men crying out. Examined and given a label like a kid on a Sunday school outing, then handed a Dorothy bag for personal possessions. Bags made at voluntary sewing parties by good ladies at home. Eight inches by 12 with a drawstring at the neck — mine was pink with a pattern of tiny flowers on it. Put wallet, fountain pen, little pocket bible and other oddments in it. Orderly took my pack away — with greatcoat, tobacco, fuse cap I'd found at Arras and French paperback *La Femme Amoureuse* — and labelled it, saying it would be sent on to me. Never saw it again."

He was taken once more by ambulance to the rail station at Achiet and lifted on to a waiting train, still wearing his lice-ridden khaki clothing. "Somehow these were removed and found myself lying between cool clean white sheets and covered by a clean blanket. Angels in white appeared but disappeared to shelters when air raid siren sounded. It was dark when train pulled up at Rouen. It was an old French hospital — I never did learn where I lay in Rouen. I can see the ward now. My bed was in a corner facing a doorway through which doctors and nursing sisters came and went. Given hot drinks. Rouen is a city of bells. In the hospital their notes rang out through the quiet ward. In the morning the nurses wiped our hands and faces with moist cloths and cool, fresh towels. Took temperatures and provided soup and hot drinks but no solid food for gas cases." While Bunnett was on board a hospital ship slipping down the river Seine on the way home to England, Len was fated to remain in the "city of bells".

Ground that had been so hard won at Bourlon Wood and defended at such cost was "very regrettably" given up to the enemy in a strategic withdrawal to what was termed a main line of resistance for the winter. It had dawned on the high command that artillery and men were caught in a death trap and they began pulling back on 4 December. Army GHQ later took the unusual step of producing a pamphlet entitled *The Story of a Great Fight*, which was a tribute to the troops who repulsed those determined assaults of mass German infantry on 30 November. It noted, "At the end of this day of high courage and glorious achievement, except for a few advanced positions some of which were afterwards regained, our line had been maintained intact. The men who had come triumphantly through this contest felt, and rightly felt, that they had won a great victory, in which the enemy had come against them in his full strength and had been defeated with losses at which even the victors stood aghast." German burial parties would still be on the slopes below Bourlon Wood in January.

Scrooge — The Skinflint at the picture house and *Dick Whittington and His Cat* on stage in the seasonal pantomime lent an air of normality to Christmas time in Lincoln. A store-owner was fined for flouting blackout rules and a mother of ten was in court for flinging a bag of sugar in the face of a shopkeeper who had refused to give her more than her ration. It was a dark and cheerless Christmas in blacked-out Avondale Street. There had been no more letters from Len. If he could have lifted pen or pencil, Amy knew he would have sent word.

Weeks had gone by since his last note. The hospital chaplain had spoken of some improvement but mention of Holy Communion made Amy fear the worst. The only way they would have found out more was if Annie had travelled to France to be at her husband's side. Mothers and wives were sometimes granted this privilege, usually in cases where a man was not too horrifically injured but had little hope of recovery. A year earlier, as Frank lay on his deathbed, the War Office had stipulated no visitors. Annie had taken every chance to be with Len those fleeting weekends when he was still training at Morn Hill near Winchester. If the army gave her the opportunity, she would surely have wanted to be with him. But even if she did make that lonely journey from south Wales to the base hospital in Rouen it is doubtful if Len would have had the strength to hold her hand, let alone tell her what he had been through. Before 1917 was out, there was one more letter from France addressed to Mrs Amy Beechey.

29 December

Dear Mrs Beechey
I am very sorry to have to tell you your son Leonard died here this morning of the effects of

his wounds. He was unfortunately far from well at the time he was hit; tetanus set in about ten days ago and he got gradually worse. He had Holy Communion on Christmas Day and once before while he was here. He is to be buried at St Sever Cemetery, Rouen, tomorrow. May God bless and comfort you and grant him rest.

Yours very truly, Stanley Hide
Church of England Chaplain

CHAPTER
SIXTEEN

The worst of fortune

Len had loved, cared for, entertained and amused
Annie. At forty-one years old and widowed for a second
time, Annie must have known her chances of finding
such happiness again were remote. She travelled to
Lincoln, a sad and forlorn figure. Edie remembered her
mother trying to comfort her distraught daughter-in-
law as best she could, while Annie mumbled over and
over, "There's nothing left — there's nothing left, you
see."

After being plunged into the appalling battle for
Bourlon Wood, it might have been something as
seemingly harmless as Len's toenail surgery of a few
months earlier that contributed to his death. Tetanus
bacteria, which flourished in earth contaminated by the
detritus of war, penetrated wounds and thrived
particularly on nail lesions of the foot. Doctors in
shambolic aid posts and dressing stations with no
chance of washing their hands also spread infection. By
the time they cut off muddy uniforms to reach wounds
they would be as filthy as their patient. It wasn't until
1918 that immunisation became widespread, thanks to
a pioneering Canadian doctor who produced the

tetanus antitoxin for 34 cents a dose, a fifth of what America's pharmaceutical giants were charging. A serum had been available but it was not enough to save Len, if he ever received it. Once tetanus set in, he suffered a terrible end, racked by violent spasms and burning temperatures, struggling to swallow and to breathe. Annie would not have wanted to see the face she remembered for its warmth and tenderness become a rigid mask, turning blue for want of oxygen.

Amy, a fifth son now dead, was in fragile health. Her condition could not have been helped by the small parcel wrapped in brown paper that arrived from Australian Imperial Force headquarters in London's Horseferry Road. It contained the few personal effects Harold carried when he was killed — pair of hairbrushes, language book, wallet cover, letters, three writing pads and photograph, the picture of Curly he kept close to his heart. The letters were probably from Curly as well.

Neither mother nor sweetheart would have the consolation of knowing Harold's final resting place. Today, his is one name among almost 11,000 on the walls of the Australian National Memorial at Villers-Bretonneux on the Somme. A mile or so across the fields from Bullecourt and well away from the coach tours is Quéant Road war cemetery, as immaculate and serene as any of those that grace the old battlefields. Skirted by a narrow lane, it is ringed by farm fields and guarded by two lines of trees. Close to the entrance, in the shadow of the Cross of Sacrifice, is a headstone with the words, "He died for the greatest cause in history — ever remembered". It is the grave of Major B. B. Leane, 48th Battalion, Australian Infantry, died 10 April 1917. Surrounding Ben Leane are 2,300 other graves, of which 1,400 belong to unidentified soldiers, almost half of whom are Australians. It cannot be too fanciful to imagine that one of those pale pillars of Portland stone, simply inscribed "A soldier of the Great War — Known unto God", marks the last resting place of Lance Corporal H. R. Beechey, 48th Battalion, AIF, died 10 April 1917.

There were still outstanding issues to be settled regarding Harold's financial affairs, but his brother was taking care of those in Australia. Chris had only just heard about Char's death in East Africa and did not yet know about Len.

16 January 1918
9 Holyrood St, West Leederville

Dear Mother

I got both your and Katie's letter telling us that Char had died of wounds in East Africa. I hardly expected it, like you. I thought he was in less danger. I think you are quite wrong in not applying for a pension. The idea of not benefiting from their deaths is quite erroneous as any pension they grant you will not half compensate for their loss. The loss of four sons and the loss of the feeling of security for yourself until the end of your days that you had while they were alive, especially as all of them were unmarried and contributed to your expenses, can never adequately be replaced by a pension.

I see by the papers that several of last year's mails are missing so in case you didn't hear Bertha had a little girl on 3rd Nov after a bad period of labour. The little girl was born with plenty of black hair, which is turning brown, and a typical Beechey type — she was much like Daisy when she was born. Her eyes are remaining blue and will be like yours and Len's and she has a remarkable resemblance to Harold at times. She is the joy of our lives.

We had a terribly trying heatwave last week, muggy and thundery, leaving the atmosphere as hot after the storm as before. Three days, 102, 106 and 108 in the shade. I'm still about the same — I can't do much in the heat in the exercising way as I'm dead tired at nights but I work and potter around in the garden and fowl yard whenever it's cool. I will try to write twice a month in future and hope you or the girls will write.

Love to all at home, Chris

In public schools up and down the land, patriotic fervour was undiminished by more than three years of wasted life. Hymns and prayers for the fallen rang out in the chapels while minds bursting with mathematics and classics turned to ways of honouring the dead. Char had ensured his name would live on through the cricketing trophy he bequeathed to Stamford in his will. Canon Day, the head, paid warm tribute to his late maths master, declaring, "Those who knew him here will rejoice to think that he was as much appreciated in the Army as he was at school to which he devoted the whole of his time and energies. In the schoolroom he insisted on hard work and in the games on hard play, being always ready to set the example in both. The games were his great hobby — whether it was football, sports or cricket, he was indefatigable, and would do anything to stimulate and improve them. Of a modest, retiring disposition, he was content to live for the school and in the school. Only those who knew him intimately appreciated the sterling worth of his character. There was nothing showy about him but he was absolutely sound. His dogged determination during his last days was typical. No man had a higher standard of loyalty and it was this which won the affection of his intimates and which rendered him the devoted son that he was of his widowed mother. To her we can but extend our heartfelt sympathy. Few can have been more sorely tried than she, seeing that she has now lost five sons in the war. To us the tragedy comes home when we realise that C. R. Beechey was the last survivor of the old staff, and he too has now followed the others who gave their all for their country."

Mr Rea, an older schoolmaster who had arrived at Stamford early in the war when the likes of Wood and Cowie left to join up, wrote to Amy with his condolences. "I merely wanted to tell you how sincerely I shared the sorrow that fell upon his friends at the news of Charles's death," he said. "In the short time during which I had the privilege of his acquaintance we came pretty close together, and our regular interchange of letters after his joining up had, I hoped, cemented what at my age is admittedly rare — a new friendship. Well, my friend is gone, and the world is the poorer for the loss of a good man."

It would be another twelve years before plans for a lasting monument at Stamford came to fruition — the memorial chapel was not consecrated until 21 June 1930. Charles, Barnard and Leonard Beechey are all remembered there. They are among the fifty-one masters and pupils killed in the First World War whose names are on the roll of honour carved out of wood panels on either side of the altar.

From Wotton-under-Edge, Amy received notice that Bar was also to be commemorated at Katharine Lady Berkeley's Grammar School. She was invited to supply particulars of his death "if not too painful to you, as his memory among some of the older scholars is still green". Bar, along with Frank, was to be honoured on the memorial to the fallen at St John's School, Leatherhead, as well. The names of Dorchester Grammar's lost masters and pupils are inscribed on memorial boards that adorn the staircase leading to the humanities department. Sadly missing is any mention of their discredited former first assistant master, Sgt B. R. Beechey. However, Bar was fondly remembered by his former Wotton-under-Edge teaching colleague Mary Webb, who had lost touch with him more than ten years earlier. She, too, contacted Amy, begging forgiveness "in that I, a stranger, write to you and recall to your memory many sorrowful days. I was the first mistress appointed on the staff of the KLB Grammar School and worked in the same building as your eldest son, Barnard Reeve Beechey, leaving the school in July 1907, one term before he resigned. I heard very little about him after my departure, and at length the news came to me that he had given his life. More I did not hear, though I longed to know more because he was my friend and it would then have been easier to pray for him. He is constantly in my prayers. Today at the Eucharist suddenly the idea was flashed into my mind that I might be able to visit his grave. On Wednesday next I leave England for Strasbourg where I expect to study at the university for a month to six weeks. If you feel you can do so, will you kindly let me know where he fell and was buried, so that if it is not too far for me to travel in the time at my disposal, I may go and pray for his soul there where he is at peace. I apologise for writing to you and hope I have not caused you pain. I believe that was not your only loss in the war . . ."

By the time Miss Webb travelled to France, Bar's final resting place in Flanders, if it was ever identified, had been obliterated by a further two and a half years of fighting.

Meanwhile, news of one family's extraordinary sacrifice had spread to America, whose own sons, fathers and husbands were pouring across the Atlantic in their tens of thousands. The United States declared war on Germany on 6 April 1917 and the first doughboys landed in France in June, although US forces would not be ready to take the field for almost another year. In the small town of Clifton, Illinois, the local newspaper, *The Advocate*, carried a front-page story under the heading "Knew British Heroes". Running alongside a list of the latest 148 men from Iroquois County to be drafted, it told how, "The following London news item in Tuesday's *Chicago Tribune* was of especial interest to Mr and Mrs Edwin Hobson of Clifton because they knew all the parties mentioned":

GAVE EIGHT SONS

BRITISH WIDOW FIVE TIMES BEREAVED IN WAR

The countless numbers of heroic sacrifices made by British mothers have been eclipsed by Mrs Beechey, widow of the Rev. P. W. T. Beechey, who was vicar of Friesthorpe, Lincolnshire. She has given eight sons to serve their country, five of whom have been slain. Three have been killed on the Western Front, another died at Rouen, while the fifth, Charles Reeve Beechey of the Royal Fusiliers, who was a master at Stamford Grammar School, has died of wounds suffered in East Africa. One son, Bernard [sic] Beechey, was a schoolmaster at Lincoln, and another, Frank, was a master of the Lincoln Cathedral Choir School. Three other sons survive. Of these, one has been paralyzed and the two others are still serving. All the brothers joined up as volunteers, two of them enlisting in Australia where they were farming.

* * *

"Mr Hobson made the acquaintance of the Reverend Mr Beechey and family on his first trip to England 15 years ago. Their home was just across the lane from his cousin's and the first evening he was there he attended a garden party given by their church. On later trips both he and Mrs Hobson spent evenings in the vicar's home, getting to know all of the eight boys, who were exceptionally bright and manly. The Hobsons had received letters recently bearing the news given in the dispatch published."

The *Chicago Tribune* story moved a Mr C. C. Robinson, postmaster and storekeeper — "Best Grades of Flour, Most Anything You Want" — of Hagaman, Illinois, to put distinctly flowery pen to paper, "To Mrs Beechey, Friesthorpe, England . . .

"Dear Madam," he wrote, "I have just read in one of our leading newspapers a statement that you are the mother of five sons who have died gloriously on the field of battle. I feel how weak and fruitless must be any words of mine which should attempt to beguile you from the grief of a loss so overwhelming. But I cannot refrain from writing you and from tending you the consolation that may be found that they died to save your country. I pray that our Heavenly Father may assuage the anguish of your bereavement and leave you only the cherished memory of the loved and lost, and the solemn pride that must be yours to have paid so costly a sacrifice upon the altar of freedom. Yours very sincerely, C. C. Robinson."

To "Post Master, Groceries, Dry Goods, Shoes, Hardware" on C. C. Robinson's headed notepaper could be added shameless plagiarist. His message of sympathy was a rip-off of President Abraham Lincoln's famous "Bixby Letter" to a mother who had supposedly lost five sons in the American Civil War. Another sympathiser from deepest Illinois had already sent Amy a copy of Lincoln's 1864 letter, stating, "I think your 'solemn pride' must be a wonderful possession and, as a single woman, I envy you, since it is far better to have eight brave volunteer sons, even when five give their lives, and one his health, than to have no son to give at all."

Other complete strangers sent messages to Amy, most expressing the sincere hope that her remaining sons would be spared to return to her. Young Sam, the baby of the family, started officer training at army cadet school in Trowbridge, Wiltshire, on 22 February 1918. He had celebrated his 18th birthday the previous August. Now that he was old enough, Sam saw no reason not to serve. The authorities also saw no reason for him not to serve. If his mother begged to differ, she did not intervene to try to have her eighth and youngest son exempted from military service or assigned to the home front.

A slight figure at 5 feet 6 inches tall and weighing just 116 pounds, Sam set down his preferences as first, the artillery, second, the infantry and third, the Royal Flying Corps. After being accepted for the artillery he had almost five months of training at Trowbridge followed by another five weeks at gunnery school. His temporary commission would be announced in the *London Gazette* on 18 August and a month before the war ended he would be posted to France.

The only official acknowledgement of the losses Amy had suffered came in the consoling words on the official War Office bereavement cards routinely sent out to grieving parents and widows across the land, stating, "The King commands me to assure you of the true sympathy of His Majesty and The Queen in your sorrow." They were signed by Lord Kitchener, whose own death at sea had so shocked the nation in 1916, and later by his successor as Secretary of State for War, Lord Derby. The King and Queen would soon have the opportunity to express the nation's gratitude to Amy Beechey in more personal terms. Meanwhile, Chris had almost sorted out Harold's financial affairs and was only just learning that Len, the brother with whom he had shared his school days and his mundane working life at the Railway Clearing House, had gone the way of Bar, Frank, Harold and Char.

6 March
9 Holyrood St

Dear Mother

I employed a solicitor to do all the business re Harold's estate and it is just about finished. He had £39 to draw deferred pay and about £94, which he left in the Commonwealth Bank. Solicitor's fees will come to about four guineas and I'm cabling the money left in the bank to you and all of it if I get the other in time — there ought to be about £125 or more for you. I had to miss my usual train this morning and as there's not another for two hours and today's mail day, I'm writing. I hope you all at home are well and not in any distress. I'm cabling the money in case you are in any need. I want you to use it for your own and the girls' comfort and convenience during the war and I'm sure that was the wish of Harold. Bertha and Kathleen are well and the hot nights are past for this year. The rains should be here soon and I'm thinking of the garden again.

Love to all, Chris

27 March

9 Holyrood St

I got yours and Edie's letters yesterday saying Len had died of wounds. We seem to have the worst of fortune. Give my sympathy to Annie when you write. I can't write a long letter as I'm busy before Easter and the mail goes midday. I fixed up all Harold's affairs and had the money cabled to you. In one letter I discussed your disinclination to apply for a pension; let me again advise you to do what I consider both moral and just and do it straight away.

I hope you are bearing all these losses well. Considering their disposition it seems inevitable that they all should have gone. I feel the greatest longing myself, staggering about as I do, to be in it again, especially as the Big German Push has started. I'll send a photo of baby soon — she'll be a regular little Beechey, only brown hair with your blue eyes.

His mother was reluctant or too proud even to claim the paltry war pension she was due for each of her unmarried sons who had died. When, at Chris's behest, she eventually applied for what was rightfully hers she had to enlist the help of the Liberal MP for Lincoln, Charles Henry Roberts, to prise the money from the government. She was to find a staunch ally and friend in the MP's wife, Lady Cecilia Roberts, daughter of the late 9th Earl of Carlisle whose estates included Castle Howard in Yorkshire and the Barony of Gisland, comprising twenty manors in what is now Cumbria. They met for the first time when they stood side by side, the 62-year-old silver-haired bereaved mother and widow from a terraced house in Lincoln and the titled lady of immense wealth and property, to be introduced to King George V and Queen Mary.

The royal summons arrived at Avondale Street, dated 5 April 1918. It reached Amy despite the unhappy knack the authorities had of sending vital correspondence to her neighbours — this time it was addressed to number 15, instead of 14. Even poor Harold's parcel of personal possessions had been sent to number 28. Headed "Royal Visit", the belated invitation said, "The Mayor desires me to inform you that subject to your approval he proposes to include your name in the list of those to be presented to Their Majesties at the Guildhall at 11:45 a.m. on Tuesday next. Kindly let me know if this is agreeable to you. Those who are to be presented should be at the Guildhall by 10:45." Amy had three days to prepare for her big day. Edie and daughter-in-law Mary insisted on taking her out to buy a new hat for the occasion.

On the Tuesday morning, 9 April, the King arrived in Lincoln by royal train wearing the undress uniform of a British Field Marshal. The Queen wore blue with a feather toque of the same colour. She had on a diamond brooch, which had been a wedding present from the county of Lincolnshire. The day began with a flying visit to an aircraft factory, then it was on to a tank testing ground where the King demanded to be taken on a joyride over the most awkward terrain. His Majesty clambered through the tiny door in the side like an excited schoolboy and the machine lurched into action, scaling slopes with its nose to the sky and then plunging down a drop on the other side. After a quarter of an hour, the King emerged to cheers from the large crowd and informed the Queen, "The motion was nothing like so bad as a destroyer in a heavy sea. I have been able to judge of the conditions under which the officers and men man the tanks in action. We all owe them admiration and gratitude for what they are doing."

From tanks, it was on to the Guildhall where half an hour had been set aside to meet fifty worthy citizens, including Amy. She was introduced to Their Majesties as "the widow of a Lincolnshire clergyman who had eight sons, five of whom have been killed during the war, one maimed and is helpless for life; the other two now serving". Her slim figure, all in black, topped by her new hat which was rather reminiscent of those worn by Tower of London Beefeaters, was captured in a photograph that appeared in London's *Daily Graphic*. Behind her stood a gaggle of onlookers, unashamed "rubber-neckers", stretching for a glimpse of the mother who gave five sons for King and Country.

It was almost a year to the day since Harold was killed at snowswept Bullecourt. She had lost two more sons since then but if she felt anger she did not show it when Their Majesties thanked her for her sacrifice before moving on to Lady Baker of Dunstable, who was next in line. A week later it was Amy's sixty-third birthday, remembered from far away by the other son she would never see again.

> 16 April — your birthday
> 9 Holyrood St

The first of your birthdays I remember was 1890 when someone mentioned it about teatime I think the first day we got to Friesthorpe. So you see I can look back 30 years. I've got most of your letters lately. I hope long before you get this that you have received Harold's money.

I trust you are well and have got over the shock of all these losses. How are the girls? They don't say much about themselves. Is Sam still in England, has he got his commission? I often feel ashamed of myself jogging along out here in safety with plenty to eat. I suppose it wasn't my fault I didn't see it out longer but I somehow feel that I ought to be where an occasional bomb or shell falls just to show my contempt of them, their frightfulness and all their filthy ways of fighting. Hitting below the belt as we say.

11 July
9 Holyrood St

I got Edie's letter saying you had been presented to the King and Queen at the Guildhall, Lincoln, and wrote to a firm of newspaper importers asking them to keep me some with any reference to or pictures of the presentation. Love to all at home — hope you all are well and not in much distress. We all three are well.

Love from Bertha, your loving son, Chris

15 August
9 Holyrood St

I'm glad to hear you are all right as regards food, especially the gooseberry pie. We hardly ever see English gooseberries out here. I cabled Harold's money three or four weeks ago. I'm glad that the MP for Lincoln has taken up the question of your pension (Mr Roberts, isn't it?).

Sam finished his officer training on 17 August. "A very fair cadet — not quite up to average standard," was the somewhat harsh verdict at the end of a report studded with "Good" and "Very Good" for the various disciplines. He was gazetted the following day and joined the Royal Garrison Artillery as a second lieutenant. With talk of a German peace offer in the air, his mother took comfort in the string of letters from him postmarked "Hampshire". But in October her heart sank with the first correspondence from her youngest boy marked "On Active Service".

21 October
BEF, France

Dear Mother

As you see by the above address I have arrived in France. We went to a camp just outside the town where we landed and went through gas and drew tin hats. We stayed there Thursday and Friday and on Saturday morning 8a.m. started on a railway journey. We were not told where we were going and got to the wrong place. It was now 11.40 at night so we scraped a meal and went to sleep in the train. I think I was one of the few who saw anything funny in it all. Then the train started again and we went back to a place we had passed about 12 midday the day before. So here we are waiting to be posted. I expect we shall leave here tomorrow or the following day.

We are here at the 4th Army Reinforcement camp and living in tents. It's not a bad life. There is a cathedral in the town supposed to be one of the best in France but nothing compared with Lincoln. One or two shells have hit it but it's not badly damaged. But it is nearly hidden by sandbags. We are doing nothing at all here but waiting for orders.

Well, au revoir. Will write when I get an address. Tons of love, your loving son, Samuel

24 October
168 Siege Battery, 68 Brigade, RGA
BEF, France

Dear Mother

At last I have arrived at my battery after a week mucking about during which time I have not spent two nights in the same place. I was overjoyed to discover that my battery was having a rest. We are doing absolutely nothing just at present, which suits me. Please send all the things I have asked for in my various letters, chiefly socks. Also suggest to Edie that I am very partial to cigarettes. I hope Doris got home all right. Please tell me how you like her as I am anxious to know.

Please write as soon as you get this and as often as possible afterwards. Arrange the family in shifts so that I get at least one letter from home per day. It will be quite easy because it will mean each of you writing only about once per week.

We get very good food over here — white bread whiter than I have seen for years and also unlimited sugar and butter, so you see we don't do too badly in that respect. The villages round here are comparatively intact. There are even civilians living in the houses. There is a family living in the house where I am billeted. I say "Bonjour Madame" and she gives me a cup of coffee in the morning when I roll out about 9a.m. Well goodbye muvver dear.

With lots of love, your loving son, Sam

November 3
168 Siege Battery
BEF, France

I haven't yet received any letters but I hope for one every post now. Life here isn't at all bad. It calls for very little bodily exertion. We get about two days' work and three days off. Today is one of the off days. I am very well except for a bit of a cold. The weather has changed and the last day or so has been cold and damp. If I don't get a letter soon I shall strike. I must have written about twenty to different people since I left England and haven't yet received one.

I see Turkey and Austria are out of it and I give Fritz credit for enough sense to see that it's not much use going on much longer.

"Fritz" in fact went on for a further eight days, as did the killing on both sides. Sam's next letter, dated 9 November, arrived on the day of the armistice. It was accompanied by a cheque for his mother to cover the consignments of socks she was sending out to France, and included news that Sam had at last received a few letters from home.

Anxious days passed during which Amy heard nothing more. As she fretted, the rest of the nation celebrated. After fifty-two months of hostilities, one

Lincoln local weekly newspaper was understandably carried away by the prospect of peace. "Sunshine gilded all. It shone on the grey cathedral towers. It danced on work and home. The Witham flashed and sparkled. All nature rejoiced," it twittered on the day of the armistice. "Wives who had lost husbands, mothers who had lost their sons joined in the rejoicing — the sacrifice was crowned with victory."

Amy, her daughters and Len's Annie might not have agreed with the sentiment. The victory flag was raised over the Guildhall in Lincoln and the mayor addressed the throng from a window. Cathedral bells rang out and the band of the Lincolnshire Regiment led the celebrations, playing "Tipperary" and "Mademoiselle from Armentières". All day, an airman buzzed the city, looping the loop in triumph. The newspapers were happy to record that there were none of the "bestial orgies" that followed the relief of Mafeking during the Boer War.

With the backing of her MP, Amy had been granted her war pension and had written to Lady Cecilia Roberts to thank her for her support. The MP's wife was too "overwhelmed with influenza anxieties" to reply immediately. A Spanish flu pandemic had claimed more than 2,200 lives in London alone in October, more than all the German air raids during four years of war. It was sweeping the world, including the Western Front, where it would kill more of the recently arrived American troops than German shells or bullets. Before running its course it would bring further distress to the Beechey family.

From her London home in swish Holland Park, Lady Cecilia confessed to "My dear Mrs Beechey" how she had been worried about one of her own girls who had been struck down by the deadly flu but was now on the mend. "The pension," admitted Her Ladyship, "is miserably small. I wish it were otherwise. You are very brave and very gracious over all that concerns you — you set a great example to us all."

Lady Cecilia also recognised how the end of the war was sure to bring its own tribulations . . . "This time of peace is in some ways a very hard one for those to bear, who have lost those they love — you have been so kind to me that I make bold to write and say what all will feel, that the fallen that have died for us live more in our hearts even than the living, and that we honour them with a reverence and homage too deep for words. I am glad that the bright, attractive boy I met at your house will be safe." She was talking about Sam.

On the eleventh hour of the eleventh day of the eleventh month the guns had fallen silent, although the occasional rogue blast was heard as batteries competed to fire the last shot of the war. From France, dated a week after the armistice, came confirmation that Sam had survived his three weeks or so in the front line.

18 November
25 Siege Battery
BEF, France

Well, Mother dear!

The war is over at last and I hope it won't be very long before peace is declared and I get home.

I suppose I may not tell you why I have been changed from 168 Battery but I am pleased I have been — it may mean that I get out quicker. I told you that the fighting would be over by Christmas. I am writing to Edie, Katie and Winifrede — I spend quite a lot of time writing letters cos Doris sends me one <u>every day</u>.

18 November
25 Siege Battery
BEF, France

Dear Winifrede

Many thanks for your two nice letters. We had a thanksgiving service on the 14th, the whole of three brigades of RGA were there and it was a very impressive service except the padre couldn't preach for nuts. Also the service was a bit of a mongrel — you see they daren't have a proper Anglican service for fear of offending the heretics who were there. So glad you liked Doris . . . So Billy and Frances [sister Fanny and her husband] are coming but there's one thing I disapprove of. Mother should not sleep in the attic. It's cold up there and she'll have lumbago and all sorts of things. Let Billy and Frances sleep up there — it won't hurt them.

Ever your loving Bro', Sam

He wrote to his mother again a few days later to thank her for a parcel containing yet more socks and for the letter dated the 11th. "<u>Great day, the 11th</u>. What would

I have given to have been in England . . . but I suppose I shan't get back to Blighty for a month or two." That forecast proved optimistic. Sam had hoped his transfer to another battery would lead to an early demobilisation. But he would be sending letters from France with a growing frustration for several months to come. Rather enviously, he noted how soldiers in England were receiving twelve days off for Christmas while the earliest he could expect leave was the following March.

For the first time, Amy would have none of her boys with her at Christmas. The military authorities seemed in no great rush to reunite her with her two surviving sons still serving in the army. Eric, stuck in Salonika, had a wife and family waiting for him. He, too, would have to sit and stew until well into 1919 before they sent him home to acquaint himself with the son and daughter he recognised thanks only to the treasured snaps Mary sent him during the years he was away. As well as his children, Spanish flu would also be waiting to greet Eric when he got back.

CHAPTER
SEVENTEEN

In proud and grateful memory

Fifty-two months of killing were over but Sam's Royal Garrison Artillery battery remained in France on salvage duties or, as often as not, doing absolutely nothing — "The easiest five shillings a day that was ever earned," he called it. As the unit's newest officer and still only nineteen, he was usually left to hold the fort while his seniors went off on jaunts to Brussels and other places that were bursting back into life. In January 1919 Sam wrote to register for a course on commercial or industrial chemistry at university in England, hoping to wangle an earlier discharge from the army as a student. Within weeks, it was being whispered that his battery would be shifting to the Rhineland as part of the army of occupation, in which case Sam told his mother he would stay on in Germany and go to college in Cologne, if possible.

In March, his battery did indeed move on, either to guard the Rhine bridgeheads or into Belgium. Sam was not sure which, but they left him behind in France to bemoan the lack of correspondence from the rest of the family. Brother Eric, in particular, could not win. When he did write, Sam complained it was "about the first letter in which he hasn't assumed I was still 15". When he didn't write, Sam urged his mother, "Just remind him he's got a brother, will you?" But his affection for the brother he had once been keen to poison in days gone by at Friesthorpe was apparent as he confessed to Amy, "I am getting quite anxious to see him — still, I s'pose we shall all be demobilised sometime."

Both were home by the time Chris wrote again from Australia on notepaper headed "The Returned Sailors', Soldiers' and Nurses' Association of WA — Leederville Branch, Hon Secretary: C. W. R. Beechey". On the other side of the world, the reality of the land fit for heroes was as harsh as in Britain, and Chris, despite his disabilities, became active in battling for the rights of those returning from the war.

28 May 1919
9 Holyrood St

Dear Mother

I made all sorts of resolutions that I would write every week after the armistice was signed. Like most of my New Year resolutions I didn't keep it. We had some excuse. Quarantine regulations have been very strict in the West. Successfully so, as we have kept the flu out for the last six months and we are still free from it. We've had wharf trouble here too at Fremantle as no doubt you've read in the papers. Another thing, I'm head of the Returned Soldiers' Association. We are not getting a fair deal. A lot of distress and disappointment here and only half our men back. Promises by the public and employers not kept and preference to returned soldiers not carried out while slackers and stay-at-homes are in cushy jobs. We are having a conference and ballot now as to whether we shall enter all industrial disputes in which returned soldiers are concerned and whether we shall become a political organisation. I think both are sure to be carried in the affirmative.

Fortunately for me I have been in constant work since I came out — still a temporary clerk in the accounts branch of the state railway. When I tell you that although five permanent salaried officers in our branch have been killed on active service and one has retired at age limit and that I applied to be the first to be appointed permanent and was told officially that the position would be reviewed when all are back and was told unofficially that there was no vacancy on the permanent salaried staff, you can see even in my case the need for a Returned Soldiers' Association.

To come back to domestic affairs, Kathleen is just about 18 months and as pretty as can be. She has your blue eyes and laughs and talks to herself all day. Curly Bailey said that Harold in several of his letters spoke highly of me and showed that he held me in much affection. I suppose those excerpts formed part of his love letters to her and I didn't ask for them to be shown me or extracted from the bodies of the letters though they gave me great consolation and happiness when I read of his death in the paper. She has since become engaged to a rather elderly admirer and no doubt destroyed his letters.

If it's not too much for you, will you let me have our war record? I mean the rank, number, company, regiment, where served, when wounded or killed, from Bar down to Sam, as I have no complete record. Though my memory is good now it wasn't when I left England and maybe I shall forget them without having them in black and white. I would like to think that a memorial was put up in Friesthorpe Church but would like it to include Father, who in my opinion was the greatest man of all.

Though only seven years older than Harold, I felt in a sort of way a youthful guardian to him. I went away with him, saw him frequently and will always regret that I was not in the same brigade when he went west. I can assure you he was a white man right through. Some day, if it meets your approval, I will write a record of him in the form of a brochure from his enlistment in September 1914 to his death in April 1917.

Love to all. Your loving son, Chris

If Chris ever did write Harold's story for posterity it has been lost over the eighty-five years since he set down his intentions. In common with his other two brothers who came home from the war, he rarely, if ever, spoke of those times.

Eric was taken ill almost as soon as he returned from Salonika. Whole swathes of the population were being wiped out by the so-called Spanish Lady, including men who survived more than four years of war only to die of influenza. Undertakers ran out of coffins to bury the dead, estimated at between 150,000 and 200,000 in Britain. When Eric's flu turned to pneumonia, the family feared the worst. Mary, who still had Katie around to help keep domestic order, had only just got her husband back. It was touch and go whether she would lose him for good and whether Amy would be robbed of yet another son. But Eric pulled through and his path to civilian life turned out to be smoother than that of many other ex-servicemen. After recovering he joined a dental practice in Yeovil and moved his family to Somerset. Sister Katie only left them when they uprooted again, this time to Bridgwater. It was after the start of another war that they settled in Trowbridge, Wiltshire, where tragedy would once more strike with the death of son Tom from pneumonia.

In later years, Eric liked to show visiting nephews and nieces around his surgery, sitting them in the dentist's chair and declaring, "Now I just want to have a look at your teeth. I don't get much opportunity to look at other dentists' work." Eric only spoke of his brothers in connection with happier days at Friesthorpe rectory. He never talked about his years in the army and he would never watch films or plays or read books about the war. He could not bear even to hear the old songs from that time, recalled his daughter Joan.

In Australia, Chris's tireless work on behalf of ex-servicemen and women earned him a place on the Returned Sailors and Soldiers Imperial League state executive. Two years after Amy Beechey was presented to the King and Queen in Lincoln, Chris, representing the league, was introduced to the future King Edward VIII, who stopped off in Perth in July 1920 at the climax of a hugely popular victory tour of the colony.

In Western Australia, there had been the same initial euphoria over the end of the war with parades, speeches, flag-waving and much singing. "We'll Hang the Kaiser from a Sour Apple Tree" competed with "God Save the King" and "Australia the Fair" for most popular ditty on the day the armistice was announced by the mayor of Perth from a window at the *Daily News* offices. But rejoicing had long since been replaced by rancour and industrial strife. Butchers, civil servants, tram workers and lumpers, who loaded the grain ships at Fremantle docks, all went on strike.

The arrival of the "Digger Prince" rekindled some of the old comradeship and patriotism. Edward had become a favourite with the Australian troops he met during the war while serving as a staff officer in the Grenadier Guards in France and Egypt. His official duties while in Perth included presenting the mother of one of Harold's officers with a bar to the Military Cross — in effect, a second MC. Captain D. G. C. Cumming of the 48th Battalion had won it at Bullecourt. He was killed at Monument Wood, Villers-Bretonneux, in 1918.

Chris was one of 3,000 old soldiers, mostly Great War survivors but some going back as far as the Indian

Mutiny of 1857, packed into His Majesty's Theatre, Perth. "It had the atmosphere of a reunion of old friends," according to one commentator. The prince was met at the stage door by the president of the returned soldiers who guided him along the line of the league's state executive. Chris, supported by his sticks, clearly held no grudge because he wrote and told his mother he very much liked the look of the Prince of Wales and was impressed by his "unaffected manner" when they shook hands.

General Sir Talbot Hobbs, representing the AIF, remarked that the prince had been admitted to the honourable fraternity of diggers, "than which no higher mark of esteem and affection could be paid". As Edward rose to respond, he got three huge cheers and a rousing rendition of "For he's a jolly good fellow". He told the massed ranks, "I am first of all very grateful for the address presented to me on behalf of West Australian branch of the Returned Sailors and Soldiers Imperial League of Australia, of which I am very proud to be patron-in-chief ... I think your president has been rigging me rather and I have not yet been long enough in Perth to get my own back! I am very glad of the opportunity of seeing so many diggers. I think this is not the first time I have met many of you. I am sorry I cannot shake hands with all of you but that, you will realise, is impossible. Let me congratulate you on your war behaviour. The fact that nine West Australians gained the Victoria Cross [in fact there were ten] and that very many other decorations were awarded to the men of this state is alone sufficient proof of the

472

splendid spirit in which you fought. Alas, your casualties were very heavy, over 5,000 of your men being killed. My deepest sympathy goes to all relations and friends of your gallant men who fell, as well as to all of you who had the misfortune to be disabled. I hope you will always look on me in the same way as you did on active service — as a cobber." The applause almost lifted the roof off the place. Then the prince went walkabout along the aisles, shaking hands with as many old soldiers as he could. His entourage were left in the crowds as he squeezed out through a side door into a waiting car and was swept off for lunch with the state governor.

The heavy workload at the railway offices forced Chris to give up his campaigning for returned soldiers for a while, although his health was now better than at any time since he got back to Australia. He was pleased to tell his mother: ". . . jerky movement less marked and natural balance slightly better and, except for very rare occasions, I am free from the terrible inflammation of bowel pain I had when I first returned. Aspirins I use so seldom that we forget where we put them last."

He had also moved up in the world, selling the little clapperboard home in Holyrood Street for £420 cash after paying 11 shillings to advertise it in the local newspaper. Bertha, who was expecting again, chose a bigger, more modern brick bungalow 200 yards away from the old one but closer to the station so Chris did not have as far to walk. It cost £850, with Chris putting down a £200 deposit and sinking the balance of his £123 War Gratuity Bond into the new place, after allocating £2 from it to the Deceased Soldiers' Children's Scholarship Fund and investing £10 in the Returned Soldiers' Co-operative Society. The rest of the cost was covered by a favourable War Service Home loan from the government. With Kathleen flourishing, life after so much death was continuing to improve for the Australian Beecheys. But Harold was not forgotten. Chris sent a War Gratuity Bond application form to his mother so she could claim her entitlement for her late son. Though far from home, he took on the responsibilities of oldest surviving Beechey brother and did his best to spare Amy further pain. He wrote to the officer in charge of base records at Melbourne asking that Harold's war medals be sent to him because of the precarious state of his mother's health caused by the loss of five sons.

In 1922 Bertha gave birth to their second daughter, whom they named Daphne. Chris found the stamina to resume his secretarial duties with the Leederville sub-branch of the Returned Sailors and Soldiers League and became an even more committed activist, fiercely expressing his solidarity with the working man and a "violent hatred and contempt" for those who didn't need to work thanks to the obscene profits they made from the war. "We still have a lot to do to induce people to give the returned digger a fair deal . . . we also have a fair amount of local distress," he told his mother.

Giving away his English public school background, Chris was equally heated about his daughters' education. He was worried they would end up speaking like Australians if they went to state school ... "something nasal and cockney and a mispronunciation of the letter 'O' — as in 'gow on' — first word rhyming with cow." Writing home in May 1923 he talks about enclosing some family snapshots taken on the lawn by Curly Bailey — Chris was still getting confused by her name. It is his last mention of Harold's girl.

Sam returned from the war and, rather than going off to university, became an apprentice chemist at the firm of Battle's in Lincoln. Eric's wife Mary recalled how handsome and fascinating he was and lost count of the number of girls to whom he became engaged. The "Doris" who had written to him every day without fail while he was On Active Service soon vanished from the scene. But he did eventually marry one of his many admirers and had six children, the first of whom was named after Harold. His wife, Dorothy Fisher, had a modest family inheritance, which they sunk into a chemist's business that collapsed in the 1930s and left them almost destitute. Dorothy died of breast cancer in September 1943 when their youngest child was still an infant. Sam shocked the family by marrying again before October was out. Later in life he went to university and gained a BSc in economics at almost fifty years of age.

The last surviving son of the Rev. P. W. T. Beechey died in 1977 at the age of 77. He had outlived most of his older brothers by sixty years. After Edie had set down her recollections of life at Friesthorpe, Sam was moved to sum up those who had sacrificed everything in the line of duty. Bar was simply "brains", Char "sterling character and respectability", Leonard "sweetness of nature", Christopher "almost superhuman physical strength", Frank "versatility and athletic prowess", and Harold "a young Grecian athlete".

Sam's own children were forbidden to play with toy soldiers, although young Harold overcame the ban by refusing to take some particularly revolting medicine when he was ill until his father promised to buy him a toy. After keeping his side of the bargain, the youngster demanded and received his first soldiers. Recalling his own childhood at Friesthorpe when he was able to hoodwink his elderly and rather gullible father, Sam could only chuckle at the lad's ingenuity. Harold, like his doomed uncle, ended up living in Australia.

Avondale Street with its unhappy memories of buff-coloured War Office envelopes dropping through the letterbox was left behind in 1920. Amy moved to a new post-war housing development in Lincoln. She kept her faith and devoted much of her later life to local church affairs, becoming known as the Mother of St Giles for her dedication to the building of a new church in the area. Soon after the war, she returned to Friesthorpe with two of her daughters for the unveiling of a pair of marble tablets commemorating those who had fallen.

The tablets are in St Peter's church, where the Rev. P. W. T. Beechey presided for twenty-two years until so ill that he took his last service seated in a chair in the aisle, delivering a sermon on the end of the world. The tablet on the right bears the inscription: "In proud and

476

grateful memory of Sgt Barnard R. Beechey, Pte Charles R. Beechey, Sec-Lieut. Frank C. R. Beechey, Rfm. Leonard R. Beechey, Lance-Corpl Harold R. Beechey, who laid down their lives in the Great War — Beloved sons of the late Rev. P. W. T. Beechey, sometime rector of this Parish." The second tablet commemorates two other sons of Friesthorpe, John Wilson and William Forman, killed in 1914-18. The memorial was dedicated and unveiled by the rector of neighbouring Wickenby. The beautiful voice heard soaring above all others as they sang "Oh God our help in ages past" belonged to Amy Beechey, who all those years before had played harmonium, led the hymns and blushed with embarrassment when her husband flourished a scarlet hanky from the pulpit.

At even more remote and scattered Snarford, two miles away, the little church is tucked away among trees with not another building in sight. On the far wall opposite the entrance is a simple Roll of Honour. It includes the names of the five rector's sons who, in winters past, used to roast chestnuts on the blazing stove next to their pew — a memory that must have warmed them years afterwards as they sat around braziers in frozen trenches. Later came the unveiling of the main war memorial in Lincoln where the city fathers also struck a special bronze medal, which they presented to the mother who had lost five sons; six, counting Chris, who was too far away to see his brothers commemorated. If he ever went back to Dowerin, Chris would have been proud to find his own name on that remote wheat-belt town's roll of honour.

Of his younger brother there is no mention. When the townsfolk put up a cenotaph to the sons of Dowerin shire who laid down their lives, Lance Corporal H. R. Beechey was overlooked.

In the following years, Chris remained in touch with sister Edie — by now Mrs Mucklow after marrying one of Sam's colleagues from Battle's chemists and opticians. When the Second World War was raging and Britain was being blitzed by German bombers, Edie wondered whether Chris and Bertha would be willing to provide a home in Perth for her daughter, Josephine, then ten years old. Chris wrote back that he would be more than happy to take in his niece and treat her as one of his own.

2 September 1940

Dear Edith

It's difficult to advise you about sending her out here, but I do consider Western Australia a haven from war, especially so for children. Its freedom from nerve strain, which must inevitably affect young girls for the rest of their lives, is assured. We live mostly out of doors. The climate is the best I've ever met. The beaches are close and handy and the sun, the wind and the salt-water bathing. We have our droughts and heatwaves like the other states, but the droughts are few and far between and the heatwaves break into cool sou' westerlies in four or five days, not like the interior. I feel the cold more and more each year because I do no work but desk office work and sit too still all day, but even I can sleep out on a verandah most of the year with plenty of blankets. Josephine would enjoy sleeping out on a big verandah at the side of the house overlooking the lawn, protected from the front and the street by the brick garage. In regard to what you said about Philip [Edie's son, age 14], preferring to stay and learn to dig trenches and use a rifle, tell him "Atta Boy" from me. I'm proud of this nephew of mine.

Sometimes I feel aggrieved that I'm out of it again like the last two years of the last war on account of war disability. I feel that I should like to be at home if only to defy the enemy whether on land, sea or air and to shake a fist at them, however impotently it might be. But it takes me sometimes all the weekend to get fit for the next week's work.

Before closing I may say we're within 100 yards of a bridge over the railway and the Perth Modern School (mixed) is just over the bridge — I'll make enquiries about enrolling her if you do decide to send Josephine.

Love to all, Chris

Now in her seventies, Josephine admits she was terrified of the idea at the time "because you did not come back from Australia; you didn't have the money then. If I went, it was for good. What a different life it would have been for me. My parents felt it might have been a better life but they would have lost their daughter." She stayed in England and Chris continued to write to her mother.

Eve of Whitsuntide 1941

The war hasn't made much difference to us — a slight increase in cost of living and a little extra taxation and more to follow, I suppose. I still feel that I should like to be in England to do something even in an office capacity but that's well nigh impossible, for one thing I don't think I could make the journey and, for another, if an HE [high explosive] exploded near me I would probably die of shock and then be absolutely useless. Tomorrow's Whit Sunday, my birthday, I'm 58.

He also dropped a line to sister Daisy.

5 May 1942

Funny how we always remember relatives and people as we last saw them. Imagination can't ever visualise them into what they've grown into. As for me, I'm thin, grim and anxious looking (so people tell me) and have lost a lot of teeth and most of my hair. Bertha says that my scowl is only a habit and I'm really cheerful and happy considering that it does take me a long time to get around and straighten my back up.

His daughter Daphne's best friend, Tess Simpson, remembers how Chris talked fondly of the small farm he had before the first war. He was like a father to Tess and walked her down the aisle on her wedding day. His balance worsened with age and when summoned before the war pensions board in less enlightened times he was surrounded by doctors and told to climb up on his chair. When Chris tried to explain it was beyond him, he was ordered, "Stand on that chair." He tried to and crashed down in a heap. Only then were they satisfied that he was not a malingerer.

With another war over, Chris sympathised about food shortages and provided Edie with a few glimpses of the brothers they had lost more than a generation earlier.

1 May 1946

In regard of your husband's account of food rations, I have felt ashamed many times of not sending food parcels but there are seven on my side of the family and three on Bertha's so if we sent to all ten it would cost about two weeks' income. We've even destroyed dripping because we could not give or send it away or have it properly sealed for overseas transport.

You ask personal questions about your elder brothers. Well, little white-haired younger sister, don't ask too much. We are all what we are made or what we made ourselves and some exhumations of bodies and spirits are not always wise. However, in odd moments I will try and put on paper memories for you and post them on. In regard to Barnard's white hair — he was born with a big white or grey patch and after he got the sack (I think he was hitting the bottle a bit heavy) and was many months out of work, he worried a lot and finally took a very humble job with the county education department. I didn't see him when I was home on leave from the Australian General Hospital but mother told me how he had thanked God when they raised the age of enlistment and he could join up and get his manship back (is there such a word as manship? I hate the hackney word manhood). He did get it back at Loos.

Char was more of a philosophical and self-contained nature. I did meet him on leave. He was trying to assure himself that it was his duty to look after mother and not to join up as all the others had done, but he failed and joined up with the London Fusiliers, composed of equal numbers of public schoolboys and labour battalions, just to show his contempt of class. He got his Calvary, as you know, in East Africa. Have you ever thought of getting a Mercator's map of the battlefields of 1914–18, marking the spots where they are buried and connecting them by straight lines to see what geometrical figures they make?

Of course, they both fell in love. After many years of mature thought I have come to pity those parsons' sons and sons of middle-class people on scanty income who went through Oxford and Cambridge and took a degree. We would all have been better put to some trade or profession. Eric, Harold and Sam were the only truly trained boys among us. Bar and Char had nothing but years of schoolmastering before them. Very few secondary schools provided living quarters for junior masters and their wives and families, and headmasterships were hard to obtain without taking [holy] orders. Though both fell in love, neither proposed or were able to marry. This is enough of family reminiscences for this letter, others perhaps at a later date.

Bertha and I are both well and like to live quietly on our own at home. I couldn't have gone on working much longer but I sleep out on the verandah all the year now and take my nap every afternoon.

Love to all, Kris

On 9 November 1949, he informed Edie, "I always consider you my best correspondent and the nearest in thought and feeling. Perhaps it is because you are still within sight of Lincoln Minster and within reach of Friesthorpe and Snarford." A few years later Chris reached a milestone that hardly seemed likely after his brush with death at Gallipoli. On 1 August 1953, he told his youngest sister, "I was seventy two months ago and only Katie remembered it and wrote to me about it. It's a great achievement on my part I consider and I never thought I would make it. I was in and out of the Repatriation Hospital for nearly thirty years and near the pearly gates (so I think) several times." He blessed his good fortune in another letter soon afterwards.

At three score years and ten to be retired and on easy street and no financial worries is much to be thankful for. I sometimes think of my early days at Friesthorpe rectory and wonder. It seems to have been another life altogether and hardly to be remembered. On review my life seems to have been divided into three parts:

Early life and young manhood until I left for Australia.

Four years working in the Bush out here and my life in the forces and in military hospitals.

My return to Australia, thirty-nine years in a railway office and building a home and family leading to my present retirement and quietly growing old.

We drive down to Albany on the cool south coast on Tuesday and will stay six weeks during the school holidays with a woman who boards four high school girls during term time.

Brother Eric died of cancer in March 1954, a month before his sixty-fifth birthday. Writing to Edie on Palm Sunday, Chris says, "I was shocked and surprised when I got Sam's cable. I had such a cheery letter from Eric about September last year and thought he had well got over his illness of two years back and that both he and Mary would live long and be happy. It's a strange thing that Eric should have been the first of the eight boys to die a natural death. Bertha and I are keeping well but feel old and tired, like driving with the handbrake on all the time." Ten years later, he tells Edie, "I was eighty-one last June and seem to get more tired every month." And then the final words from Chris to his sister . . .

26 June 1967

I've got beyond writing letters as I used to do. Like the London charwoman, I want to do nothing forever and ever. I walk very slowly with a stick and a calliper and Bertha just as slowly with one stick. However, Daphne comes in two or three times a week and does our shopping and makes the beds and does other odd jobs for us. The grocer and the baker and the milkman call regularly and we don't get out much.

I don't enjoy the TV much. It's a lazy way of hearing the news. Bertha watches ballet and listens to opera. Neither means a thing to me. The programmes get worse every week. We both get very tired and I'm getting near the last round-up, as Bing Crosby sang many years ago.

Chris died at the age of eighty-five in September 1968. His eldest daughter Kathleen in her own final years recollected that "he never forgot Harold or the others". In England, Edie also never forgot, slipping an "In Memoriam" notice in the newspaper each Remembrance Day, just as her mother had done while she was alive . . . names, numbers, ranks and regiments. She wrote fondly of their days at Friesthorpe, describing all those big brothers who went away to school or university or to work and who came back to make a great fuss of her. She had adored them and, with her mother, had been their enduring link with home when the war took them away. She was usually there whenever the postman or the telegrams arrived with terrible news. She was, as Eric had remarked, "officer in charge of parcels" and, after her mother's passing, she preserved the letters that today keep their memory alive. Her daughter Josephine remembers Edie deciding many years ago that she was going to type them all up for posterity. "When she told me," she said, "I just thought, how boring!"

Edie, by then the last surviving Beechey child, died in 1992. Her ashes were interred in Friesthorpe churchyard and, eighty years after her father's death, her name was added to the headstone commemorating the Rev. P. W. Thomas Beechey with the inscription "His Thirteenth Child".

As for the rest of the Beechey sisters, Frances, the eldest and so often a second mother figure to the little ones, also lived into her nineties. Her husband, Billy Hay, had come through the war and they had a son and a daughter. Katie, the Beechey sister who had been farmed out to help Mary cope in wartime and to ease congestion at 14 Avondale Street, remained with Eric's family for many years before becoming a secretary at a London bank. She later converted to theosophy — a mystical religion espousing spiritual ecstasy and universal brotherhood — and went to live in India, where she died aged seventy-seven. Margaret, prettiest of the girls, also never married although a mysterious admirer named Kaminski was said to have worshipped her. She contracted TB in her early twenties and was a semi-invalid for much of her life. She, too, had a spell in India as companion to her intrepid Uncle Charlie's daughter. She died in 1958 and is buried in the secluded garden of a Staffordshire nunnery. Winifrede worked for many years for the BBC in London and, at fifty-five, became the wife and then widow of a Major Wingate-Marsh. She was eighty when she died in 1976.

Amy Beechey, who had been refused life insurance when she was thirty because of her supposedly weak heart, lived on into her eighty-second year. As well as devoting herself to church work at St Giles, she consoled herself reading her sons' letters and keeping their pictures in pride of place at her home. There were also special mementoes, such as a poem in tribute "To Lieut. Beechey who died November 13th 1916" (in fact, Frank died on 14 November), written by someone identified only as HWP.

Write we his name, whose loss we now deplore
Upon the roll of those who come no more,
His course is run, he did, he gave his best,
And passes thus with honour to his rest.
As on the field of sport he played the game
And faced with cheerful mien whatever came,
So in the sterner game of war he died,
Still playing, not for self, but for his side.
Many will miss that ever-smiling face,
Regret serves not to fill the empty space.

★ ★ ★

Amy had outlived Frank and most of her eight boys by twenty years. She was taken ill at Christmas 1936 but assured all the family who had gathered around her, "You can go and have your Christmas dinner; I won't die till Boxing Day." She was as good as her word, passing away peacefully on the morning of St Stephen's. Her funeral was at St Giles, the new parish church so dear to her heart, which had only recently been completed. On Christmas Day the vicar visited her and, with a real sense of joy and fulfilment, she told him, "Well, I have seen the church." Her body rested in St Giles overnight before the day of her funeral.

With her sons lying in foreign fields from Flanders to Dar es Salaam in what was then Tanganyika, formerly German East Africa, Amy chose to be buried not at Friesthorpe but close to other boys who had laid down their lives. They were the young men from as far away as Canada and Australia, the sick and the wounded, who spent their final days in the military hospital in Lincoln and would never return home. Contemporary accounts tell of Amy's burial among the soldiers, but that was three years before a second war came along and the military corner of Lincoln Newport cemetery was extended to accommodate another hundred young men. The mother who lost five sons is no longer in the midst of the war dead. But as the sunlight flickers through leafless trees on bright November days, the long shadow of the Cross of Sacrifice still brushes the grave of Amy Beechey.

488

Sergeant Barnard Reeve Beechey, 2nd Battalion the Lincolnshire Regiment, killed in action 25 September 1915, aged 38. No known grave. Commemorated on the Ploegsteert Memorial, Hainault, Belgium.

Second Lieutenant Frank Collett Reeve Beechey, 13th Battalion the East Yorkshire Regiment, died of wounds 14 November 1916, aged 30. Buried at Warlincourte Halte British Cemetery, Pas de Calais, France.

Lance Corporal Harold Reeve Beechey, 48th Battalion Australian Imperial Force, killed in action 10 April 1917, aged 26. No known grave. Commemorated on the Villers-Bretonneux Memorial, Somme, France.

Private Charles Reeve Beechey, 25th Battalion Royal Fusiliers, died of wounds 20 October 1917, aged 39. Buried at Dar es Salaam War Cemetery, Tanzania, Africa.

Rifleman Leonard Reeve Beechey, 18th Battalion the London Regiment (London Irish Rifles), died of wounds 29 December 1917, aged 36. Buried at St Sever Cemetery Extension, Rouen, France.

At the going down of the sun and in the morning, we will remember them.

Epilogue

The story of the Beechey brothers took me from Friesthorpe to Western Australia, but would never have been told had I not lost my way cycling through the Cotswolds one summer's day. Instead of reaching Bourton on the Water, where I was hoping to dangle my feet in the river, I found myself at Great Rissington, one of those honey-coloured villages of stone cottages, huge churches and great manor houses that hug the Windrush valley beyond Burford like golden charms on a bracelet. I thought about a pint but the only pub was bolted and barred so I rolled on down the lane and came to the church, which, if it couldn't provide lager top, at least promised relief from the melting heat of the afternoon.

Within its ancient walls, all was cool stillness and silence. I perched on a pew and watched specks of dust from down the ages pirouetting in a slash of sunlight. In the musty shadows I noticed a marble tablet on the wall with a British Legion flag drooping in front of it — a memorial to the dozen or so sons of this Gloucestershire village who laid down their lives in the Great War.

Below it hung a plain wooden frame containing individual photographs of the boys; pictures taken especially for sweethearts, wives or mothers before each of these young men went off to die. Some of them appeared more nervous of a camera than anything they might have to face in the front line. Frozen in sepia-tinted time, they all looked so proud and scrubbed in their uniforms. It was simple, evocative and profoundly moving.

I looked at those young faces and at the names beneath each picture. One was repeated over and over. Souls. Five lost Souls — Frederick George Souls, Albert Souls, Walter Davis Souls, Arthur William Souls and Alfred Ernest Souls, five brothers who all fought and died. *Saving Private Ryan* had recently been winning Oscars and stunning cinema audiences everywhere. That was a story about three American brothers being lost and the mission to pluck a fourth from the Second World War battlefields of Europe. The world also knew of the Fighting Sullivans, five brothers who all went down with the USS *Juneau* when she was torpedoed at Guadalcanal in 1942. They, too, inspired a Hollywood movie. A battleship and convention centre were named in their honour. The fighting Souls brothers, in contrast, were barely remembered even in their home village, except when their names were read out on 11 November each year.

I spent eighteen months trying to find out about them, but more than eighty years after the events, it was a mostly frustrating and unrewarding search. I clung to the hope that a relative might magically appear with a

491

treasure chest of memories that had been hidden away in a dusty attic. I did find a wonderfully sprightly gentleman called Victor Walkley, who was a nephew of the Souls boys. For years he had been firing off letters to prime ministers and Buckingham Palace asking for some kind of formal recognition for the family's sacrifice. The replies were always polite. Although there appeared to be an honour for every sporting personality and contributor to party funds, there wasn't one that could be suitably bestowed on a long-deceased mother who had given five sons for King and Country. At least Victor had his uncles' medals, including the Military Medal won by Arthur Souls in April 1918. Arthur was posted as missing presumed dead in the action on the Somme, where he was singled out for gallantry. His twin brother Alfred had been killed in Flanders a fortnight earlier. Albert, Fred and Walter Souls had all been killed in 1916. Their mother and father, Annie and William Souls, had another son, Percy, who was too young to fight. He died of meningitis after the war. The whole male line had been wiped out.

The boys, who had never married, had three sisters: Iris, Kate and Hilda. Victor was Iris's son. The medals, once kept in a glass case in pride of place in his grandma's house, were handed down to him, but there was nothing else. I found Katherine Hall, Kate's child, still living in the same village where she was brought up by Annie Souls like her own daughter. Katherine was born outside of marriage when her mother worked in service in London and remembered being pushed around in a pram by a figure in khaki — one of her doomed uncles home on leave. A candle was kept burning in the window of the family's four-room cottage in case the oldest boy, Fred, lost in the Battle of the Somme and with no known grave, should one day come home. Annie's bitterness over such loss only surfaced whenever "God Save the King" was played. She would neither stand nor sing, much to the young Katherine's embarrassment at the time. When a neighbour was heard to remark that old Mrs Souls must be well off with the war pensions from five dead sons, the family moved to nearby Great Barrington.

All the family papers — letters, postcards, any photographs and probably the citation accompanying Arthur's Military Medal — went on a bonfire that burned for two days in the 1950s. None of the boys' military records survived the Blitz during which Hitler's bombs destroyed three-quarters of the service papers of First World War soldiers. Even their school life was a closed book. The Great Rissington records disappeared into a skip never to be seen again when the village school was refurbished to commemorate its centenary.

I gave up tearing my hair out and wrote an article about the Souls brothers, which appeared in *Saga Magazine* and the *Sunday Telegraph* for Remembrance Sunday 2001. The number of old soldiers left from 1914–18 would not even add up to a half a platoon as I write this — thirty or so out of the millions who put on a uniform for Britain and Empire. Yet the letters I received in response to the Souls piece showed how much that conflict was seared into the national consciousness. It is now more than ninety years since the Great War began but people still grieve for fathers they never knew. At the eightieth anniversary commemoration of the Battle of the Somme on 1 July 1996, I wandered away from the crowds and dignitaries, and the last few survivors in their wheelchairs at Thiepval. Among the graves in the great shadow of the Memorial to the Missing of the Somme I stooped to read a small home-made plaque with the words: "To my Unknown Soldier — I never knew you, darling dad, your photograph was all I had." The gravestone was that of a man killed in October 1916 and the plaque was signed and dated, "Joan, 1993 — my thoughts with you till my life ends." At another cemetery, with a great wall of names of the dead with no known graves, someone had left a small cluster of poppies with a message attached, a simple, heartfelt poem to a long-lost father, killed in the Battle of Arras in April 1917:

> I still think I'm dreaming, I can't believe it's true,
> That I can go on living without ever seeing you.
> And when my life is through
> I pray that God will take my hand
> And lead me straight to you
> Your loving daughter, Olive

When I wrote the articles, I thought nobody could have given more than Annie Souls. The Imperial War Museum and the Commonwealth War Graves Commission knew of no greater sacrifice. But another mother *had* given as much.

494

Her name was Amy Beechey and her five lost sons have been similarly forgotten by history. But the youngest of her six daughters, Edith Emily, never forgot. She kept a small brown case of family papers and photographs, which she passed on to her own daughter when she went into a nursing home. It lay hidden away and unopened for years. Then, in response to my story of the lost Souls, a picture of the Beechey family was printed on the letters pages of *Saga Magazine*, with a short note about them from a relative in Somerset, Mrs Ann Beechey.

I contacted her but she knew little else. I looked up the Beechey boys on the Commonwealth War Graves Commission website. Two of them had no known grave, one was buried in modern-day Tanzania and another on the Somme. The fifth and last to give his life lay at rest a couple of hundred yards from young Walter Souls. Both had died of wounds and were now comrades in the same battalion of the dead at St Sever cemetery, Rouen, northern France.

In all my Souls' searching I had found just two surviving letters, one with well-meaning platitudes from a chaplain and the other from the matron of the same hospital, telling of 24-year-old Walter's final hours. "Dear Mrs Souls," she wrote, "I much regret to have to tell you that your son died very suddenly about nine o'clock yesterday evening. He came to us with a wound in his left leg, and on Tuesday he had to undergo an operation, but he rallied and seemed to be better. He was quite cheery, and then the next evening he suddenly collapsed and died instantly from an embolism (or clot of blood) in the heart. I am enclosing a postcard he wrote on the day he died. He will be buried in the little British cemetery just outside Rouen where lie other brave lads who have fallen in this dreadful war ...." As I read those words from a microfilm screen in Cirencester public library, I was whirled back in time to August 1916, to a stone farm cottage in Great Rissington where Annie Souls, short, plumpish and silver-haired, clutches a picture postcard of fresh-faced Walter with the simple legend "Forget Me Not" as she mourns another lost son.

That sorrowful matron's letter was one of the few fragments I found while piecing together the story of the Souls brothers. The Beechey breakthrough was sudden, spectacular and as unexpected as those achieved all too rarely by Great War generals. Ann Beechey kindly sent me a copy of the picture she had submitted to *Saga Magazine* and casually mentioned that someone else had been in touch about it, a Mrs Josephine Warren, who was a niece of the Beechey boys. She was the daughter of Mrs Edith Emily Mucklow *née* Beechey, and somewhere in her attic was that case of memories handed down from her grandmother to her mother and then on to her.

Josephine's duties with the Royal Horticultural Society made her a difficult woman to pin down during the spring and summer months. But one May Bank Holiday Sunday I travelled to Devon and was welcomed into her home to find the case lying open on the dining-room table. Elastic bands, some perished with age, held together bundles of letters composed on any scrap of paper a son in the trenches could lay his hands on to write home. I picked up the top pile and as the rubber band disintegrated out dropped a small yellowing envelope with the words "Killed In Action" scrawled across it. Josephine, her husband John and son Martin left me to it.

There were around 300 letters — some pages long, others just brief notes hastily scribbled to acknowledge the desperate news from home that another brother had been killed. A short message from one of the boys as he lay dying was meant to reassure his mother. But the weak, childlike, spidery handwriting could only have broken her heart.

There were kindly, regretful messages from commanding officers, comrades and chaplains as well as the bald, impersonal official Army Form B.104-82 that every wife and mother dreaded, beginning: "It is my painful duty to inform you . . ." It is a remarkable legacy of one family's suffering, borne with courage and dignity.

I drank Josephine's tea and read out snatches of the letters to her. John disappeared and every now and then came back with a box file or brown envelope, which he had rummaged round to find. There were the writings of Josephine's late mother, who had left a touching and charming memoir of her upbringing, surrounded by big, strong brothers. And there were the family photographs — the Beechey boys in their uniforms; their mother, grey-haired with proud, aquiline features; their elderly father, who died of cancer before the war took his sons; faded pictures of what seemed a perfect childhood in the Lincolnshire countryside.

Without Josephine Warren, this book would never have been written. I thank her and John not only for entrusting me with the family treasure, which they have preserved so immaculately, but also for their unfailing hospitality, kindness and encouragement.

Acknowledgements

In my pursuit of the Beechey story it became clear that the brothers who survived the war had been reticent to dwell on those times in later life. Chris lived with the physical pain and distress of Gallipoli to his dying day but was as reluctant as Eric and Sam to talk about the war. When their sister Edith wrote her family memoir, it was not about the tragedy that overwhelmed them but about idyllic days at Friesthorpe rectory. Her favourite brother, Frank, spoke of "the huge Beechey tribe" in one of his letters. To the sons, daughters, grandsons and nieces I tracked down, the Beechey sacrifice had always been largely a matter of unspoken pride.

I have acknowledged elsewhere the debt owed to Josephine Warren. It was chiefly through her that I was able to pursue other members of the "Beechey tribe" who were usually happy to contribute their time and any memories they could to what must have seemed a lost cause after so long. My thanks go to Mrs Janet Mandeville, Eric's daughter, who adopted a completely new Christian name owing to the glut of Joans in her tuition group at school; also to Josephine's brother, Phillip Mucklow; Sam's son, Harry Beechey; Frances's grand-daughter, Janet Ridings; Chris's daughter, Mrs Kathleen Hector, and his grandson, Nick Mayman.

When I set off on a Beechey digging trip Down Under in March 2003, I was fortunate to have already made contact with Bill Edgar, archivist and curator of Hale School in Perth. His knowledge of Western Australian military history and his enthusiasm for the subject, so apparent in his own book, *Warrior of Kokoda*, have helped and inspired. In return for his company and guidance on trips to Blackboy Hill and the "backblocks" of South Ucarty and for taking the time to read and comment on my words, pie and chips at the Dowerin gas station diner seems scant reward. Pete Pitman was also a good sport and guide to a bush country that seems as inhospitable today as it must have been almost a hundred years ago. Gus and Robbie Hagboom, whose family still live off this most brutal of landscapes, proved anything but inhospitable.

I am grateful to the awesome Australian War Memorial in Canberra, where Emma Jones and Robyn Van Dyke ensured I made the most of four short days. Strolling the broad sweep of Anzac Way, past the rows of silent monuments lining the avenue up to the domed memorial, compares with standing at the Menin Gate for the "Last Post". London's Kennington Road does not stir quite the same emotions but the Imperial War Museum is just as much of a national treasure. My thanks go to archivist Anthony Richards and his colleagues in the Department of Documents. I am also indebted to the National Archives, the British Newspaper Library, the Bodleian Library, the National Army Museum, the Leeds University Liddle Collection, the Guildhall Library and the Dorset, Oxfordshire and Lincolnshire county archives. Gerard Foley was my enthusiastic guide to the resources of the Battye

Library, Perth, Western Australia. Thanks also to: Val Hutch of the Royal Western Australian Historical Society; Paul Bridges and Norm Wells of the Army Museum of Western Australia in Fremantle; Les McLeod at the Department of Planning and Infrastructure at Midland, WA; Bret Christian and George Williams of Post Newspapers in Subiaco, Perth; Jenny Kohlen of the "Can You Help?" column at the *West Australian* newspaper; Jeanne Iles, Margaret Philippson and the terrier-like research team at the Western Australian Genealogical Society; Alan and Jill Revell in Sydney; Gwen Treasure of Como, WA; and Geoff Pocock, historian and archivist for the UK arm of the Legion of Frontiersmen of the Commonwealth.

The initial spark for this book came from Sheila Young of Winchester, after she had read my piece on the Souls brothers in *Saga Magazine*. Mrs Ann Beechey of South Petherton, Somerset, was similarly moved to write to me about her husband's distant family and I bless her for putting me in touch with Josephine Warren. My researches have taken me back to school, to those fine old establishments with draughty corridors and eccentric plumbing and equally eccentric masters where the Beechey boys taught and were taught. A-pluses go to Sally Todd of St John's School, Leatherhead; Dot Mariner and Tracey Butler of Christ's Hospital School, Horsham; Kevin Norman of De Aston School, Market Rasen; and John Craddock, archivist of Stamford School. Alex Spillman, churchwarden at Friesthorpe, has been the font of all local knowledge for that corner of Lincolnshire. Ernie Tonkinson of

Albany, Western Australia, brought Harold's girl, "Curly" Boyce, to life in words and pictures.

The fact that none of my family starved during the research and writing of *Brothers In War* is largely down to Lee Clayton and Lee Horton of *The People*, two of "Fleet Street's" finest. Thanks also to Mirror Group lawyer Rachel Welsh for her continued common-sense advice long after the champagne ran dry.

At Ebury Press, I am indebted to Jake Lingwood for giving me this chance, to Andrew Goodfellow for seeing so clearly how the story should be told and to Mari Roberts for stripping away the barbed wire with her skilful and sympathetic editing. Above all, I salute Ken Barlow at Ebury who championed *Brothers In War* from start to finish. This is Ken's book as well as mine.

Finally, I am not the only one who has lived in a war zone for the past three years. My wife, Julie, has put up with the chaos of paperwork, the bedlam of box files and book stacks, the frequent absences and — even when I was at home — the days and nights when it seemed I was married to a laptop instead of to her. She has also been a valued proofreader and, together with Gillian Betterton, a meticulous transcriber of letters and tape recordings.

The Patriot's Progress

Henry Williamson

A starkly powerful novel of one man's experiences in the First World War, *The Patriot's Progress* captures the grim experiences of an ordinary man caught up in a conflict over which he has no control.

John Bullock is a common soldier, fighting out of blind patriotism for a cause he does not understand, living through the bewilderment of his brutal initiation into army life, and finally facing the terrors of trench warfare on the battlefields of France.

Illustrated with the original lino-cuts of William Kermode, this book draws upon Henry Williamson's own war experiences. The combination of the text and illustrations creates a vivid and unforgettable portrayal of the war machine.

ISBN 978-0-7531-7708-2 (hb)
ISBN 978-0-7531-7709-9 (pb)

A Woman in Berlin

Anonymous

Begun on the day when Berlin first saw the face of war, the anonymous author of *A Woman in Berlin* describes life within the falling city as it was sacked by the Russian Army. Fending off the boredom and deprivation of hiding, she records her experiences, observations and meditations in this stark and vivid diary. Reports of the bombing, the rationing of food and the overwhelming terror of death are written in dispassionate, though determinedly optimistic, prose.

It caused huge controversy when first published in German in the 1950s. In 2003, over 40 years later it was republished in Germany to critical acclaim — and more controversy.

Newly translated into English, this is an astonishing and deeply affecting account of a woman fighting for survival amidst the horror and inhumanity of war.

ISBN 978-0-7531-9376-1 (hb)
ISBN 978-0-7531-9377-8 (pb)